Praise for

IN THE
ZONE

'Clyde Brolin truly captures the passion I experienced and
translates it into words… *In The Zone* is one hell of a book!'
Edwin Moses, *double Olympic 400m hurdles gold medallist
who went unbeaten for nearly ten years*

'This is a good, good book. It's broken up into three parts –
Conceive, Believe and Achieve – and it gets better the more
you dive into it.'
Chris Evans, *BBC Radio 2*

'The mind is such an untapped resource in both sport
and day-to-day life. *In The Zone* gives you the tools to tap the
true power of your brain.'
Anthony Watson, *professional rugby player for Bath,
England and the British and Irish Lions*

'*In The Zone* is an amazingly inspiring book! This was clearly
a labour of love and I feel humble compared with the other profiles,
not least Alex Zanardi.'
Roz Savage, *the first woman to row solo across the three big oceans*

'Remarkable stories and insights… *In The Zone's* fascinating
collection of interviews draws out the simple attributes required to
achieve incredible results.'
Andy Green, *World Land Speed Record Holder and driver
for Bloodhound SSC*

'It is an honour to be a part of this book. It is very well written
and it can help change people's perceptions and ultimately their
lives in a positive way.'
Pieter du Preez, *four-time Paracycling World Champion and the first
quadriplegic triathlete to complete an Ironman*

'Clyde Brolin's *In The Zone* is a very insightful read. When you're in
the Zone, it's impossible to make a wrong move!'
Ryan Doyle, *the first World Champion Freerunner*

IN THE
ZONE

HOW CHAMPIONS THINK
AND WIN BIG

by CLYDE BROLIN

BLINK
bringing you closer

Published by Blink Publishing
3.08, The Plaza,
535 Kings Road,
Chelsea Harbour,
London, SW10 0SZ

www.blinkpublishing.co.uk

facebook.com/blinkpublishing
twitter.com/blinkpublishing

Hardback – 978-1-911274-55-1
Trade Paperback – 978-1-911274-82-7
Ebook – 978-1-911274-56-8
Paperback – 978-1-911274-57-5

A CIP catalogue of this book is available from the British Library.

Typeset by Envy Design
Printed and bound by Clays Ltd, St Ives Plc

1 3 5 7 9 10 8 6 4 2

Every reasonable effort has been made to trace copyright holders of material
reproduced in this book, but if any have been inadvertently overlooked the
publishers would be glad to hear from them.

Blink Publishing is an imprint of the Bonnier Publishing Group
www.bonnierpublishing.co.uk

For dreamers everywhere
(past, present and future)

CONTENTS

PROLOGUE   1
INTRODUCTION   9

CONCEIVE

1. VISUALISATION   31

BELIEVE

2. COURAGE   61
3. RISK   91
4. CONFIDENCE   119
5. ATTITUDE   147

ACHIEVE

6. FOCUS   177
7. RESILIENCE   203
8. TEAMWORK   231
9. PASSION   257

CONCLUSION   285

ACKNOWLEDGEMENTS   305

ABOUT THE AUTHOR   308

INDEX   309

PROLOGUE

W hat was he thinking? It's the Indianapolis 500, the biggest spectator event in world sport, the very last corner of the final lap. For 799 corners out of 800, JR Hildebrand looks anything but an Indy rookie, in the lead and easing towards headlines as the first American driver for 84 years to win on their debut. The neural pathways honed over JR's years of throwing fast cars around do their job immaculately. Then, with home glory beckoning at the historic race, something in the mechanism freezes.

With the chequered flag in sight after this 500-mile epic, JR has to make one last choice: 'go high' up the oval racetrack's banking to lap Charlie Kimball's slower car or back off and hope the loss of pace doesn't allow any of his challengers through. He chooses option one, having earlier nailed a similar move at the same corner. But this time as he leaves the comfort of the racing line his worn tyres are less forgiving, as is the concrete as he veers wide and hits the wall.

The mass gasp of over 300,000 fans packing the track's miles of grandstands easily drowns out the crunch of the carnage and the screaming engines. Yet JR may get away with it even now: the momentum from his crash keeps him scraping along the wall towards the yard of bricks marking the Indy finish line. He slams his foot to the floor in a desperate attempt to keep his remaining two wheels moving for the last few hundred yards. In the end he crosses the line well clear of his rivals, all bar one.

Picking his way past the wreckage comes Britain's Dan Wheldon for the most dramatic victory in Indy history, on its 2011 centenary to boot. At the line Dan is just 2.1 seconds ahead. Talk about luck. Or is it? It turns out he was close enough to profit from JR's late mishap only because of a finely tuned piece of machinery that has been firing on all cylinders: his brain.

'Those last 20 laps were incredibly quick,' Dan told me. 'People were on different strategies and in my case it was about making sure every lap was the best it could possibly be. I had to drive flat out. But when you're in the Zone – especially in a confident time of your career – you do things and it's like... really?

'The team later told me I'd made an adjustment to the weight jacker and anti-roll bars at every single corner for those last 20 laps. And I didn't know it. In fact I didn't believe them. I thought I'd been adjusting them quite often but knew it wasn't that many, no way. So they showed me the data. I did it without even knowing. When you get in the Zone you have the ability to do things totally naturally.'

This 'natural' ability is the holy grail of performance at the highest level. This is the big payback – when all the years of graft come flooding back out in a torrent of pure, blissful execution. Hard work may lie behind any outstanding feat, but when the moment actually arrives, it can feel effortless, as if it requires no input at all.

Of course the weight jacker (which switches weight between the front wheels) and anti-roll bar (affecting the suspension) don't sound the most 'natural' element to racing a car. They are hardly as ingrained as using wheel and pedals to control speed and direction, but they are crucial to oval racing where these monster IndyCars lap at over 200mph. If you reach this level of competition, it's assumed you're driving a car to its limit; these set-up changes push that very 'limit' ever further.

How hard can it be to go round and round in circles? Ask Emerson Fittipaldi, a Brazilian who won two F1 world titles in the 1970s before winning the Indianapolis 500 twice too. Fittipaldi faced the wrath of diehard fans for daring to drink orange juice to celebrate instead of the traditional winner's bottle of milk, but by then he didn't need to be told how even the tiniest change can have a major impact in IndyCars.

'Oval racing seems easy but people don't see how technical it is,' he says. 'It may not look like it but it's more sophisticated to get the maximum out of a car if you keep turning left than turning both ways on a road course. It requires more fine-tuning than Formula 1 to be on the edge at that speed. You have to set up all four corners of the car as every tyre has different pressure and camber. The limit varies on every inch of track during a race as the tyres and balance change. Each turn is different from the one before, so you have to feel how the car is changing, how much to save tyres, how far to carry the car at the rear if it's not handling. The way you turn the steering wheel has to be progressive: you can't make a sudden move and be inches from the wall.

'Even clouds in the sky have an effect – and if you're not careful about the wind you can lose the car. At Indianapolis we regularly check the windsocks even at 240mph. If you are downwind at turn three, the car understeers (keeps going straight). If you go into turn one with a headwind, the car will be loose (the American term for oversteer, when the rear end is always trying to jump out). So you have to anticipate what an IndyCar will do before it does it. Like any sport, the key is to be consistently fast without making mistakes. To focus and to be able to be on the edge, you have to go over 100 per cent. You can go to 101 or 102 but if you go to 103 per cent you crash. That's the kind of edge that you are always trying to find.'

If that's the standard scale, Dan Wheldon must have been at 102.99 per cent in 2011. During his late charge he let his natural self handle the busy process of using up every last inch of road at speeds inconceivable to most of us. By also making so many micro-adjustments on the hoof, he gained time that would prove invaluable come that fateful final corner. With 15 laps left, Dan was 20 seconds behind JR, who was having to ration his fuel to reach the finish. By the last lap the American leader was in sight. Dan's team hadn't expected JR's fuel to last so long but they kept urging their man to be ready to capitalise if the rookie ran out. Dan was still busy passing lapped cars when his rival ran out of road instead.

'I didn't actually see JR hit the wall as soon as everybody

else because I was making sure I'd cleared a couple of cars,' said Dan. 'Then out of the corner of my eye I noticed he had come into contact with the barrier. I wasn't sure what he was going to do next. The Indianapolis 500 is such a big event, I didn't know if he would turn back across the track to try to take me with him. I wasn't sure where the debris would land. There were still cars to clear. So it's about 100 per cent focus. When I saw the side of JR's car was pancaked and he was just going to continue straight with two wheels on his wagon, I concentrated on avoiding the debris and making it across the line, which fortunately I did.'

Dan was fortunate in that he was the first Indianapolis 500 winner to lead the race for just one lap out of 200. But luck doesn't tell the whole story. Despite all their years of training, when it comes to the biggest stages, even sport's greats don't peak as often as we might imagine. Dan made sure he peaked. A planner by nature, he would always compulsively ensure his overalls were folded and laid out even after his races. But he paid just as much obsessive attention to his mind.

'It starts before the race,' he said. 'Typically you have obligations for sponsors which they do as close as possible to the race so everybody's in town. After that I like to take ten minutes to be on my own: not necessarily totally alone, but around people I'm comfortable with. Then I visualise the race. I go through it, thinking how my car has gone in practice, the changes I've made to the anti-roll bar and the weight jacker, what I've done to make it better in traffic, what's made it worse, how many pit stops we'll have. It's about looking ahead and making sure you're prepared for anything.

'Once the race starts it's just complete concentration. At the speeds we do anything can happen quickly. There are times when the car will all of a sudden snap, particularly on the ovals. It's about being able to react quickly to that. If your mind's elsewhere, if you're not 100 per cent in that Zone, the car will go. If you hit the wall, yeah it's incredibly hard. It could potentially put you out of racing for ever. You don't want to be out of that seat. So it's 100 per cent concentration. You think nothing other than making sure you're driving the racing car as hard as you can.'

JR Hildebrand knows all about the Zone too, even if he couldn't – quite – keep it up on his Indianapolis debut: 'When you're in the moment, when you really feel at your best, it's almost a subconscious experience,' he tells me. 'You allow your natural instincts to take over and seek that moment of total control – not just physically but a comprehensive grasp of all the variables at play. When you find that rhythm, you just execute and adrenalin gets pumped into your veins that you remember afterwards.

'It's a big part of why we keep striving to do this at a high level. When you overlay speed and the element of risk, it's a feeling that's hard to replicate anywhere else. But frankly I've had it more in recent years than when I was a rookie, when a lot of it was still new: whether paying attention to fuel economy or making sure you don't screw up in the pits, you don't have the muscle memory then. As a rookie I found myself much more consciously aware of what was happening.'

What was he thinking? Why was he thinking, more like… It's no surprise this 'conscious' state hindered JR when it mattered most. The Zone arrives when a life of practice is allowed to do its job uncluttered by the stream of superfluous information, doubts and worries dreamt up by the conscious mind. Stemming this flow of mental detritus is far from easy, as JR found while Dan Wheldon cleared his mind and flew. Weeks later Dan still seemed without a care in the world as his grin gleamed and his insights flowed, as we spoke at the Goodwood Festival of Speed.

Tragically, neither of us knew the centenary Indy 500 would be the last race Dan would ever win. Within weeks he was caught in another accident that was not his fault: a 15-car Las Vegas pile-up in which his car was one of several sent flying into the catch fencing. This time there was no way out, no surprise glory. He died from his injuries.

Dan's life and death prove just how far the plunge can be from peak to trough. But here's what I learned from Dan during the all-too-short gap between his extremes: even though most of us don't dare dream of scaling such heights, they await anyone who truly craves the climb. To win a glimpse of the view from the ultimate peak – the Zone – it's really not about luck.

INTRODUCTION

At the 1976 Olympic Games the Romanian gymnast Nadia Comăneci produced an uneven bars routine so flawless it left the judges no option but to award the first ever perfect ten. The moment is assured an eternal pedestal in sporting mythology – and it came about due to the strength of the steely mind driving this slender body.

'When things go perfectly it does feel magical,' Comăneci tells me. 'All your accomplishments and all the work you've done go into an imaginary bag. Then when you're out there you have to focus to get the routine you've done over the years out of the bag. In gymnastics the ultimate is the Olympics, but it's a psychological moment when you have to perform there because it only comes every four years. You have a minute for each event so you have to be the best at that particular time. It doesn't matter how you were ten minutes ago, you have to be the best right now.

'It's a tough job but that's what makes us unique. Everybody has a dream and you want to reach that target. If it works you go back and remember all the hours you put in. Of course it is hard; if it was easy, everybody would be an Olympic champion. But it's so worth it.'

A life of training is crucial for any aspiring Olympian just as it was for Dan Wheldon or anyone aiming to master a complex skill. Everyone from musicians to circus performers must put in this time because no one comes out of the womb able to juggle or play the piano. To learn requires a process starting with a deliberate decision to go for it, then continual conscious affirmations that it's still worth dedicating all the necessary time and effort. But all this conscious exertion is really aimed at filling the subconscious 'bag' until it is equipped to take over on the biggest stage. What sifts gold from dust is the ability to pull it all back out again when it counts.

A friend of mine who regularly topped the Cambridge University engineering exams described a similarly enviable ability: the minute he stepped into the exam hall, every single thing he had ever learned about a required topic came flooding back to him. For everyone else in that room or anyone who dreads this summer torture such a knack must seem unsporting. But when someone concentrates totally on their 'bag', it is possible to break through conscious thought and out the other side. The result may not seem magical to the protagonists themselves – indeed it may feel the most natural thing in the world – but it sure seems magical to the rest of us.

There is no age limit to the magic: while most children don't take this level of focus beyond Lego and dolls, some go much further. Gymnastics has a long history of young athletes performing terrifying manoeuvres, most notably in the former Eastern Bloc. To fill her own bag of tricks Comăneci spent six hours a day amassing countless back flips on balance beams while her friends were busy just being kids.

The Romanian gymnastics team employed psychologists to help these young girls visualise their entire routine until they could do it without thinking. Finally, to ensure there would be no problem competing in front of hostile crowds, their coaches even brought people in off the street and asked them to cause as much commotion as possible while their charges practised. Along the way Comăneci learned that pulling it off when it matters comes down to the workings not of the limbs but the brain.

'You have to be in the Zone,' she insists. 'But everybody has their own way of getting there. In my case I'd stay in a room by myself to go through every routine and skill piece by piece and remember how to make it right. In gymnastics it's easy to get out of the Zone as there are distractions, perhaps if there's music playing or someone else is performing. So you have to prepare for that in advance. Even though you have four routines to do, you have to think of each event at a time. You can't think of one while you're doing another one. You have to be in the moment.'

These last seven words are the basis of spiritual traditions such as Zen Buddhism. Acting on them is deceptively hard but those who push to extremes get a head start in unearthing such fundamental truths. Given this was a girl in her early teens, Comăneci's level of mental control was mind-blowing. She even faced occasional crass criticism for not seeming to be enjoying herself enough. Little did anyone know this young athlete had already raised the uneven bar in terms of the focus required to perform.

Comăneci hit her glorious peak in 1976 – at the age of 14 – but history tends to overlook the fact she did manage to 'follow that' by reaching perfection six more times on bars and beam that week, leading to three gold medals. Four years later she added two more golds. Such was the Romanian's supremacy, she now admits the rare occasions when she got it wrong are what stick in her mind: 'Time does slow down, especially when you make a mistake and you just want to go back and do it again but you can't. When something doesn't quite go perfectly it stays with you because it makes you aware of what you have to work on. I didn't have too many times when I made mistakes but I remember those times.'

There are downsides to being known all over the world for a single event in your life, regardless of how exquisite or pioneering it is. No matter what else you achieve from that point on, the world has already taken its snapshot of you: 'People always remember exactly where they were when they saw my first ten,' smiles Comăneci. 'But they don't know how many medals I won.'

Gymnastics has now changed its marking system so perfection, sensibly, is no longer an option. But that doesn't matter a jot to those chasing this special version of inner perfection. Great Britain's Max Whitlock, who took two golds in the space of an hour on floor and pommel horse at Rio in 2016, describes the experience as 'surreal', adding: 'You've trained so long for that one moment, a massive amount of focus and effort has gone into it. So you make sure you are in that Zone. That's why I don't watch any other gymnasts,

I just focus on my job. I understand what Nadia Comǎneci says about the "bag" but I try not to think like that because it can put pressure on you. If I've had a good build-up I'm happy. No matter what I do now, I couldn't have done any more. I try my best and if I do a good job great; if I don't I'll go again next time.'

What is most surprising about those who make it to the top is that the ultimate satisfaction tends not to come from the moment of triumph but their visits to the Zone along the way. For anyone who spends all their time striving to win a round piece of metal you'd think that – or at least the public acclaim that accompanies it – would be what they treasure most. Instead this very private ecstasy may be the real payback.

Of course Comǎneci's brutal training regime seems far too much too young to most, a fact apparently borne out by her 1989 defection to the West. She still lives in America, working for charities helping underprivileged children around the world. As a child prodigy herself, Comǎneci knows the kind of start that works. No matter what anyone else thinks, she looks back on her upbringing with joy and insists it was her choice to follow her passion. Moreover, making it all the way to the top means she is one of few people who can state with authority that the journey beats the destination.

'When you're a kid, you're a boat with no direction,' she adds. 'You can't choose what you want to do and you don't know. Kids want to be unique; they want to be defined by what they do. That's why they have to find something they are good at and stay with it. This is not only in sport but a general idea of how they can be the best. We should give kids opportunities and they should go with what they like most.

I started gymnastics when I was six, but I had good people around me who gave me a couple of options and guided me.

'In today's world if somebody wins an Olympic silver medal the next question is: "What went wrong?" People quantify your work by results. But it's not about the result. I always tell kids you have to learn the process. You should accomplish little things and focus on being a little better every day. That way you may get to the big one, but you'll end up being happy anyway because you'll learn a lot on the way. Of course it's nice to get a medal round your neck, but the process is more important. If you lose the passion and love for what you do, you're not going to feel satisfied.'

•

Whether it's painting a picture or building a tower, children have a natural ability to concentrate totally on what they're doing – as long as they love it. Yet this is also the age when they face an onslaught of negativity by well-meaning adults, much of it for essential well-being and safety. Starting with the first time a baby sees the alarm on a parent's face as they crawl near the top of the stairs, the words 'no', 'can't', 'don't' and 'mustn't' are an ever-present refrain. If this keeps up it can not only extinguish dreams at source but ingrain itself so totally that by adulthood we police ourselves to avoid any step outside our comfort zone. Then we must resort to mental trickery to coerce ourselves back to the 'can do' state where great performances flourish.

By contrast Dan Wheldon's family always told him 'you can', hence his weekly trips round the UK to race karts before he hit double figures. He loved filling his 'bag' too. Having grown up watching father Clive race, when Dan got his own chance he'd wake his parents by knocking on their door with his overalls already on. Soon he was winning, all the way up to the karting world championship, embedding the path to the Zone in his young head. As he told me: 'It feels magical when you've got a lot of confidence, your car's not quite right yet you still extract the fun out of it. That is the magical moment for me: to nail that perfect performance.'

Over a decade in IndyCar, Wheldon regularly nailed it, winning the 2005 championship along with its showpiece Indianapolis 500 and twice coming second. Magical as these moments are, it is during the harder times – which dominate most lives no matter how glorious they seem – that the real learning goes on. Before they went careering in different directions, Wheldon and Jenson Button were the closest of rivals as they toured the British karting circuits. Button later endured years of (relative) hardship at the wrong end of the Formula 1 grid, a common complaint in a sport where machinery always plays a critical role. His perseverance paid off when he found himself in a dominant 2009 Brawn car, winning the world title he'd spent 21 years dreaming about. 'You can learn a lot from someone like Jenson,' said Dan. 'What I admired most is that through the difficult times he was able to stay very positive. He continued to believe in himself.'

Such a positive attitude can be infectious. Racing drivers rely on their car, but these are designed, built and maintained by humans too, each of whom has a chance to find the Zone – or not – in everything they do. When a group working together peaks en masse, the sensation can be amplified to a whole new level, one that sport's great managers are forever trying to generate in their teams.

Incredibly, Dan didn't even have a full-time drive in

2011, instead making a one-off return at Indianapolis. Yet he drew on his inner driving force to turn motivator for the engineers and mechanics looking after his car: 'I had a lot of quiet confidence even from the first day,' he recalled. 'The team were surprised by my confidence. They'd had a hard Indianapolis the year before and they were more worried about just qualifying for the race. After the first day I said, "Listen guys: we can win this race, there's no doubt. But the way you're thinking won't allow us to win the race because you're more focused on just trying to make the race."

'I've never really told anybody about the confidence I had. But there are times when you know you're going to have a good one. I'd always had a very good feeling in the pit of my stomach that something good would happen at this Indianapolis 500. I didn't know what that was going to be: if I was going to win or come second. It's one of those things you never tell anybody, you keep it to yourself. Visualisation doesn't always mean you're confident. You can visualise not doing well. So it's visualisation with confidence. That, for me, is what completes it.'

•

Visualisation, confidence, the Zone? In my experience they don't teach you about any of this in school. Modern education offers us the skills to become dutiful workers and model citizens, happily telling us how and what to think. Yet it doesn't even broach the subject of how to 'not think' when it matters. Indeed I could have made it through life without even hearing about this special natural level of performance – but for my early passion for watching the world's top sports stars do their thing.

INTRODUCTION

At its best, sport is beautiful. Whether it's a dipping volley into the top corner, a 147 break, a home run, a nine-dart finish, a whipped backhand onto the baseline, an athletics world record or a hole-in-one, such moments make us all gasp. When anyone approaches this kind of excellence on the biggest stages, it can lead not just to victory but annihilation. Pity we only get to admire the view from the outside. What I wanted to discover was not just how it looks but how it really *feels*. Thankfully one legend was particularly eloquent about what went on inside his head as he worked his magic.

Motor sport's definitive peak experience came on a very different track from the big sweeping left-handers of Indianapolis. During qualifying for the 1988 Monaco Grand Prix, Brazil's Ayrton Senna lapped the tortuous streets of the Riviera harbour one and a half seconds faster than a field featuring world champion Alain Prost in an identical McLaren. Such supremacy is unheard of in motor racing and rare in sport, comparable to Usain Bolt's performance at the Beijing Olympics in 2008.

Senna didn't reveal how he had dazzled under the Monaco sun until years later when Canadian journalist Gerald Donaldson coaxed out an account that is now part of Formula 1 folklore. A misty-eyed Senna explained how he had undergone an apparent out-of-body experience, gazing down on himself as he flew: 'I was already on pole and I was going faster and faster. One lap after the other, quicker, and quicker, and quicker, and I suddenly realised that I was no longer driving the car consciously.

'I was kind of driving it by instinct, only I was in a different dimension. It was like I was in a tunnel. I was just going,

going – more, and more, and more, and more. I was way over the limit, but still able to find even more. Then, suddenly, something just kicked me. I kind of woke up and I realised that I was in a different atmosphere than you normally are. Immediately my reaction was to back off, slow down. I drove back slowly to the pits and I didn't want to go out any more that day. It frightened me because I realised I was well beyond my conscious understanding.'

This account was what first piqued my interest in peak performance, inspiring my decade of research for *Overdrive: Formula 1 in the Zone*. As I tracked down the greats of F1, I soon realised the Brazilian was not alone in flying so high; most racers had found this blissful driving perfection in some form. Even since the book's 2010 publication, I haven't managed to stop myself quizzing sport's elite about it. Global interest in the story flew even higher with the movie *Senna*, whose filmmakers were adamant the Monaco footage would survive their mammoth cutting process.

'For all its deletions there were a few things the film had to include and that lap was foremost,' writer Manish Pandey tells me. 'What make it work are Senna's own words about that "place" he reaches when he touches perfection. When I heard them it's no exaggeration to say I had goosebumps throughout. That's what the film is all about: man touching perfection within himself, walking on still water.'

This apparently mystical area of ability is not limited to travelling at ludicrous speeds round a racetrack. The Zone comes in all shapes, depending on the activity. In more cerebral pursuits it can lead to moments of inspiration. When I pushed, Pandey admitted even he found hints of it during his seven long years of work on the movie: 'When we were working on the very first outline the story wasn't working out,' adds Pandey. 'Then I was on a treadmill in the gym, which had a rhythm to it. I'd stopped thinking about the film when suddenly: bang. It just hit me. Why does he drive? He drives to be with God. That was it. That was the "Big Bang" moment for me. I realised what the film was really going to be about: a man's journey to God.'

Such a journey is not for everyone but it was a key component of the copious charisma that was amplified by Senna's early demise. First on the scene to treat the Brazilian's fatal injuries at Imola in 1994 was Professor Sid Watkins, F1's long-time doctor. I was lucky to quiz Watkins at the premiere of *Senna*, which moved 'the Prof' to tears a year before his own death in 2012. A brain surgeon by trade, even this man of science was lost for a rational explanation of what happened to his close friend in Monaco: 'I don't think it was a neurological phenomenon,' Watkins told me. 'I think it was a spiritual phenomenon. Someone else who experienced that was military officer TE Lawrence (later to find fame as Lawrence of Arabia). Asked why he liked to go so fast, he said: "Because when I go fast my spirit is in advance of my body." That's exactly what Senna felt. It's very strange. But TE Lawrence was a mystic and so was Senna.'

•

Senna's quest for external glory to match this internal heaven was dominated by an oft-bitter rivalry with France's four-time world champion Alain Prost, who gleefully mocked this apparent 'God Complex' in a bid to destabilise his usurper as the era's finest driver. But here's the next Hollywood twist. When I spoke to Prost I discovered he found the Zone too –

flying around the very same Monaco streets two years before he was trounced by Senna.

'I did almost 200 races in Formula 1 and maybe only four or five times in my career did I really feel this magic experience that the car and you are as one,' he says. 'It's hard to explain and when you're very demanding of yourself, you don't have this kind of experience very often. But at Monaco in 1986 I remember the whole weekend was like this, including the race. I was really flying and I could not see the speed. The speed meant nothing: to me it felt like I was driving at 30mph. I wouldn't describe it as a trance, because that implies you're not in control of everything. It was almost the opposite. Your mind is still focused but it's really happiness. It's happiness. And you are fast. You know both you and the car are under control. Yet you are quick. Even if you decide to go slower it doesn't make a big difference because it is so easy.'

Prost's account includes many classic constituents of the Zone experience. It was effortless yet it was under total control. The confines of time and space started to bend: everything slowed while his body extended until he felt at one with his car. Moreover, it resulted in a stunning performance that was clear to all, not least the dispassionate timesheets. Still he admits his reaction to this magic moment is less evocative than Senna's, stemming not from wizardry but from plain hard work.

'Everybody has their own feeling: especially Ayrton, who was a different type of driver and a different type of person,' adds Prost. 'So I wouldn't like to compare to him – or anybody else, because honestly it is a very personal feeling. Ayrton spoke in mystical terms, but for me it was the opposite. For me it was really practical. If you're like me you're curious about everything: you work hard on set-up and this work led to the result, not this sort of trance. It's an achievement which does not happen often, but for me it was more pragmatic: that's why it was maybe a bit boring...'

Prost's approach may not carry the same flamboyant attraction as his rival's but both led to the same outcome – even if only on these rare joyous moments. Such a work ethic, similar to Dan Wheldon's, is common in motor racing where attention to detail is ubiquitous. Even Senna was a control freak, raising the bar for fitness training and engineering feedback. Still it didn't dim his awe at the 'mystical' side of his craft.

The Brazilian's depictions of his inner spirit captured the imagination of many young racers – not least a compatriot of Prost's who would be crowned 2016 IndyCar champion: 'Ayrton is the reason I got interested in racing,' Simon Pagenaud tells me. 'He's been my idol, really my life model since I was a kid. He always had this special aura around him. His ability to go deeper in his thoughts and concentration level was very intriguing. I started experiencing it early on, albeit not on purpose, in my go-kart. But I was still a bit too emotional and excited.

'When I began racing cars I figured out the mental side was the most important. Your brain commands your body, so you need to train your brain to do what you want. Something I've been working on for years is to channel my energy, to find the path to ultimate concentration. Meditation is one of the tools I use. It happens more and more after all these years of practice. When you have confidence in your team it is easy to trigger. It's discipline that gets me there. But it takes many, many years to control it.'

This sensation is paradoxical in that it is about total concentration, while at the same time letting go to allow your natural ability to take over. The complexity doesn't end there, as we will hear in the course of this book: while there are many patterns to the experiences, there are different levels to the magic, just as there are different ways to get there in different fields. Few can truly claim to have mastered this elusive slice of Earthly heaven to the point of controlling it at will – and even those who get closest don't always develop the mystical aura of Ayrton Senna as described by Pagenaud. But they are guaranteed to enjoy every second of this internal bliss.

Of the many drivers Senna inspired, one has gone on to surpass many of his idol's Formula 1 records: Lewis Hamilton. 'Over the years I've had some incredible experiences,' he tells me. 'I don't know what Ayrton went through when he was on the edge but I've been on as much of the edge as I can be – and over and beyond. One of those edge moments is when you hit the wall, one is when you put an incredible lap all together. That's what keeps me going. There have been moments, particularly in Monaco, where it does almost feel like an out-of-body experience. You can't believe you're driving where Ayrton and the greats of the past have driven. It's mind-blowing how you are able to keep that car out of the barriers at the speeds you're doing.'

The out-of-body experience sounds fanciful. It's certainly at the top end of the scale of the sensations reported in the Zone, but it's more common than we'd think. If the conscious mind takes a back seat, it seems we really can fly. Finland's double F1 world champion Mika Häkkinen once described feeling like a 'bird of prey' looking down on his car. This sounds surreal enough to unsettle anyone, let alone when you're throwing a racing car around at the limit of adhesion. To clarify, I asked Häkkinen if he had ever taken his 'Flying Finn' nickname literally and watched himself race.

'Yes, that is the feeling you get,' he says. 'You become so much in control of what you're doing, it's really like coming out of your body. You actually start to see more than just forwards. You learn to understand exactly what's happening in front, in the back and at the side. You can sense everything. It comes with confidence, 100 per cent concentration and knowing exactly what you're doing. There is nothing else in life other than that moment. Everything becomes like slow motion – even though you're going at unbelievable speed round the Monaco track. It's an amazing feeling but it didn't just happen at peak moments, it happened often. The more you can stay yourself and under control, that's the best way to do it. I'd say you have to reach this level if you want to be a champion.'

•

With such highs on offer, no wonder racing drivers keep risking the ultimate low. It's not just the all-time greats. Some days, it transpires, really are 'your day'. 28 November 2010 was Filipe Albuquerque's day as this young Portuguese racer emerged from obscurity to defeat a line-up of legends – including Alain Prost, Michael Schumacher and Sebastian Vettel, who have collected 15 F1 world titles between them – to take the Race Of Champions crown at his first attempt.

Ho hum, not bad. But this was my day. I don't believe you can ask Nadia Com□neci or Usain Bolt for a piggy back to get a close-up of what they do. Yet here I was, one year later, lapping the same racetrack inside a Düsseldorf football stadium at the 2011 Race Of Champions – in the passenger seat as Albuquerque revved the very KTM X-Bow he had used to defeat Vettel.

I was soon in no doubt about how seriously Albuquerque was taking this. Even on the supposedly gentle run to the start line he ensured the car rarely felt like a car at all. As he put heat in the tyres with a series of weaves and burnouts, the X-Bow would suddenly feel unsettlingly light as if we were on a hoverboard. By the time we were waved away for the actual timed laps I admit to losing circulation in my knuckles: mercifully this was to be a short run or my typing days were over.

As the lights went out and we lurched forwards I knew I had to suspend every idea I'd ever cultivated about the speed that corners should be taken. They came thick and staggeringly fast, and I quickly accepted there was no alternative but to put my total faith in the ability of the young charger manhandling the open-topped car while its two inhabitants exhibited wildly contrasting mental states.

The track featured a specially-built 100-tonne crossover bridge linking its two loops, like a giant Scalextric set. I now get why bridges do not feature more widely in motor sport: on the entry, all you can see is the top tier of the stands. As we launched skywards at full throttle all evidence suggested our inevitable final destination would be Row Z. Yet as soon as the laws of physics overcame any brief moment of 'air' my nonchalant chauffeur was on the anchors for the next right-hander.

With the reflex of self-preservation beaten into submission, I focused the rest of my simpering mental capacity on the majesty of Albuquerque's skill. That was not hard because racing at the top level is an art. He didn't just hurl the X-Bow round the track, he danced. Every time the back end skipped out, this leading man teased it back in line and away we shimmied round the floor, whirls seamlessly blending into reels and pirouettes. Too soon it was over and I let fly with the whoop I'd been stifling for fear of breaking the concentration of the maestro beside me. Some chance...

'Being a racing driver is all about chasing the perfect lap,' says Albuquerque. 'Getting to the limit gives us the pleasure. When all this comes together the feeling is unbelievable. You feel arrogant... "Damn I'm good" – not meaning no one can beat you, but this was a perfect lap, one you'd like to show your friends. You don't need to see the data to know no one will beat you because the car really goes beyond the limit. You think: "Wow. If someone beats me I'll shake their hand." Sometimes even I can't explain how I do it, but the secret is to let it happen like you think it will. Be yourself in the car, be natural and just do it. If you go faster, awesome. If not, keep trying.'

To make it big you have to nail this perfect lap when it matters. Albuquerque was racing in an unglamorous Italian series when he won a regional qualifying event for the Race Of Champions. That's when he grabbed his chance, blitzing the world's best. Nine-time world rally champion Sébastien Loeb confirms he was beaten fair and square by this relative unknown in the Grand Final: 'I gave everything and did a good race but he was a bit faster. He was just flying...'

•

The dream machine that really powers these superstars to glory has no wheels – but it is the inspiration for this book.

It was in a quest to understand the true scope of human potential that I took on a seven-year tour of world sport. Along the way I've spoken to hundreds of champions – including Serbian tennis players, South African triathletes, New Zealand rugby players, Italian Paralympians, Jamaican sprinters, British rowers, Moroccan hurdlers, Brazilian skateboarders, Dutch footballers, Australian surfers, Northern Irish golfers, Japanese pilots, Ukrainian pole vaulters, German rally drivers, American swimmers, Kenyan runners, Spanish motorcyclists, Indian cricketers and Austrian skydivers. The best part of this privileged exploration of such great minds? All of them are desperate to share out the magic and help the rest of us find the Zone too.

The message from the select few who have been to the very top is disarmingly simple yet astonishingly consistent: we have a much greater influence than we dared imagine on the big wide world out there. It may sound way too good to be true but the elite are only too happy to let us all in on the secret they routinely unearth during their ascent: the true creative power of the human mind is limitless. We are – without exception – dream machines.

Every champion who ever lived started out as a dreamer. They dare to dream then merely follow their instincts to ensure they live their dream while the rest of us look for excuses to avoid ours. The first step is to recognise what that dream actually is. That's not as easy as it sounds. We are all bombarded by conflicting messages and advice from cradle to grave, which can cloud anyone's reverie. This dream is not the image projected onto us by family, friends, media, government or anyone else, but the private ideal that comes from deep within and simply won't leave us alone.

INTRODUCTION

We all have a dream. You have one. I have one. It doesn't have to be anything as extreme as aiming to become the best in the world. It might be as commonplace as to fall in love, raise a family or write a song. However mundane it may seem, each is a work of pure beauty, individually tailored and unique to us. It's the inner voice that won't shut up and go away, because it's embedded in our heart not our head.

Going for it is another story altogether, as we will hear. But whether in sport, music, science or anywhere else, the greatest dreamers trust their intuition and hone it into a vision. Then they dream up the many smaller steps to this picture-perfect future, the first of which usually tells any sporting wannabes to get down the gym. No matter if it takes years or decades, they must fend off all doubts and keep the faith that it will pay off eventually. Then when the big day comes and the world is watching, they have to let go of all this conscious effort and let their subconscious shine: in the Zone.

These moments are the true driving force and inspiration behind the relentless dedication of the sports stars in these pages – the drug that keeps them going through the pain and coming back for more. When they really go with the flow on the biggest stage, the sensation is so intense, so extraordinary that it can feel like the entire universe is flying along with them. The feats look magic from outside; indeed they *feel* so magic from within that in some extreme fields they're worth the ultimate risk. Compared to that, medals, trophies, money and all of glory's other trimmings are mere trinkets.

The three crucial stages of the dream machine can be summed up as Conceive, Believe, Achieve. It's as simple as CBA – easy to say, much harder to bring into play when each letter is shorthand for an epic battle with our own minds.

Of those who do get as far as C, the vast majority won't make it past B. It takes special mind control to manage even a shot at A, which is the process of following a dream – the real victory – not its completion. Even greater trickery is required to get beyond CBA to the big Z, daring to let go and find the Zone when all you've ever worked for is on the line.

Conceivable? Believable? Achievable? Absolutely. Easy? Dream on…

CONCEIVE

1

VISUALISATION

I f anyone dreamt up the idea of the TT (Tourist Trophy) today, they would be laughed off the Isle Of Man. This madcap 37.73-mile dash on a motorcycle round the iconic Snaefell Mountain Course's everyday roads – past houses, walls, trees and assorted equally immovable obstacles – is a rare ongoing contest where health and safety do not get a look-in. While serious injuries are no longer commonplace in Formula 1, the TT's total of 250 fatalities in 100 years continues to rise with depressing regularity.

Yet one man has ridden over the bumps and statistics that would have had him riding in the great TT in the sky long before now. John McGuinness, who became the first man to lap the track at an *average* of over 130mph, has won 23 races at the event. And counting. And, yes, his success owes much to starting young – in his case getting his first taste of riding aged just three courtesy of his father who ran a motorbike shop in the UK town of Morecambe. Just as Dan Wheldon developed a love for karting by watching Dad Clive, the ten-year-old McGuinness travelled to watch his father – also John – in the Jurby road race before the TT. He was instantly smitten with the noise, the atmosphere, the smell and the sheer unadulterated speed.

'It was always the start of the school holidays,' McGuinness tells me. 'And our holiday was to go over there and watch Dad race. We'd watch TT practice then come home when the racing was on. I'd come back kicking and screaming, crying my eyes out, wanting to go back to watch the TT rather than get on the boat back home.

'It was like that for a few years. Then I suppose it was anything I could soak up. I'd just read the books and look at the pictures. When I was about 12 a video called *V Four Victory* was released, featuring on-bike footage of TT legend Joey Dunlop for the first time. Now it's all HD but then it was a bit more agricultural. They just put a big old camera on the handlebars and away he went. But I watched it over and over and over again. I'd just sit there watching the telly, mesmerised by it. It gave me an insight and from then I always knew I wanted to do it. I just had a dream – more of a pipe dream, to be fair – and ambition to do it. I never knew how it would all pan out.'

The repeated viewing of this video had the effect of cementing the 200-corner TT route firmly into the subconscious of the 'mesmerised' young McGuinness. That's not just how his dream was born, but how he began a lifelong process of preparation for his dream career. Of course there's a big gap between sucking up the knowledge and using it in real life, but it was a gulf he was determined to bridge.

There followed a laborious process requiring McGuinness to 'beg, steal or borrow' from his family to get his racing career off the ground. He still appreciates the support and the 'always positive world' they showed him as he tried to turn his pipe dream into reality – despite the hardships involved in watching a loved one in a potentially lethal sport. McGuinness eventually did some British Superbike racing when he was 18, realising he needed experience before taking on the big one.

'You need to grow up a bit before you do the TT,' he insists. 'You're braver when you're younger but you need to be a bit more mature and understand what bikes do. You also need to know how hard the ground is if you hit it and that trees and walls are not going to move for you. I entered my first TT when I was 25 and just took it easy. I came in under the radar. I wasn't a high-profile rider. I was just enjoying riding motor bikes. We finished the race 15th and went away happy.

'I already knew where the corners were from the video – just as you can play a PlayStation game to learn these days. But you don't get to know the undulations, the cambers, the bumps, everything that comes with it. That only comes with experience. It took me four years to win my first TT. It was never going to happen overnight, but it was about time I won one in 1999. I'd learned my way round, ridden some good bikes and I was now on the best bike on the track. When I did win it, I broke a nine-year-old 250cc lap record but still it was more like relief than elation. It's weird but when you win one, you don't think you've made it, just: "What's the next challenge now?" I suppose the rest is history but I never thought I'd last here for 20 years.'

The odds are weighted heavily against any such run.

Despite the importance of experience in learning every nuance of the track, no one can assume their skill will be enough to see them through. Joey Dunlop, who still tops the all-time stats with 26 TT wins, proved the value of his accumulated knowledge by taking his last three victories at the age of 48 – four weeks before his death in an obscure Estonian road race. McGuinness, now a father, knows just what level of respect the course is due.

'Joey's wins when he was a "grey-haired old man" show there's no substitute for experience,' adds McGuinness. 'If you've still got the fitness, strength and the will to win then you can definitely still do it. But I never get cocky. I've seen some nasties around there. The place can really bite you and when it does, it bites hard. So I never get sure of it. I treat it with the utmost respect. I know more or less every bump now, but things change. Bikes change, tyres change and the engines get faster so you arrive at corners quicker. You ride different bikes – Superbikes, Superstocks, 600cc, 250cc, 125cc, everything – so there are a few curve balls that get bunged at you. But even if I get nervous I go there dead cool and calm. Racing's selfish sometimes and I work the TT around myself really. There's no secret ingredient, no magic wand, it's just a case of going there with good people and good bikes and going for it.'

A 'creature of habit', McGuinness minimises the impact of the ever-changing landscape by keeping as much consistency as possible off-track with mechanics and tyres he knows. But new challenges remain even so. It took him until 2012 to win his first Superstock race, finally removing any lingering suspicions his record was down to having the best bike. The experience brought out yet another similarity to Dunlop.

'Some people have race faces,' smiles McGuinness. 'We were all in trouble if Joey had his race face on. I don't really have a race face; usually I just look around, yapping on to people and waiting to go. Yet some people say I had a race face on for the 2012 Superstock race. Apparently before the start I just looked down the road and looked really up for it. I didn't realise. But I'd been trying to win the Superstock race for ten years and I had come second before, so I was determined to win it. That race is always a level playing field because you can go to a shop with ten grand, buy one and away you go. So to win on that was quite satisfying.'

As pipe dreams go, McGuinness hasn't done too badly. And it was all kicked off by a mesmerised young lad watching his favourite video over and over again. Still, if *V Four Victory* was the catalyst, he acted on it and took the many steps necessary to turn his dream into reality. The years may now be catching up with him, but even into his forties McGuinness has twice appeared to struggle all week at the TT only to dominate the final showpiece Senior race. So high is his level of concentration that if anyone could hold on to his motorbike long enough to stick a pin in him, he insists he wouldn't feel a thing. The key is the sheer level of data accumulated both before his debut and over the years of chucking himself around this unique location.

'During my time I've built up a library of knowledge to use when it's needed, but you do it as a subconscious thing really,' says McGuinness. 'You do it by feel, by engine vibration, stuff like that. Once you set off, the clutch is out, you go apex, apex, jump, fourth gear, third gear, 120mph, brake, feather brake, light brake, half-throttle, quarter-throttle. There's so much going on but it just happens.

'I don't prepare for the TT any differently. I just go through life kicking about with the kids. Then when the TT comes along I concentrate as hard as I can on it and take things step by step. You can't make a plan with that place, there's so much going on. You can't make a TT win up. I've tried to win TTs in different ways but you can't say: "Right. I'm going to go fast now and beat everyone." You've got to get in a good rhythm, start breathing properly and just try and get into the Zone. Then you try not to use too much energy so if it comes to a dogfight at the end you have a bit left. It's definitely a completely different world out there.'

•

American writer Ernest Hemingway famously rated motor racing as one of only three 'real' sports alongside mountaineering and bullfighting; the rest are merely 'games'. America's Pikes Peak hill climb conveniently blends the first two as racers speed up to an altitude of 14,000 feet on a 12-mile toll road that snakes around sheer Colorado cliffs. Features such as Bottomless Pit and Devil's Playground give a flavour of this 'Race to the Clouds' where mistakes can lead to the end of the road.

American motor racing legend Bobby Unser, a triple Indianapolis 500 winner, is also the most successful driver ever at Pikes Peak with 13 wins between 1956 and 1986, back when it was a dirt track rather than the comparatively luxurious tarmac in place since 2011. If the big secret to success is to live the dream, Unser took this even more literally. He attributes his success to a peculiar dedication to the cause as a kid. Not in a kart, not even on a pushbike, but in the comfort of his bed.

VISUALISATION

'When I was eight years old I'd go to sleep every night thinking about Pikes Peak,' says Unser. 'This is how I learned the Pikes Peak road, all 150 turns of it. Later I read that scientific tests had shown the subconscious mind works all the time when you're sleeping. I was already doing that, so I thought: "I was right." Your body gets its proper rest in sleep but your brain doesn't have to sleep. So it should pick up and usually it will discover something. Your subconscious mind is really important and it really works. It's one of the most powerful things there is for a racing driver. I did that throughout my career and I still do it today.'

It was during Unser's era that doctors started investigating driver performance, attaching heartbeat and blood pressure monitors to observe the body's reactions at the limit. Even though Unser's cars were heavy to handle, leaving blisters on his hands, his heart rate would not change – a sign, he reckons, that his subconscious mind had done its job.

'It works all the time,' smiles Unser. 'If you're in business, think about your business the same way. Get some sleep but think about it before you go to sleep and your subconscious mind just carries it on. It's a free thing and it has its own energy, it does its own thing. You don't wake up the next day feeling: "I thought about the car all night, I'm so tired." It isn't the case. You can do it all year round. Learn to live that way. Think about it. It always works. The subconscious mind does most of the work and it does it all free. You'll find that no matter what you do, it will be better.'

There was occasionally, though, a downside to Unser's bedtime routine. Much of his work was to improve the performance of the cars he drove, and when he drifted off thinking about that, his subconscious could get so 'radical' that it woke him up at 3am with an idea. He started keeping a notepad by his bed so his inspiration didn't get lost by his less efficient conscious mind – jotting a couple of words to jolt his memory in the morning. Team boss Roger Penske appreciated these nocturnal insights and Unser reckons they led to a measurable gain 70 per cent of the time. But the primary purpose was to keep his mind at the limit as he raced.

'When I used to watch Indianapolis, all the cars would go fast in the first half of the race then out of the blue a guy would just bin it,' he adds. 'That's a total lack of concentration: he's daydreaming. If you lose your concentration for even one second, you're history. So the idea is to learn how to concentrate. How long would you guess we can concentrate on anything, say the prettiest girl imaginable? The answer is about two and half minutes. My concentration had to be at the top for three and a half *hours*. My driving doesn't have to be at 110 per cent all that time but my concentration has to be. That comes completely down to mental training.'

In an era before sports psychology even existed, Unser would seek out every opportunity he could find to train his mind. Tyre testing and development work were golden tickets to sharpen his head and his concentration. After a lifetime of studying the subject, he reckons such 'brain tuning' is what separates out the best in any field.

'If a racing driver has the desire to get into the Zone he has to put a lot of work in,' adds Unser. 'Anyone can get there for a little bit: call them a fast qualifier. But the drivers who really stay at that peak are running at 110 per cent all the time, even if it's more important when there are problems. It's when things are worst that you produce most, so when everything goes to hell you have to produce that 110 per cent or you're not a Stirling Moss, a Jackie Stewart or a Mario Andretti. In the old days it was very dangerous to stay at 110 per cent, but the best live that way all their lives. You can't be conservative and be successful, no matter whether it's business or any kind of sport. I used to study all kinds of people and the ones who become successful and famous can go to that 110 per cent; they can live there and they can do it all the time.'

•

The world's most decorated Olympian, Michael Phelps, collected 28 swimming medals between 2004 and 2016, 23 of them gold. The foundation to his success was a brutal training schedule of countless repetitions – averaging seven miles a day, 365 days a year. He started young too: by the age of 11 he was swimming two and a half hours every day. He was just 15 when he made his Olympic debut at Sydney in 2000, reaching the 200m butterfly final but missing the medals. Just months later he broke that world record and the deluge began. His individual total now ranks him ahead of more than 150 nations in the all-time Olympic medal table.

Phelps was fortunate to grow up into the perfect physique for swimming – a long trunk and a wide arm span – but it's in his head that he shines brightest. Such a staggering, history-altering career would never have come to fruition if Phelps hadn't worked tirelessly to create vivid images of his races in advance, then steer his future accordingly. Thanks to rigorous mental training with coach Bob Bowman, he learned to write his goals down, specifying each target time to a hundredth of a second. Even in his early teens he soon found himself hitting them precisely.

'I started visualising when I was about 14,' Phelps tells

me. 'It was all about thinking how a race could go, how you want it to go and how you don't want it to go so you're ready for anything. I found it could really help me to prepare. Visualisation is important so you don't have any surprises. That means you can always stay relaxed. That was a big key in everything we did. Starting it at a very young age really helped me throughout my career.'

Visualisation is not just about being prepared for anything; it's about shaping the future to fit the mould of your private vision. It helped that Phelps was also taught never to believe in limits. As such he always dreamt big, not settling for gold alone: 'It's crazy when I look back on my career because to me it feels like I've been living a dream come true,' he smiles. 'This is everything I thought about and dreamt of as a kid. It's like: "This is real?" And it's wild. Everything I've been able to accomplish is something I've always wanted and I've done everything I ever wanted to achieve. I wanted to change the sport of swimming and take it to a new level – and I have.'

Before his racing retirement, Phelps, now a father, started his own foundation aimed at promoting water safety: 'I still swim but now it's more for peace of mind, to clear my head and get away; I'm at home in the water. But there is still a lot I want to achieve. Spending time with kids is a passion of mine. Putting a smile on a kid's face and seeing them having fun always puts a smile on my face too. Now I want to help kids accomplish their dreams.'

The fact these successful 'dream achievers' are so keen to share out the secret is a lesson in itself. They start with a big vision, then they map out their route towards it by dividing it into smaller, more manageable goal-sized images.

British athlete Denise Lewis, who won heptathlon gold at the 2000 Sydney Olympics, insists: 'I always dreamt big. I always wanted to be an Olympian, I didn't have a Plan B. So I tried to give myself the best possible chance to make it happen – by learning the trade, asking the right questions, following the sport to the best of my ability, keeping learning and wanting to take myself forward. Then, when you are one of the 20 best athletes in the world, it's about the desire, the hunger, repeating the execution and the visualisation, which plays a big part in sport.

'After my first global title I knew I'd arrived where I wanted to be. It was then about how to re-enact it, keeping the momentum going to become Olympic champion. It takes a while to understand the big occasions and grandioso stadiums are the reason you went into sport in the first place. I relished being in that environment. Yes, it was nerve-racking at first because you know it matters, but there is nothing better than those moments. That's what lit my fire when I was a kid.'

There is one higher setting on the pressure cooker. Jessica Ennis-Hill is one of the 'lucky' few to have sampled a brand of hysteria reserved for the media-appointed 'face' of the Olympics. Ahead of the 2012 London Olympics, an image of the Briton's face was even plastered over an area the size of 15 tennis courts near Heathrow Airport. Instead of crumbling under this intense focus, she thrived on it.

'It's the most surreal experience,' admits Ennis-Hill. 'I was a bit overwhelmed at first but pressure is good: you always feel nerves when you have expectations from yourself and other people. But you need that to help you perform. When you have the crowd 100 per cent behind you it brings that extra performance out. Not every athlete has experienced it, so I feel lucky I've had that chance. Nothing will compare to that.'

It's all about fixing a firm vision of excellence in the mind, a technique Ennis-Hill used to make sure she found the Zone in front of an expectant nation and planet. She was usually twitchy ahead of big events, but on the morning of her first day of competition she felt a strange sense of calm. Before a capacity crowd of 80,000 she duly went out and set an individual British record of 12.54 seconds in the 100m hurdles. The only camera angle the delirious home fans didn't see was the all-important view from inside. By contrast the athlete herself wasn't new to this footage: she'd seen it all in intricate detail long before she even set foot in the stadium.

'It takes a lot of time and mental rehearsal to get yourself into that state,' adds Ennis-Hill. 'I went through every event and made sure I pictured the perfect event. So my technique and everything was right. But I didn't let myself think about the podium and I never ever visualised winning. I didn't let myself think too far ahead; I had to stay focused on each event. I always break it down and picture the perfect race, the perfect jump and let it build that way.

'When I stepped into the Olympic Stadium for the first time I was completely ready. I had no injuries, no problems and my mind was completely focused on what I was setting out to do. That's an amazing feeling as an athlete, when you know you're 100 per cent ready. When you've got a crowd like that, nothing can stop you. When I saw my time in the hurdles I couldn't believe it. It was an incredible start. Then I was on a roll: one of those moments when things just roll on and it gets better and better.'

It snowballed from there – and Ennis-Hill's vision played out to perfection all the way until she took the tape in the next day's 800m to seal glory in style.

•

Within sport the use of visualisation – now common at the highest level – dates back over half a century. The first nations to make it a formal part of their training regime were in the Eastern Bloc during the Cold War. Then once its effects became apparent the practice spread. But even these apparent pioneers were late to the party.

'Visualising successful outcomes is nothing new,' says sports mind coach Don MacPherson. 'In fact there is evidence of our cavemen ancestors using it to bring on a successful hunt for food. Paintings of speared wildebeest were placed near exits to be the last thing they saw before venturing outside the safety of their cave. The reason we don't find pictures of cavemen being eaten by wild animals is because it is always better to visualise what you want to happen, not what you don't.

'Your imagination is your brain's Sat Nav and it can drive you to your dreams and goals. What you can "see" you can "be". A golfer should visualise the ball flying gracefully through the air then bouncing down the middle of the fairway, rather than a mental picture of the water hazard. The world's most successful golfer, Jack Nicklaus, would never hit the ball until he had enjoyed what he called his "Hollywood movies". Visualisation lets you be the producer, director and the hero of your movie.'

The simulators used to train pilots and astronauts are based on these principles – hence why Formula 1 teams now invest in picture-perfect recreations of the world's tracks. But visualisation requires no equipment other than what we have between our ears. Formula 1's youngest ever world champion, Sebastian Vettel, spent his childhood filling his subconscious mind over countless practice laps in a kart. But there is a final piece of revision needed, as I found when I met the German during his run of four straight world titles. As he sits in the garage before each qualifying lap, Vettel shuts his eyes and settles down to imagine a preview of what lies ahead. This is how he tops up his subconscious until it is primed and ready to take over.

'Qualifying is all about the one lap, so it's more intense than racing,' Vettel tells me. 'The speed is higher, too, as you have got new tyres. In the race you have to take care of the tyres and think about a lot of things at the same time: How long does the stint last? What's the objective? It's busy in a different way, whereas qualifying is very raw and just about that one lap. So you spend time going through the lap. What are the key points? Where do you have to improve compared to the run before? What do you have to look out for? Once you start the lap you are busy and there is no time left to think about anything else. So you clear your mind and you really have to be in the moment. Even if you make a mistake it's important not to think about it when you arrive at the next corner. You just focus corner by corner – and ideally let it flow.'

This aim to live 'in the moment' seems a key factor in peak performance. This also sums up an anomaly about visualisation, whose essence is to focus on the future, taking attention away from *that* present moment. That's a mind-bending philosophical puzzle to unravel, but visualisation's real-world effect is hard to dispute: somehow it lodges in our heads and steers us down the desired path when it matters.

When that path heads straight up, the stakes fly even higher. The Red Bull Air Race claims the title of the world's fastest motor sport, with planes speeding at up to 250mph between a series of pylons just 25 metres above the ground. The pilots take it in turns to set a time, similar to F1 qualifying, enduring forces of up to 10G (ten times the force of gravity) as their planes dart and twist around the course. Before each run they mentally rehearse in the calm of their hangars – spreading their hands in front of them to act as wings, swinging from side to side through a maze of drink cans laid out to represent pylons. Canada's Pete McLeod has mastered the art to the extent that when he runs through the course his entire body now reacts as if he was in the sky.

'When I'm pulling G, I don't really feel it any more because I'm so used to it,' he says. 'But to combat these high G Forces we do strain manoeuvres inside the cockpit. We've been doing them for years, so even if I mentally put myself under 10G now, my stomach muscles and my legs are automatically going to clench. It's like if you think of something that automatically gives you the shivers, it's a muscle-memory thing. It shows your brain is pretty special: after a while it will do things automatically.'

It's one thing keeping a jumbo jet level at altitude, but to race so close to the unforgiving ground requires the super-computer lodged firmly inside the human head to become the ultimate autopilot. At its best this processor still thrashes anything the technical world can throw at it. But to reach such a level, first it needs to be filled with the right data, then it needs all other programs to shut down while it focuses on the job in hand. McLeod begins this process when he is sent the map of a new track weeks before each race, evaluating the shortest lines and key challenges. Then the detailed work on what he terms his 'self-made virtual reality' takes place during practice runs in glorious 3D. He later hones his image by analysing timing screens and videos both of himself and the other pilots.

'When you first go on the track you're just trying to make it through, watching where the gates, trees and surprises are,' says McLeod. 'After that it becomes more of a subconscious thing. You don't just turn your brain off, you're paying attention to the finer details. Maybe you were at capacity earlier, but as that's put into the auto-run file you fill it with even more. That's why times get quicker from training to race day. If I want to make a change in my line I need to reprogram it all over again. So now you're doing something you haven't done before. When you come to a gate at 200mph there are thousandths of a second to make that decision. But you don't have time to think: "I got through that gate, now what's next?" It's automatic.'

•

Ground level offers extreme challenges too, not least in rallying where road-legal cars speed through anything from deserts to snowfields. Unlike F1, the drivers don't race round the same circuit lap after lap. Instead they continually face new terrain, which they learn during a brief 'recce' with their co-driver. That makes mental preparation crucial – indeed it can help you to the very top, as Walter Röhrl proves.

The German won world titles in 1980 and 1982 during the Group B machinery era which featured the most spectacular rally cars of all time. These high-powered monsters were outlawed in 1986 on safety grounds due to the increasing trail of death and destruction they left in their wake, yet Röhrl tamed them. He is still rated one of the all-time rally greats due to his apparent sixth sense in all the terrifying conditions his sport throws at its competitors. Rallies take place night and day on everything from mud to gravel to ice in weather ranging from wind, hail and snow to Röhrl's true speciality: fog. One 1980 special stage round the forests of Portugal's Arganil has gone down in legend, summing up his genius…

'I knew every year it was foggy in Arganil so I was specially prepared,' Röhrl tells me. 'Normally I would go through a recce twice, but this time I did the stage six or seven times. When I got back to the hotel I lay on the bed with my stopwatch and closed my eyes. The difference to the time I'd done before was six or seven seconds. Then I was sure I knew the stage so I started hoping the rally would be foggy. It was. When I went out everything was under control and there was not one corner where I had any kind of awkward situation. I beat the second-placed driver by four minutes 59 seconds. The rest of the 15 drivers were within 30 seconds of each other.'

Röhrl was streets ahead with the art of visualisation too. While the rest of the world's elite relied exclusively on the information coming in from their co-driver to tell them what lay ahead, he was on a different wavelength altogether.

'Every time there was fog I was so much faster than everybody else,' he adds. 'That was to do with my photo-graphic memory. If you can remember a lot, that is a big advantage in rally driving. If you think you can go fast in a Group B car with just the information from the co-driver, it doesn't work. You have to have it in your head. That way you can choose the right line, otherwise you are not perfect. My advantage was that I had whatever was going on in my head already. That meant the information from Christian (co-driver Geistdörfer) was just a helpful reminder.

'I would always prepare like that for an important stage. Sometimes you might come to the start and the stage was not ready yet so you had to wait. The other drivers would get out and chat but I stayed in the car, took the notes from Christian and read through them: "This corner has trees on the right, this one is 100mph." Then after 20 minutes they jumped into the car but I was one minute faster than everybody else.'

With special stages up to 50 miles long it's a daunting prospect even to try to lodge so much information, but Röhrl was relentless in his dedication and grateful that the demands of the period's powerful machinery made it crucial to have a 'connection between the right leg and the brain'. The relatively stable competition was another plus, enabling him to win the Monte Carlo Rally four times in five years, each time in a different car. Still Röhrl is shocked at footage of himself pelting at speed through crowds in an era where spectators would routinely line the track as they do at the Tour de France.

'This shows the power of the mind, which people don't really grasp,' he says. 'It was a big help in my career that I was able to concentrate just on rallying. Nothing else in my life was important, only to have success. If I think back to my career I never felt I had one good day, then the next day less so, except perhaps if I was sick. I didn't have peaks and troughs: in all my life I was always focused and at the same level. As soon as the countdown went "Five, four, three, two, one", I forgot everything else.'

This power doesn't have to diminish with age either. A long-time Porsche test driver, in 2013 Röhrl was in the team setting a production car lap record at Germany's iconic Nürburgring Nordschleife, a monster circuit known as the 'Green Hell' that was taken off the F1 calendar in 1976 after the fiery accident that nearly killed Austrian driver Niki Lauda. The outright mark of 6 minutes 57 seconds was set by 33-year-old German Marc Lieb but Röhrl was just seconds behind around the 13-mile behemoth – at the age of 67.

'This can transfer to other fields too,' Röhrl adds. 'For skiers it's the same. If they can really remember every jump and every compression, it's a big help. I still do it today. The Nürburgring is fun for a rally driver because it's not a normal race track. It goes up and down with compressions and jumps. That is real car driving and I love it. Of course after 20 years' testing I know every corner and every stone. But while I lie in bed in the morning I do a lap. I know everything: where I shift gears, where I line up with the trees as I go over the brow of a hill. All these things I have in my head.'

•

Of course you don't need an engine to go fast: gravity alone offers more than enough power if you give it half a chance. Franz Klammer never needed any extra oomph to reach unfathomable speeds on a hill: just give him a pair of planks attached to his feet. Klammer prevailed over a golden era for skiing, sealing a record five World Cup titles plus gold in the blue riband men's downhill at the 1976 Olympics after a truly wild ride. The secret to 'The Kaiser's' success, which included one matchless run of ten straight wins, was that he didn't consider his opponents to be his rivals. No, his main adversary was about a thousand times taller.

'I won every race in one season – except one when I lost my ski,' he gleefully recalls. 'That means you have to be better than the best one of the others. You always know one of these guys will have a very good run because they're all after you. But I'm not racing against any person, I'm racing the mountain. For a while when I was winning all the races, you just knew you were ahead of everything. So you're the boss in the ring. You know how you want to do it and you can just conquer the mountain. Then you get into the Zone. Otherwise you never get there. This happened to me a lot, and those moments almost always led to victory because you're the leader. It's not the skis or the mountain telling you what to do. You're mastering the mountain.'

It takes a big man to take on nature, but Klammer offered his mighty rival the highest respect imaginable. He didn't just show up on the day and expect mastery to fall into his lap; rather it was a steady accumulation that began in the privacy of his mind.

'The most important thing is to figure out what you have to do to perform,' he says. 'It's not up to you when you have to race so you have to be totally consistent. If the race is at midday on Saturday you cannot afford not to be on form then. You have to be spot on. So I had a mental build-up during the week, like gradually pulling back a bow and arrow. When I arrived for the course inspections on Wednesday I started pulling the bow back, building up the tension more and more until I was ready to go. Then on Saturday I let the arrow fly.

'I always used to visualise the course too. When I went to

bed I lay down and went through the downhill, then again the next morning, visualising what I was going to do. You learn that as you go through your career. Once you really have the feel the hard bit isn't the turns, because you're always in action, but the flat. If a flat section takes 20 seconds you don't know how long that takes without a clock. Still, when I was really in my heyday I could imagine the whole course within three or four tenths of my actual racing time. Then when I got to the start I'd do it all differently because if you stick to the line you are too slow...'

When Klammer raced he always seemed to be balancing precariously on the edge – of the course, of adhesion, of sanity itself. But it was this mental preparation that allowed him to push these limits when it mattered. If anything, his ability to time his visualisations accurately in advance is even more remarkable given that when you truly peak, time itself can start to feel like a fluid concept.

'For me being "in the Zone" is when everything is in slow motion so you have all the time in the world,' adds Klammer. 'In skiing you have certain crucial sections of the course when you really have to get it right. Afterwards it is flat, so if you make a mistake you will lose a lot of time and you won't win the race. But when you're in the Zone, you have a very clear picture ahead of you and you see all these little details. So you can go for it. It's a special feeling when you're in full flow. Sometimes it's a bit harder but you still have to do it. It's a sort of confidence; it's everything you have.

'I can only agree with Ayrton Senna who said when he pushed to the limit he could always find more. You have to push it constantly. Let's say one year your limit was here. Next year you have to move it out further. Otherwise you won't stay on top. True champions have that mental side sorted, being prepared and knowing what the body needs to be successful. The likes of Senna and Muhammad Ali knew exactly what they needed to perform that well. That comes both from your genes and all the experience you collect throughout the years. It's not about skill. Of course you have to have some ability, but basically it is the will. It's also crucial to have no fear of defeat.'

Even those for whom defeat is the standard diet can sample the same highs as their apparently indestructible competitors. British Olympic skier Graham Bell never quite mastered the mountain to the same extent as Franz Klammer in competition, but he shared a similar recollection of the good days, even if they were harder to forecast.

'When you do one of your best runs, you sometimes think everything is easy and time feels slow,' says Bell. 'I've had that when you do everything perfectly, but I never found a way of predicting when it would happen. In my case it was an effect rather than a cause, happening once you've got it right instead of the other way round. Even when it does you don't feel elated; because in skiing it's all over so quickly, you try not to think of anything before you get to the finish. That would distract from the sensation of being "in the moment".

'So you deliberately try to forget any mistakes. You can't start worrying about what you've just done or how much time it's cost you, because you've got other things coming up ahead. But it's important to remember the run later, particularly in training. So while you're on the run you spend the whole time forgetting what's gone before. Then you get to the finish and you've got to try and remember it again. It can sometimes take ten minutes. You can be driving back in the van to the hotel when you think, "Whoa, that's what I did!"'

Bell now works as a TV presenter and while he still takes to the mountains holding a television camera, the trips to the Zone have disappeared. He reckons you have to be in training and at the top of your game to find it. Indeed he smiles as he admits when he goes that fast these days he's just 'really, really scared…'

•

Generally no bad thing and certainly nothing to be ashamed of, fear is often our inner minds simply kicking in to keep us safe. But visualisation is one key trick we can use to quell our natural inner panic and steel ourselves ahead of a major challenge.

Britain's Andy Green must have more effective tactics than most. In 1997 he became the first man to break the speed of sound on the ground, clocking an average 763mph over two timed miles in opposite directions at Nevada's Black Rock Desert in the jet-propelled car Thrust SSC. Green remains the world land speed record holder but he is not ready to slow down yet. Now into his fifties, he is collaborating with the Bloodhound SSC Project in a bid to pass the next big milestone: 1,000mph.

Wing Commander Green is used to such speeds from his day job as an RAF fighter pilot, but even test pilots have a few thousand feet spare to attempt a recovery if something goes wrong. Phobias of flying and heights may be common but altitude is really a luxury in disguise. The fundamental principle remains that people don't kill themselves in the air; it's the ground that does the damage. That's why in a land speed record bid the load on the spinning wheels, which will reach 10,000rpm at full speed, is matched by the load on the spinning mind of the human inside.

'Getting into the Zone is a fairly common phenomenon with anyone who does high-performance racing or indeed high-performance flying,' says Green. 'The way you generate the ability for your brain to work at what appears to be abnormal speed is to remove an awful lot of the uncertainty. For the Formula 1 driver, it's about doing the same lap or at least driving the car on the total limit, thousands of times. In flying you do an enormous amount of study, simulation and practice. It doesn't happen on your first sortie, it happens when you've got a thousand hours.

'The tricky bit for a land speed record driver is that the car may only run a total of 50 times over the course of two years. So my actual practice is going to be very limited. What I need to be able to do is tap into real-world skills outside the land speed record: flying and driving – but particularly flying. I can't build up familiarity in this environment but I can give myself an artificially large capacity by tapping into the ability to do other things that look and seem familiar.'

Green's military background and range of experience ensured he shone in the selection process for the original Thrust SSC drive, which involved being thrown into all manner of demanding and unpredictable situations. On one run, he suddenly found steering left took the car right. That's hard enough to cope with on a clown's bicycle, let alone when you add a couple of zeroes to the mph column. That Green can keep a state of mental calm despite impending disaster is down to his extensive, exhaustive groundwork. Robbed of physical practice, he settles for watching endless rehearsals in the comfort of his own imaginary movie theatre.

'It's about simulation, study and mental preparation,' says Green. 'You think through all the variables so you've got a tightly tied mental picture of exactly what you expect to see. If you go to the cinema, when you haven't read the script and you don't know the story, you've got to grasp all that the first time. Normally it's the third time you watch a film that you start to see the details. I need to see them first time. So it's about trying to see the film before you go into the cinema. You read the script and watch the film in your mind, then you see how they've made it and see the differences. After you've pictured it all in your mind you can spot tiny differences because you're effectively seeing it for the second or third time.

'I'll go through the profile in detail several times so I know it, including the specifics of when I'm going to press each button. Years ahead I'm already visualising: "What will it be like? What can help me? Which display technology and helmet? Will my head be leaning forwards when I'm accelerating at 2.5G or do I need an energy-absorbing head pad? You think it through in advance so you have the right technology in the car. It's all part of picturing every aspect so when you get to the cinema the seat fits you, you're sitting in a nice place and the popcorn is ready to go.'

Short of donning a pair of slippers, Green makes it all sound rather cosy. But this mental movie-making needs to be done well in advance because the final run-up has its own demands. Land speed records are far from an individual glory run and the support team needs to work in harmony too. On the day a 'gentle momentum' builds to make sure

Green's team keep their own mental focus, to avoid either a mad rush or anyone twiddling their thumbs. Even starting up Bloodhound SSC takes ten minutes with three different engines, computer systems, hydraulics, telemetry and a range of sensors to check. Then there are minor details like the air ambulance, which Green touchingly insists is not just for him as others work in close proximity.

'Nothing happens until we've got all that into the right place,' says Green. 'There's a sequence for getting it right and it develops a life of its own. It's like the countdown for the launch of a space rocket. Over many years NASA developed the ability to stop countdowns part way through, but they never like doing it because you never pick it up seamlessly. We can do it but it's about developing that smooth flow.'

If the tick of the countdown clock is relentless, that's nothing compared to the onslaught Green faces when he begins his run. The timed mile itself lasts a mere 3.5 seconds, but that is just one part of a brutal two-minute acceleration and deceleration. He is not just holding on for grim life but monitoring a bewildering range of systems, any of which could suddenly destabilise the car. As he builds up speed, Green must also build up his mental capacity beyond average human standards – to a point where time apparently runs slower than normal.

'I need to break the run up almost second by second,' adds Green. 'That's to see how it is constructed, work out what I need to do in each moment and disregard the things I don't have to do. Do I have to watch the engine oil temperatures or all the pressure sensors in the rocket? No, the car can monitor those and find out if there's a problem. There might be a critical moment 15 seconds into the run when it becomes relevant, but until then I can turn my attention elsewhere. At that point I need to stop what I'm doing and check the pressures. If they're fine I can ignore them for 15 more seconds. It's about working out a sequence so I appear to be doing 15 things at a time when I'm really doing one thing at a time, very quickly one after another.'

This sequence is a hard enough feat when the movie sticks to the script. When a hair gets stuck in the gate or lines get fluffed, that's when the mental capacity of the leading man is pushed to the ultimate limit.

'The least stable we ever ran Thrust SSC was on the day we set the supersonic record,' says Green. 'We accelerated flat out and got up to 760-odd miles per hour, but trans-sonic the car kicked left. I put in 90-degrees steering lock and the car still wasn't responding, so I started throttling back to the minimum afterburner to regain control. As the car started sliding sideways it went just over 50-feet off-line. Those two figures – 90-degrees steering lock and 50-feet off-line – were the absolute limits of what was manageable in my mind and I hit both at the same time.

'There was a moment's pause: is that safe? The car was starting to respond, so the answer was yes. At that moment I realised I was 50 feet off-line so I was driving up the track I would be coming back down on 45 minutes later (land speed records involve two runs in opposite directions within an hour). But I had the spare capacity to realise that wouldn't matter, I'd be slowing down under a parachute by this point. That was the sort of analysis I was able to do at over 600mph, accelerating at 25mph per second. That's because I'd gone through all the various things that fitted together. I managed to assemble those within a second or two and make the decision.

I literally said "On the run line, don't worry about it, car's correcting."

'All this time there's a piece of my brain running a little mental clock saying: "In four seconds you'll have to look ahead for the measured mile because it's coming up. Four seconds later you have to check the speed. Meanwhile you have to check the fuel pressure." So I've got all that stacked up in the back of my brain. If I can generate that spare capacity in Bloodhound, which will be accelerating twice as fast, I'll be very comfortable.'

Despite his cool façade Green does admit to a buzz at the limit, but insists it is dwarfed by his excitement at the prospect of the millions of schoolchildren he hopes Bloodhound will inspire into engineering. He crams his subconscious mind with every feasible scenario so he can apparently slow time down when at the limit, yet he retains the soothing reassurance of an airline pilot over the intercom even as he grapples with a supersonic prototype going haywire.

The first step to finding the Zone, then, seems to be all about the dream itself. Elite performance begins with a vision, even if it may initially be nothing more than a blurry outline of some distant ideal. No matter how extreme the chosen endeavour, it is when a human mind takes it seriously that the fine-tuning really begins. The mind builds up an inner momentum of its own, bringing the image into sharper focus with each step we take. Once we truly conceive a plan, we're on our way.

BELIEVE

2

COURAGE

' The last second is what's most special and addictive: when you stand on the edge, you look down and you still have the chance to turn around and walk away. That last second when you step off. Then you know you are on the way. You cannot return. You pick up speed and you accelerate so fast. You can hear the air creating a really strange noise, especially when you jump from a big cliff. A couple of moments later you pull your parachute, you land, you look back up at that big mountain and you're still alive. For me this is total freedom.'

Some people really do seem born to fly. As a child Felix Baumgartner would climb trees to enjoy the view from up high and endlessly pester friends and family to throw him into the air. When he was just five years old, he drew a picture of himself parachuting to Earth with his mother Eva watching on from ground level. Felix gave Eva the drawing, only for her to hand it back to him in 1986 when he did his first real skydive, aged 17, at a club in his home city of Salzburg, Austria.

Baumgartner learned the basics of parachuting from instructor Roland Rettenbacher, whose wife was old friends with Eva. Then Baumgartner spent five years in the Austrian Army's parachute exhibition team, jumping almost every day and building up his mastery of freefall. After he left the military he worked as a motorcycle mechanic to support his skydiving. In a bid to make a living from his stunts he switched to BASE jumping: an edgier, even more extreme pursuit that involves jumping not from an aeroplane but from the Buildings, Antennas, Spans and Earth of its acronym.

Few of Baumgartner's fellow BASE jumpers shared his freefall expertise, but he recognised every leap in his new discipline carried major risks, involving locations from which no human of sound mind should really consider taking the fast way down. So he aimed to jump as rarely as possible but with maximum publicity each time. The haul of records soon began. Baumgartner's 1999 leap from Kuala Lumpur's Petronas Towers was then the highest from a building, and his jump from Rio de Janeiro's Christ the Redeemer statue in the same year was the lowest. For a decade he jumped off ever higher buildings as they sprung up around the world, along with feats like a wing suit crossing of the English Channel. His skill level kept rising, as did his self-belief. This constant quest for ever greater challenges led the Austrian to his big finale: the world's highest ever freefall.

•

Despite his life at the limit, the 'Fearless Felix' moniker that will follow Baumgartner for ever is not – entirely – accurate.

We all share an evolutionary instinct for survival that tells us whether something is likely to earn an early introduction to our Maker. It goes by many names such as 'inner critic', 'judge', or 'Self 1' to borrow *Inner Game* author W Timothy Gallwey's expression. The most evocative of all must be 'Monkey Mind', how Chinese Buddhists have long described the nagging voice in our heads that flits from thought to thought, like a monkey swinging from tree to tree in the jungle.

Even the daredevils who spend their lives chasing Baumgartner's concept of 'freedom' know this voice, which acts as an automatic sprinkler system for our more outlandish flashes of inspiration. That certainly applies to all the previous aspirants to the existing freefall record, set in 1960 by America's Joe Kittinger. When Kittinger jumped out of a balloon 19 miles up, his prime motivation was not entertainment or glory; he was part of an American government research programme into pilots ejecting from the US Air Force's new range of high-altitude aeroplanes. With no such formidable funding and backup, other record attempts had since ended fatally.

Nonetheless, when Felix Baumgartner first heard about the feat he was hooked, not least by one tantalising detail: during his descent Kittinger had reached a speed of 614mph (988 km/h). Just shy of the speed of sound.

To become the first human being to break the sound barrier without an engine, Baumgartner would have to go even higher – 24 miles – and raise the stakes to similar heights by resisting any temptation to resort to his stabilising 'drogue' chute. Kittinger used one of these to tame the horizontal spins that inevitably result during a plummet through the stratosphere's thinner air. If the rotations get too fast our blood apparently starts to exit the body through the only way out it can find: our eyeballs. That doesn't sound like an instinctive basis for survival. So Baumgartner's first challenge, long before he could have any chance to use his skydiving know-how to tame any outward spin, was to learn how to bring his spinning Monkey Mind under firm control.

'You should never override your inner safety mechanism,' Baumgartner tells me. 'That's one thing I would never do, which is why I'm still alive after 25 years of this. The big fear was that I would hurt myself. That's always a part of my jumps: no matter how much you prepare there's always a good chance of hurting myself. That's why I always try to find the right people to work with. I listen and learn from them to ensure it's not going to happen. The people who failed in attempts to break the speed of sound in the past tried to go from zero to hero. But I'm a big fan of preparation: the more you prepare, the better you perform. Like any athlete a skydiver has to work out and be disciplined. I have lots of skills and lots of discipline. I would not go in for just one jump because it's overwhelming. That's why we did a lot of jumps to build up.'

Five long years of preparation for Baumgartner and his Red Bull Stratos team may seem excessive for any mere 'stunt', but this is the discipline required to go to the limit and beyond. Felix worked his way up with practice runs from 15 and 18 miles, while his team twice sent his capsule up to the record-breaking height without anyone aboard. Eventually there was only one remaining unknown: what would happen to a human body as it crossed the sound barrier without a vehicle.

Of course, such a gradual build-up also allows the Monkey

Mind time to lodge a protest. The main problem with taking human beings to such heights is the so-called Armstrong Limit: an altitude of about 11 miles named not after astronaut Neil but US Air Force doctor Harry George Armstrong, who identified the point where the body's fluids start to vaporise with deadly effects. That's why pressure suits are essential.

During one 1960s high-altitude test flight in an unpressurised F-104 fighter, the pilot gave the matter-of-fact radio message: 'My glove came off. Goodbye...' before he lost consciousness and died. Keen amateur New Jersey skydiver Nick Piantanida was ascending on his third bid for Kittinger's record in 1966 when his face mask apparently depressurised nearly 11 miles above Minnesota. His ground crew hastily brought his capsule down but Piantanida fell into a coma from the brain and tissue damage and died four months later.

Still, for Baumgartner the very pressure suit that would be keeping him alive turned into a major issue. He looks like an action hero should, all chiselled looks and a forearm tattoo reading 'Born To Fly'. Yet for a skydiver craving 'total freedom', the suit severely limited his movements and even made him claustrophobic. Felix hid the problem from his team until it became so extreme that he once drove to Los Angeles airport in tears and flew home to Austria – all to avoid a scheduled practice in the suit.

'In the beginning it was not a big deal because I only had to spend an hour in the suit,' sighs Baumgartner. 'But later in the project we had a full dress rehearsal in a pressure chamber so we could simulate altitude and temperature. The main goal was to spend five hours inside the capsule practising the procedure, pushing the dials and buttons.

But I knew I could not do five hours in the suit because when you put your visor down, you're locked into your own little world. The only thing you can hear is yourself breathing – and after a while I would get anxious. I did not know who to talk to because I was supposed to be the hero, but I was already getting a big problem on the ground inside the suit. So I needed help.'

It can take even more courage to admit to such a weakness. Baumgartner had never turned to anyone for help before, but he ended up meeting sports psychologist Michael Gervais. Felix claims they did nothing special, just 'talking and talking', but part of the process was getting him to make friends with the suit, three of which had been tailor-made for him at the cost of $1.8m. After all, it would keep his blood from boiling. Nonetheless it took three weeks to build up the minutes and hours until he could finally endure enough time in the suit to play the lead.

Once that worry was safely behind him, the Baumgartner Monkey Mind could really let rip with all the others. Even leaving obvious risks aside, the entire event was going to be televised live around the globe, from before he stepped into the capsule until he hopefully landed back on terra firma. Most Monkey Minds get jittery about appearing in public but few have an audience stretching to millions.

'If you do something like this and everybody's watching, you lie in your bed and you roll around the night before,' he admits. 'You think: "Tomorrow I'm doing something that takes about seven hours and the whole world is watching every move. Everything I say is going to be observed by a lot of people." This is pressure.

'Of course you have doubts in quiet moments. Before we

went up I had two hours to wait because of a delay caused by too much wind. I was in the locker room waiting, and you sit there and think about things like the friends you have lost and the failures we had while we'd been working on this project. You think about it and you hope it's not going to happen today. You prepare for the worst and hope for the best. Then you put everything out there and you hope it's good enough.'

The final build-up to a mission like this is invariably fraught. Even on the big day itself the two-hour ascent was dominated by Baumgartner's struggle to deal with an apparent problem with mist on his visor that could have left him blind on the way back down. The live audio feed was cut while technicians in Mission Control at New Mexico's Roswell Airport – including Joe Kittinger himself at the age of 84, the only voice Felix could hear over the intercom – reassured him about his electrically heated faceplate. They finally persuaded him to unplug the main power supply to prove it would automatically revert to the 'High' setting under the sole energy of the batteries in his chest pack. Even then, only through his methodical approach was Felix able to overcome these final internal battles.

'When you're inside that capsule in a pressure suit you're locked in and so limited,' he adds. 'If anything goes wrong there's not much you can do. We prepared for many scenarios, but the reality is if it happens you're screwed. So I knew I had to lead every situation. That's why I addressed the problem with my visor early on. Once you get outside the capsule, if the visor is not working you have to do the whole thing blindfolded. As long as I was inside I had time, I was pressurised and I had protection. That was why we took so long sorting this out, to make sure you're always one step ahead. If it gets out of sequence it's like standing on somebody's toes in dancing, so we always try to get back into the sequence as fast as we can. When you're the leader of the game you perform well. During the ascent I was always leading.'

This leading man also knew the script dictated he was committed to diving as soon as he left the (relative) comfort of his capsule because once it was fully inflated, his spacesuit would no longer fit back through the door. Show time...

•

When Felix Baumgartner took one small step out onto his capsule's external platform, he found himself gazing down on Planet Earth from 24 miles up. But this was no time to stand and stare. He uttered a few pre-crafted words: 'Sometimes you have to get up really high to understand how small you really are...' Then he jumped.

Seconds later he was frantically working to tame a violent horizontal spin that could have resulted in him passing out. Whereas skydivers get used to reacting to the feel of air rushing past, with less of it about in the stratosphere it was 'like swimming without feeling the water' and Baumgartner had to wait to see in which direction he was pushed before he could react. Thanks to a life spent in the skies he eventually regained control. As the air around him thickened his speed gradually slowed to standard terminal velocity (about 200mph), and Baumgartner sailed home to nail a mission that had taken five years to prepare but under ten minutes to complete. With a top speed of Mach 1.25 (843.6mph) he had become the first human to break the sound barrier under his own steam.

Four decades on from the last Moon landing, Baumgartner's 2012 feat may rank as the 'one giant leap' moment for two entire generations. Before his jump, the Austrian – born in 1969, the year of Apollo 11 – even dined with Neil Armstrong to compare notes and enquire about what goes through a man's mind at such a moment. In the last year of his own life, the veteran astronaut insisted he had been so focused on doing every manoeuvre by the book there was no spare time for any extraneous thoughts or emotion. That only kicks in when you later look back at the footage and realise what happened. Prescient, as it turned out. The question Felix Baumgartner is most often asked is: 'What was it like up there?' but the view was the last thing on his mind. He was in the Zone.

'When you're at the exit point you're so focused and determined you don't see or hear anything around you,' says Baumgartner. 'In the first part of the jump I spun five times anticlockwise and 22 times clockwise. I did not think about anything else because I was so focused on stopping that spin. It was a lot of work and took almost a minute. For the rest of the flight I was more relaxed because I was just trying to fly in the right direction, towards my rescue teams on the ground. While I was flying down my visor started fogging up but luckily it did not get too bad. At 5,000 feet (1.5km) I had to pull my parachute. Then I realised I'd broken the speed of sound.'

Sounds simple. But that's because 14 October 2012 was far from the first time that Felix Baumgartner had gone through the sound barrier under his own steam. In fact he had done the whole thing many times before – just not in the public gaze.

'I visualised this jump from the moment I heard about Joe's original record,' Baumgartner tells me. 'I have done this jump a thousand times in my mind – just like every other jump I've ever done: Rio's Jesus, the cave in Croatia, the highest building in the world. I lie in my bed and come up with a proper game plan. I'm really good at pre-programming my mind and I always do this. I think about how it will feel, what it will look like. The more I think about it, the more it becomes reality. When I finally do it for real, 99 per cent of the time it works exactly like I'd visualised and it feels the same way it felt in my mind.'

As we've already heard, the aim of visualisation is more than just preparation; it's about taking control of the future and tailoring it to our liking. By continually dreaming of his freefall from the edge of space Baumgartner painted a vivid picture and created a momentum in his mind that made success all but an inevitable consequence.

'It's the power of will and the focus you have,' he says. 'When I was standing out there on the exterior step it felt almost how I expected. This is the key. The more you can turn thoughts into reality – from a mindset perspective – the better you are. Mental preparation is crucial: you have to ensure you find the right mindset for that moment. Then when you are finally in that position there will be no surprises. You pre-program your mind and it works exactly the way you expect. Most of the time…'

•

This process is the source of the unerring self-belief needed to do the extraordinary. Still, you or I can't just sit down and talk ourselves to the top: the mind isn't fooled quite so easily.

No matter which field we choose, the inner belief required to create history is instead born of years of homework.

What separates the stuntman from other champions is the fact they're playing for stakes rather higher than a medal or a trophy. It is entirely up to daredevils to get themselves out in one piece when things don't quite go according to plan, no matter how meticulous their mental preparation. That's why the courage required to throw yourself out of a balloon requires the backup of a life's practice. The Monkey Mind can be tamed even in such extremes – but only if it trusts that you know what to do in any circumstance, especially when the reality doesn't match the vision: 'If something goes wrong it takes a lot of skills to save that moment,' admits Baumgartner. 'If you face something unexpected it takes a different mindset and different skills.'

By the time he found the Zone and broke the sound barrier, Baumgartner was the veteran of 2,500 parachute jumps. Only with such an extensive background was he able to control his mind at the crucial moment: letting go of conscious thought while paradoxically being ready to react to any hiccup. As such, even 'Fearless Felix' is left with nothing but awe and disbelief at the intrepid achievement of the man talking him down from Mission Control, whose freefall records had lasted for over 50 years.

'You have to hand it to Joe Kittinger; I have a lot of respect for that guy,' says Baumgartner. 'When he was standing there 19 miles up he had only done 33 skydives. That's nothing: when you've done 33 skydives you're a bloody beginner. I remember when I had 33 skydives I could barely make it out of an aeroplane. Yet he's standing there at that altitude. There's not much difference between 19 miles and 24 miles:

it's a very hostile environment and if something goes wrong you will die.

'If your equipment malfunctions, you will die within 15 seconds. So we look at what he was wearing and we laugh about it these days. What the hell is that crappy parachute and that crappy spacesuit? But we have to remember Joe had the latest and greatest equipment available at the time, so they trusted it. He also had a drogue chute that came out in freefall to stabilise him – so he had a bit of backup. But still, with the little knowledge they had back in the 1960s, what he did is really big. The biggest difference to me is that with 33 skydives I would never have done it. I'd have said, "Guys, I'm still not a fully-trained skydiver so I cannot do it."'

The reality is that Baumgartner may not even have made it far enough down the line to make that choice thanks to his issue with the pressure suit. Here's the other big difference to consider: the funding for Kittinger's stunt came not from a multinational drinks manufacturer on a publicity hunt but the American military. They don't tend to wait around for anyone to get their mind in order: when they say, 'Jump' you really do say, 'How high?' Rightly or wrongly, that is what military training is all about.

The daredevils in these pages are acting voluntarily: their love for the process is what gives them the incentive to keep chasing their dream throughout its many ups and downs. This is how they maintain the energy to tame their Monkey Mind even in the face of extreme danger. But to put yourself – and others – in peril because of what someone else wants is another matter, requiring a total bypass of our inner voice. The military obsession with following orders is really an institutionalised form of Monkey Mind control, crucial in the hellish environments into which it thrusts its personnel.

After his time as a high-altitude pioneer Kittinger became a combat pilot in Vietnam, once ejecting at faster than the speed of sound when his F-4 was hit by an enemy missile. He was then tortured as a prisoner of war. All his other achievements must pale into insignificance when it comes to mental fortitude. Even so I was taken aback when a former paratrooper from the Special Boat Service, the elite of Britain's Royal Navy, insisted any of his old colleagues would have carried out Baumgartner's jump without fuss or hesitation.

Red Bull has its own pressures too: they generate publicity by showing people pushing themselves to the limit, but they know it would backfire if it were to cause serious injury or worse. In Kittinger's day there was no global audience watching live on *YouTube* or rolling news stations; indeed if it had gone wrong no one might ever have found out. During one early practice, the cords of Kittinger's parachute wrapped around his neck, sending him into a 120rpm flat spin. He fell unconscious and was jolted awake only when his reserve chute deployed 3,000 feet above the ground. Even during Joe's record leap itself his right glove malfunctioned and his hand swelled to double its normal size – but he didn't let on in case his ground crew aborted the mission. When I asked Felix if it was Joe's military mentality that saw him through, he immediately agreed.

'The military mind is the easy mind because they just function,' Baumgartner smiles. 'The military don't ask "how do you feel?" and "what do you want to do?" If you do not deliver they just ask somebody else and replace you. So this is a different mindset and different skills. I spent five years in the Austrian military, so I also had a military background but it's nothing compared to Joe Kittinger. He was in the US Air Force, he got shot down twice and he spent a lot of time at the "Hanoi Hilton" (Hỏa Lò Prison where American prisoners of war were held in Vietnam).

'But we needed guys like Joe: we call them "pre-astronauts". The skills they developed and all the knowledge they gathered was important for going into space and going to the Moon, because they were testing spacesuits. Now we know it works and that humans can survive up there we can take it to the next level. Everything they accomplished and the data they gained from it was available to us. Now we are doing the same thing. Everybody takes the knowledge from everybody else then they push it to the next level. This is why we have progress.

'They say "the sky's the limit" and that's definitely the way it is. I met a guy who was an old-school freestyle skier years ago. He became the world champion with one backflip on skis. When he said you would eventually see guys doing double and triple flips they thought it was just science fiction. These days it is reality. Remember when they did the first backflip on a motorcycle? Now they do double backflips and a single backflip is just standard. So sport will always progress. Equipment gets better and our knowledge gets more developed so I don't think it will ever stop. At some point somebody will put up their hand and say: "Hey, I'm going to kick Felix Baumgartner's ass." I just hope it's not for many years...'

What's most intriguing about pioneers is how soon they are followed down their path as others see what is possible. In fact Baumgartner's freefall height record lasted only two years before it was surpassed by self-funded Google executive Alan Eustace, although his use of a drogue chute for stability – so effective he didn't spin once – meant he didn't beat Felix for speed. Mighty as Eustace's feat is, it is easier to follow rather than lead, hence why history always hails the first to break new ground. Joe Kittinger's original freefall record is a rare exception that lasted half a century, but Baumgartner has many early pioneers to thank. Chuck Yeager ranks high in the list as the first human to break the speed of sound at all, albeit with rocket power, on 14 October 1947 – precisely 65 years before Baumgartner's dive.

Baumgartner adds: 'At the time everybody thought if you want to break the sound barrier you will die, because a lot of pilots did die trying to break the speed of sound. But then Chuck Yeager somehow went through the sound barrier. From that moment everybody knew it was possible. Then they went on to Mach 2 and Mach 3 in hypersonic planes. I call those guys mapmakers. They draw a map then everyone else takes this map and they follow the roads.

'It was always important to me to become a mapmaker. I always wanted to do something that people respect and say, "Hey cool, we never thought this was possible. Now we know we can take it to the next level." I hope I am a mapmaker. We proved to the whole world that you can survive supersonic speed in freefall. Nobody thought this would be possible but we broke that chain of thought. Now everybody knows it is possible and they'll take it to the next level.'

Most enchantingly, when you do take the plunge you don't necessarily have to chart each new route entirely under your own steam. We've played down the input of external fortune, but when you aim high it's uncanny how things sometimes just work. Even Baumgartner benefited from what appears to be pure luck throughout his career. It wasn't just during his jumps that a force of gravity kicked in: he received nudges in the right direction – starting with having his local skydiving club sponsored by Red Bull, long before they dominated the world's action sports. Right to the end there was apparent help to be had from above. A few days before his big finale, the first attempt was postponed due to strong winds. The balloon they had inflated had to be written off – so on the day of the eventual launch Felix really was in the last-chance balloon. But it could have been much, much worse...

'If we had lost our last balloon we would have postponed the project to 2013,' says a rueful Baumgartner. 'We'd have lost the whole momentum because everybody was fired up, with the media and everything. We had built a little city out in Roswell because there's nothing else there, but we would have had to shut it down. Then as it turns out we wouldn't even have been able to pull off the jump at the same time in 2013 because that's when the US Government had its shutdown: the Federal Aviation Authority was not working – and without the FAA there's no record verification.

'So sometimes it's ironic that those little details completely screw things up. We were damned lucky we didn't lose that last balloon and we were able to launch it. I don't know if it's God or luck or whatever, but sometimes you just have to have that luck. In the end we were so lucky because otherwise we would still have been sitting on our asses. 2014? Damn... Kittinger's getting old, I'm getting old. It's hard to keep that focus and attention for so many years because nobody's interested any more and at a certain point everybody says, "You know what? Screw it." So I'm glad it's over. Now I can put my focus on something else…'

•

It seems mastery of airflow is a transferable skill. One of Baumgartner's compatriots, Hannes Arch, made the most of his upbringing in Austria's mountains, climbing and taking up hang-gliding aged 15 before a switch to paragliding. Another pioneering BASE jumper, Arch was the first man to leap from the North Face of the Eiger in the Alps and the first to land a paraglider on a hot air balloon. He then allowed himself the comparative comfort of an aeroplane, going on to fend off the world's best aerobatic pilots and win the 2008 Red Bull Air Race world championship.

'If you do all those really dangerous sports you know exactly where you are,' Arch told me in 2014. 'Nobody wants to die, especially me, because I really love life. Sometimes you turn around and don't jump because you know it would be dangerous. These sports teach you to handle risk, so they are the perfect preparation for air racing: focus is the most important factor for surviving dangerous sports, but also to be fast in air racing. The interesting thing is that if you are in this mindset – focused 100 per cent on flying without having to deal with thoughts of crashing or risk – you get really fast. And when you get really fast you realise you are always really safe. When you start to risk and jeopardise safety it slows you down.'

Arch sure was fast. He won 11 races, finishing in the top three for five straight years. Elsewhere this 'lover of life' invented the Red Bull X-Alps: a punishing dash from

Salzburg to Monaco by foot or paraglider. He also used his skills as a helicopter pilot to help out with charity efforts in Nepal by ferrying supplies to remote mountain communities. He was flying a helicopter from a hut in his beloved Austrian mountains when he crashed and died just shy of his 49th birthday in 2016.

It all serves as a moving reminder that flying will always carry risks, no matter who is at the controls. Even to attempt an air race up against those odds seems reckless, yet, as Arch points out, the irony is that the act of seeking 100 per cent focus makes you both fast and safe. Air racing is such an extreme sport that it forces pilots into clearing their minds – fast – and it's the same with all who push to the edge.

This is why daredevils tend to share remarkable disdain for the term 'adrenalin junkie', insisting the meticulous planning behind their exploits proves how far that is from reality. Felix Baumgartner even prefers the term 'risk manager', which makes it sound like he spent all his time working in a bank. He now uses his hard-earned skills to manage risk in everything from helicopters to racing cars.

When I asked Baumgartner to sum up his primary message to children; this is what he said: 'I think it's important to have discipline and patience. You should focus on the goal and you should not let go of it, no matter what it is – and you should not listen to anyone who says you cannot do it. You just have to make up your mind, think about what you want to do and make sure you don't lose the vision of your goal.

'It's not just kids but adults too. It's never too late to do something different. Many people have goals, then when they face the first or second problem they say: "It's too difficult. Forget it, I'll find another goal." Ten years later they've had ten different goals and never accomplished anything. So you have to focus on one goal and make the judgement: "Is it really important to me? Am I willing to invest all the blood, sweat and tears to reach that goal? Am I willing to go the extra mile?" If the answer is yes, go for it. That's pretty much what I did and this is where it brought me. Everyone said I could not break the speed of sound. But I proved them wrong...'

•

You don't have to take to the skies to know how tough our inner mental battle can be. For a seeker of the true limit of the mind's power, there is surely no higher arena than a boxing ring. Step through the ropes, then look into the eyes of someone preparing to pummel you into submission. You're soon guaranteed to find out who would win the scuffle between the positive and negative sides of your head.

'Marvelous' Marvin Hagler is one of the sport's all-time greats, having been a major player in a vintage era for middleweight boxing in the 1980s that featured the likes of Roberto Duran, Sugar Ray Leonard and Thomas 'Hitman' Hearns. Even in this supreme physical contest, Hagler insists the mind is a crucial component.

'I really believe boxing is the toughest sport in the world,' Hagler tells me. 'It is a game where you have to be both physically and mentally ready. It doesn't work one without the other. Boxing is a fancy dance where you show them what you can do with your hands – but it's also about using the mind. You need the mind to set up the shots, you've got to have hunger and you've got to have that killer instinct. But first you need the mind to give you the courage to put on a pair of gloves and go out there to do combat against another opponent. You're the one going into the ring and there's no backup.'

While bodily harm is a side-product of many of the sports in this book, only in boxing is it the aim of the game, with the knockout the ultimate objective. Hagler still describes boxing as an art, labelling today's Ultimate Fighting Championship 'brutal' and better suited for the 'bar room'. Yet this American had to learn the art of patience before the art of war as his first world title shot only arrived in his 50th professional fight. That leaves plenty of time for doubt to arise but Hagler never entertained the slightest scepticism about whether he would end up getting his big break – just as he instantly dispelled any attempt by a negative thought to force its way into his head during the fights themselves.

'You always have to try not to lose faith,' adds Hagler. 'I always knew my day would come one day and I never doubted it would happen. When? You don't know. So you constantly have to keep working, keeping your mental attitude together and staying in tip-top shape. Then during a fight you throw doubt out. You don't even let it creep in. I guess it starts when you first start boxing and you start to be a little cocky. That's because you don't have the confidence. Once you know what you can do with your hands and how smart you are with the boxing game, your confidence starts to come and then everything comes together.'

Hagler's distinction between cockiness and confidence is intriguing, but by his 60th fight everything came together in style with his undisputed world middleweight championship on the line for the 11th time at Las Vegas in 1985. His opponent Thomas 'Hitman' Hearns expected the typical measured start from the champ, who generally preferred to start slowly and build up. Instead Hagler gave a masterclass of unabated aggression in a first round often rated among the greatest in boxing history. Hagler later sustained a cut above his right eye that was twice inspected by the ringside doctor in the third and final round, but even that didn't stop the onslaught. He eventually floored Hearns with a left-right combination and a right hook after just 7 minutes and 52 seconds.

'The biggest rivalries and the biggest fights mean more headaches and pains so you've got to prepare yourself,' says Hagler. 'It's like when you fight an opponent in their own backyard: it's tougher so you've got to train that much harder. During the "War" against Hearns I realised you can't keep him standing. As long as he's standing he can do damage. But the biggest rewards come for winning those big fights. If you achieve it, you know: "I sacrificed and I accomplished what I was after."'

Hagler's greatest sacrifice was that he famously incarcerated himself to train ahead of his big fights. This was as much about getting his head together as his body: 'I put myself in jail during training because that's what I believe you have to do. That comes with the sacrifice – and it's about believing it will work. It's about getting your mind focused on what you want to accomplish, which is basically to knock the junk out of the other guy. So you've got to be in tune with what you're doing – and you've really got to be focused. In boxing it only takes a second and your lights can be out.'

When I asked what mental tricks he used to get in the Zone, Hagler was just as instantaneous in his reply: 'I was very easy: all you've got to do is give me the name of my opponent. That's all. From there you would start to build up a lot of hatred and take that aggression to get yourself mentally and physically ready. It's not a hatred for him personally. It's just a hatred you have to build up to win. After the fight you see fighters hug and kiss and make up. But inside the ring there is no love...'

•

Hatred is an extreme example, but everyone needs to find their own way to silence the inner critic – as even sport's most cocksure figures can be plagued by damaging self-doubt. Under Steve Waugh's captaincy around the turn of the millennium, Australia so dominated Test cricket they won a record 16 Test matches in a row – plus the 1999 World Cup. Along the way Waugh joined the elite to score more than 10,000 test runs. Yet even this steely Australian – who answers to nicknames 'Iceman' and 'Man-O'War' – admits he was forever doing battle with the Monkey Mind's demons.

'Of course doubts creep in every day,' Waugh tells me. 'It's like an internal boxing match inside your head, negative versus positive. You've got to accept that's going to happen all the time. So I had tricks. It's a matter of getting rid of the negative and bringing the positive stuff to the front when you really need it. You let the doubts creep in and think negatively when it doesn't count – in between the big moments. Then when you need to switch on you've got to say, "Let's get back on the game. You're good enough, you've done it before. This is why you're doing it. Concentrate..."'

Waugh learned these tricks the hard way after plenty of brutal bouts lasted the distance inside his own mind: 'I don't think I was mentally tough in the first couple of years. In fact I was mentally weak because I doubted myself a lot and things didn't go well. That's when you learn a lot about yourself. The key is not to go back to the bad habits. I gradually toughened up; towards the end of my career I had the mental side pretty sorted. But you can't become lazy and think it will happen because you've got a tough mind. You've got to work on the basics so that mental toughness can make that extra two or three per cent.'

Cricket offers the chance to take the edge off your opponents too. Purists may weep but Waugh's Australian team mastered the art of 'sledging', mocking opposing batsmen (who are always outnumbered eleven to two) in the gaps between deliveries to knock them out of their stride. The Aussies were dealt their fair share of abuse in return but Waugh was famous for an impenetrable, blinkered stare as he batted. In fact he had to trick himself to block out all extraneous distractions, but a useful by-product was that this often fooled his adversaries as well.

'A lot of the time it's bluff,' admits Waugh. 'Part of the mental side of sport is letting the opposition think you're tougher than you really are. Often your form hasn't been that good or you're not feeling great, but if you go out with a positive attitude and positive body language the opposition thinks you're in control of your game. In my case it was about getting onto the field quickly and having a good look around before the bowlers or fielders could get set. That meant I was putting a flag in the ground: it is my turf and you're coming onto my patch. If you walked out there slowly, it felt like you were coming in on their turf. So you teach yourself to do things in a positive way to take the initiative and get the upper hand.

'It really is a one-on-one battle out in the middle, batsman versus bowler. But if you give off that good aura, you're often on top straightaway. It's enjoyable when it works, but you don't just smile when you're enjoying yourself. The great bowlers like Curtly Ambrose never gave any indication of what they were thinking either. That's even more intimidating because it puts doubts in your mind. You're never quite sure: is he trying to get you out or actually trying to hurt you?'

India's Kapil Dev, one of cricket's all-time top wicket-takers, shared Waugh's knack of accentuating the positive with both bat and ball. 'Of course you're afraid of failure when you first walk into the ground,' he tells me. 'But once you're on the field it's never negative. Your natural ability and hard work should take over. When things go wrong or you don't perform, many sportsmen curse themselves, but I was not that type of cricketer. I never like to waste my energy. In cricket, things so often don't go your way. Do you curse yourself or say you're lucky? You take things in your stride. If you have the ability and you've worked so hard you will come to that Zone – but only if you are mentally and physically there. When the days are good, don't let them go, or that Zone. Certain days God has created for you.'

Paradoxically Dev believes it's when things are going well that you need the courage to swallow a dose of humility instead. 'When you're on top not many people tell you about your mistakes,' he adds. 'But it won't help if people keep saying you're brilliant. So I always had a few friends, family and coaches who had to tell me only what I was doing wrong: "From outside this is what we see that's negative." You need people like that who keep telling you your mistakes, even when you're at your best. When you're not playing well, that's the time you start working. Then when you're playing well, that's the time you start working harder than ever.'

Of course it doesn't take much for a good spell of form to bite the dust. When it does, the Monkey Mind is always ready to fight back with a right hook of its own. Top-class sport brings any negativity to the boil, not least because it's a world where every move is analysed *ad nauseam* – by the other players, the crowds and millions watching on TV. When things go wrong on a cricket pitch the walk back is one of the loneliest on Earth.

England test cricketer Marcus Trescothick raised eyebrows when he admitted to a 'stress-related illness' that led him to quit the international scene in the middle of a distinguished career in 2006. He later revealed the lifestyle of touring for such long periods away from his wife and young daughter triggered anxiety attacks, which he had first experienced during a primary school trip to Torquay. When he was finally diagnosed with depression it opened a debate on a hitherto taboo subject in the macho world of sport. If you own up to physical injury or illness, no problem. But mental illness? No matter if the cause is biological, genetic or a chemical imbalance, that is just not cricket.

'Full credit to Marcus Trescothick; that was a brave decision,' says Waugh. 'It really opened the door for other sportspeople to say: "I'm feeling pretty bad, maybe it's OK for me to do the same." It wasn't that way 20 years ago. You just gutsed it out; that was part of being a professional cricketer. But times have changed and for a good reason. You've got to look after the health of your players. As Australians it's not in our nature to be open about it, but I've seen players who have suffered the same things. You see they're down and they want to go home. Every sportsperson has been there. It builds up to a point where you think: "I've got to get out of here."

'After playing professional cricket for 20 years I understand that. I've had that loads of times, particularly early on. It took me 13 Test matches to be part of a winning side and three and a half years until my first century. So I had a lot of self-doubt. You spend so much time away from family, you feel really homesick when things don't go well. If you have any issue – personal or financial – you're stuck in a hotel room by yourself watching a TV show you don't enjoy, ordering room service you don't want. I remember hotels on the Indian subcontinent when you had to wait three hours for a phone call home. You're on for ten seconds, then the phone line drops out. You try to get over that the best you can but things can start getting in your head.'

•

The cause of mental torment can be indisputably physical. Waugh's fellow Australian Mick Doohan won five consecutive motorcycling world championships on the top-level 500cc machinery in the 1990s. But his triumphant run was topped and tailed by two huge crashes, the second (at Spain's Jerez circuit in 1999) ending a career that could have been curtailed by the first – at the Netherlands' Assen in 1992 before his first title.

After surgery on Doohan's broken tibia and fibula, the complications were so grave the doctor at the Dutch hospital wanted to amputate the leg from the knee down. Only the intervention of Dr Claudio Costa saved the Australian's career. Costa headed motorcycling's travelling clinic, regularly courting controversy for his determination to get riders back on the bike, broken bones and all, confident in our underused ability to self-heal. No chance this time. Costa resorted to sewing Doohan's legs together for a fortnight to allow the left leg to act as donor for the right, which had started to turn black. The eternally grateful Doohan's mindset may have helped too.

'I don't know whether the mind can make you heal any quicker,' Doohan tells me. 'But I was able to keep pushing myself forward rather than feel sorry for myself. A common thread between positive thinkers is that there are no rear-vision mirrors. Everything happens ahead of us so we can't change anything: "Let's move on, this is where I want to go..." In daily life if you're taken out by a car or some other devastating accident there are often questions like: "Why did it happen?" Motor sport leaves no doubt. We know accidents, injuries and even fatalities are a real possibility. So when they occur you don't sit around and dwell on them.'

This doesn't mean that Doohan abandoned fear altogether, far from it. After an experience like that, no one needed to remind him of the stakes every time he sat on a bike. But he didn't shy away from the reality of the risks he took. Instead he used fear as a positive motivational tool to push even closer to the limit.

'Everyone's got fear,' he insists. 'You need a healthy amount of fear to keep yourself safe. But you've got to use that fear. The more experience you have and the more understanding of what you're doing, the further that fear is pushed to the side. You've got to push to the edge of that fear boundary to expand it. If you consistently push that boundary, it keeps moving. Everybody has a different level, so you've got to know where your line is, of fear that something's going to go wrong. Then you've got to run along its edge, as close as possible but without stepping over it – that's when accidents happen – making it more elastic so you have more margin. The closer you can stay to that limit all the time, the more it keeps moving.

'Most certainly I didn't want to hurt myself or anybody else around me. A lot of people think racers need brass ones or to be absolutely crazy. I disagree. The guys with that approach generally don't go too far; they might be quick for a lap but they end up in an ambulance. So you need controlled aggression.'

You could swap the word 'fear' for 'Monkey Mind' in the above quote and it mirrors everything we've heard in this chapter. Just as Felix Baumgartner defeated his Monkey Mind by planning everything out until it gave up all opposition, Doohan paid similarly meticulous attention to detail.

'You recognise how dangerous the sport is but you prepare yourself mentally, physically and with the machine so it's almost second nature,' adds Doohan. 'It's the same with anything: if you've got no plan it won't unfold too well. In racing you are always a corner ahead so it's not a surprise when you get there. But it starts earlier: before you go to a circuit you try to recall where you hit the marks the previous year, so you're not wasting time. The night before I raced, I went through all the scenarios: "What if this happens?" You're ahead of the game all the time. If you're completely immersed in what you're doing you know you're on the edge yet it feels like you can go past it. No matter what you do, you seem to be within the bounds. The competitors keep chasing where they think you are. But if you keep moving that limit they never catch you because you've already moved on...'

Current top-level motorcycle racer Marc Márquez seemed to have moved on before he even arrived. Having been encouraged into the sport by his parents, from the age of six Márquez was throwing a dirt bike around Spanish tracks. This background helped him come to track racing with a striking style: such was his angle of lean into corners he had to wear special magnesium elbow pads because the standard ones wore down too quickly. The Spaniard won titles at 125cc and Moto2, but even he was taken aback to ride to global glory in his first year in MotoGP, the first debut winner for 35 years and its youngest ever champion at the age of 20. As the others play catch-up he has kept amassing world titles. But on two wheels not even the most precocious student can avoid hard knocks. Márquez suffered a detached retina in a crash in 2011. His ride could almost have ended there and then. Instead it took him to the next level.

'That was the most difficult month of my career,' Márquez tells me. 'That's because the doctors told me: "We don't know if you will ride a bike again." I had to have an operation but there was a chance the vision would not return to 100 per cent. That would be fine for normal life but not for riding the bike. But I was so lucky: my doctor did a very good job and gave me the chance to ride again. Now it's 100 per cent better. That changed my mentality so that I enjoyed every moment, enjoyed the races and whatever we did. When I look at this recovery, I say we need to enjoy life because you never know what will happen in the future. You need fear – but just a little bit. If you fear too much you are slow because you are too scared. The most important thing is to enjoy the moment and everything that comes with it.'

3

RISK

Mercifully for the rest of us, you don't have to jump out of a balloon or go motorcycle racing to get in the Zone. This book features some of those whose passion for speed requires endless flirtation with the risk of injury or worse, showing how far some are prepared to go in search of this private heaven. But the thrill-seeker does not have an exclusive ticket and no one has to put their life in peril to find it. Even so, to find our true calling, a step into the unknown is always required at some level – whether it's about quitting the day job or having the guts to follow a dream.

That was the choice faced by British factory worker Jamie Bestwick in the late 1990s. Committed as he was to his job, one vision just wouldn't go away: he found himself spending every day dreaming about making a living from his hobby of riding BMX bikes. All well and good, but for a minor technicality: such a profession didn't exist. He nonetheless began travelling across the Atlantic to compete, coming up with increasingly inventive stories to explain his days off. He once arrived at work with his arm in a sling pretending he'd broken his collarbone – before jetting to San Diego for the fledgling X Games, which has since become the Mecca for action sports stars.

Ditching a regular pay cheque is still hard, as any bill-payer knows, but when a bike company offered to match his salary Bestwick took the plunge and moved to the USA, the only country where anyone actually got paid (a bit) to ride. He still gave himself just one year and double-checked his factory would take him back if needed.

'Even then I didn't jump straightaway because you don't know what's going to happen,' admits Bestwick. 'If somebody gives you the chance to fulfil a dream, it's a scary thought. I still had my mortgage to pay, I had to buy food and petrol. And I just didn't think the BMX would pan out. Even when we moved, in the back of my mind I kept thinking: "What if I crashed so bad that this whole thing ends tomorrow?" There are no guarantees: that applies to anything in life. But here was a kid from a small English town making a gigantic leap into the world of a professional up-and-coming sport. You've left everything you know, all the people you love and all the safety nets in your home town – all to chase after a dream. It was a scary prospect.'

The risks were soon spelt out when he crashed in a snowy Pennsylvania field 'literally in the middle of nowhere', suffering a haematoma that made his leg balloon to three times its size. And the whole trip wasn't quite the big hurrah he'd anticipated, either. Going from a regular nine-to-five job to having to organise his own time and stay in shape was harder than he'd imagined. There was no immediate success and Bestwick continued questioning whether he'd done the right thing. By the 1999 X Games, three years after his debut, the contest had captured the public imagination and featured star turns by the likes of motocross rider Travis Pastrana and skateboarder Tony Hawk.

'I felt really good about my riding that year but it turns out I knocked myself out after 30 seconds,' says Bestwick. 'I got so angry with myself, I rode back to the hotel. When I used to turn up for work every day I was serious because there was the looming threat of being fired. But I wasn't putting the same work ethic into riding a BMX at the highest level. I had a chat with myself and made a choice to stick at it. I went to the next event and won it. That was like winning the lottery. Jackpot…

'Even after that there were turbulent times. When you get a good win like that early in your career it can feel like you're on top of the wave now so you can just ride it. You take your focus off what you're supposed to be doing. When I rolled into work and said, "I'm not coming back, I'm going to ride my bike for a living", some people thought it was funny. But I was determined. Every time I lose determination in what I'm doing, there seems to be a catastrophic result – and it usually ends up with getting hurt. I missed two X Games in a row through breaking bones the night before…'

The cumulative effect of such a battering over the years meant that a disc in Bestwick's spine eventually fragmented, and in 2006 he had an operation to fuse two together. As he went under anaesthetic the doctor told him he would never ride a bike again, and he was even prepared to accept that

– until he came round and realised he hadn't even touched the surface of what he wanted to achieve. He failed in his initial X Games comeback later that year and even vowed to quit the competition altogether, such was his anger with his performance. But another 'chat' with himself kicked him into another gear. When asked about his 'retirement' on his 2007 return, he replied: 'That guy retired but the new Jamie Bestwick has just turned up.'

Bestwick Mk II hasn't done too badly. He won his ninth straight BMX Vert title in 2014 at the age of 42, an outright record in any individual X Games event. He recalls: 'After my operation I lost my first event because something in my head said: "I'm inferior today and I can't hang with these guys." But there's no shame in losing a contest. They're just lessons. In fact it teaches you a lot when you don't bring home the gold. You go back and think, "What happened?" I had to relive those moments in my head to work out what I did so wrong to make sure I'd never do it again. Most of it boils down to not letting the massive moment you're in get the better of you.

'When you see the finished product it's the cigar moment, the end result. But what you don't see are the hours and hours of dedication to make that moment look so spectacular. I practise tricks all day long because I have so much fun doing them. Yet at the time when you're under a tremendous amount of pressure, it's pressure you put on yourself. Other guys can make an impact on the competition but all they're trying to do is change your mind. They're trying to tell you: "Those tricks you have in your head right now that you thought would be good enough to win? They won't." It's the pressure you put on yourself that sometimes doesn't allow you to pull off even the simplest tricks; things you can do with your eyes closed on a daily basis.'

Over the years Bestwick Mk II has gradually increased his command over his mental approach even further by the use of techniques including yoga. This extended level of concentration is the basis for his record run, as his head has become a fortress impenetrable from any mind games, whether inflicted from outside or within.

'Being on top of the ramp and waiting for my name to be called is a trigger now,' he says. 'That's my cue: it's my time to go unleash all the time I spent training every day and the monotony of doing the same thing over and over so I could perfect it at any given moment. When your name's called there's nowhere else in the world you want to be other than on that ramp waiting to show the world what you've got.

'That drug of competition is what I'm hooked on: to know I have all these things in place but it's not 100 per cent guaranteed that I'll do a single one of them. It can go wrong at any moment – but that's what you live for. You live for the days that you're scared and wondering whether you'll lose the competition, yet somehow you manage to keep control and keep it all together. That's a *need* now – and I'm pretty fortunate to know what that feeling's like.'

Fortunate? That's one of the favourite words used by the sports stars featured in these pages, but this is a very special kind of self-inflicted fortune. The main battle is not with any other external competitor but with the very internal rival of fear – from the fear of just starting out to the daily risks associated with breaking new ground in a sport where the ground really can break you back.

'You have risks but it's worth it,' insists Bestwick. 'There's nothing that isn't a risk these days. Going on the internet is a risk, putting a phone to your ear is a risk. I live in the world of risk and I'm comfortable with it. The rewards of risk outweigh it. It's amazing what you can get yourself to do in the moment. If there was no risk in what I do, I'd probably go and find something else riskier. If fear wasn't there you wouldn't do it. It's like when you're a kid: you're always trying to push it that little bit further and further until it bites you. Then you start again.

'So it's living with the fear and knowing that fear is your friend. Fear is a great teacher in knowing when you're taking it too far. Do I like to live on the edge in other parts of my life? I took up motorcycle racing so I'm always seeking the thrill. But I wouldn't say I'm a risk-taker. I'm much more calculated than that. I look at the whole package and I want it to be pristine – elegant, smooth, shiny, polished. That's what I want in my riding and I'm prepared to work harder than anybody else to achieve that.'

Bestwick's BMX Vert discipline involves riders flying into the air, performing a trick and landing on a half-pipe. The payback for the inevitable pain they endure in private whenever they try something new is the rush they get when they nail it in public.

'The X Games used to have a best trick competition on a 125-foot half-pipe,' says Bestwick. 'One year I was watching people repeatedly pummel themselves into this ramp thinking, "Good Lord, that looks terrible." I can remember taking off, then time stood still. I couldn't hear anybody screaming, I couldn't hear any music or the guy yelling on the microphone. I could hear the freewheel of my bike. That was it. I could hear a pin drop on the other side of the stadium. I did a backflip, whipping the bike around twice while I was upside-down. On this trick, which I was pulling for the first time, you have to let the bike rotate. So you hear the wheel working as the bike goes round. As I was concentrating, the whole world turned in front of me. It was like being at the theatre when they lift the curtain and all the cast is there for the final bow. The ramp opened up, I saw all these flashing lights and I saw the people on the deck.

'The minute I landed it was like somebody went – click – and the music came back on and the people started screaming. This is the moment when you're supposed to jump up and down and scream because you've just pulled one of the wildest tricks that you'd never think of doing, even on your craziest days. But I stood on the deck and didn't do anything. I didn't know what to do. I honestly didn't think anything had happened because I was too busy and zoned out in what I was doing. The whole thing was surreal. It doesn't happen often – usually when somewhere inside you're waiting for an almighty bang. Every time I've had a really bad wreck there's a slamming bang that seems to echo inside the helmet, then deadly silence. The bang is the last thing you hear, usually because you're knocked out. Then you know it's bad. But when the crowd come back in then you know it's good...'

•

Risk isn't just about the avoidance of pain in a quest for moments of inner perfection or outer glory. For some, a perfect life involves taking pain on in a head-to-head fight. In the 1980s Daley Thompson competed in the track and field discipline created for supermen: the decathlon, a gruelling slog through ten events over two days. Each time the Briton strode into a stadium he knew pain was on its way, whether in competition or during training as he pushed his limits. That is a sacrifice already, but when I meet Thompson it becomes clear that committing your entire life to a single activity brings another personality trait to the fore: the will to gamble.

'I'm one of those people who are more than happy to put all my eggs in one basket,' Thompson tells me. 'There's not much else going on because you don't have any other responsibilities as a sportsperson, particularly a young one. So you spend all day every day thinking about your career, doing it or sleeping. That's it. Even walking along the street I'd make sure everything was in line, aim for a crack in the pavement and put my foot down, half stopping to see how close I am. Another ten steps later the same. Everything is about wanting to go two centimetres further in the long jump. That's all you do – or all I did anyway.

'It takes a discus thrower five years to get it right. If you only spend a third of that time it takes three times longer. So the decathlon takes forever because all of us are useless at some of it. I've no idea where my patience came from but I know I had it because when I started training at 16 I had a "Daley Diary" where I wrote my aims. It says it would be nice to go to my first Olympics in 1980, make the top ten in 1984, get a medal in 1988 and win it in 1992. I was prepared for all that because I didn't see it as a short-term thing, I saw it as a career.'

Thompson hit his own targets ahead of schedule, using the 1976 Olympics as his only stepping stone to gold in the next two. Knowing he was in for the long haul, 17-year-old Daley used his time in Montreal to pick the brains of the sporting royalty around him. He then began an unbeaten run that lasted nine years despite – or because of – an intense rivalry: Thompson was faster than a speeding bullet while Germany's Jürgen Hingsen was more powerful than a locomotive. The pair regularly exchanged the world record but never any gold, which Daley hoarded.

'People see the decathlon as being too hard work,' adds Thompson. 'It is. It wouldn't have been my first choice; I'd have preferred to be the world's fastest man. They only train for half an hour a day… But I once heard no matter how hard you're training, you should never be more than six weeks away from your best performance. During those six weeks it's not training, it's more important: it's about getting your head into the right place. Even when you're out there competing in front of crowds of thousands it doesn't feel any different because – for me at least – you're there all the time and that's my normal state of affairs, not the other way around.'

This is how Thompson retained his composure even when things went against him. In the 1984 Olympics he faced losing his lead to Hingsen after two poor discus throws. Then he pulled out a personal best with his third and last effort, prompting Ron Pickering's commentary classic: 'It's a better one, it's a better one, it's a better one, it's a better one!' A big risk? Hardly. In this case Daley had thousands of discus throws in the bank; he'd never thrown three bad ones in a row 'even in training' so it didn't even occur to him it might happen on the biggest stage.

'I never got knocked out of it by a bad moment – because once it's done it's done,' says Thompson. 'It's like golf: you've got to move on. If you're in the past, it's going to kill the present and the future. Nah, you just forget it. You have to be in the moment. That's where everybody has to be. Whether they can get it or not, they have to be here and now, because this is the only one that counts. You can't wait to knock him out later, let's do it now. Because he might be really strong later...'

British long jumper Greg Rutherford, who joined Thompson in 2015 as a rare athlete to hold Olympic, World, Commonwealth and European titles at the same time, shares his elder countryman's obsessive pursuit of performance. He even had a long jump pit built in his garden so he could have no excuses not to train. 'Athletics takes up every waking minute,' he insists. 'Everything I do – what I eat, how I sleep – has an impact. When you make plans you think about that impact. Then when you walk into a stadium there's a rush of adrenalin. But you've prepped for it so much you snap into the Zone by default. Every champion is extremely driven. Their goal is to be the best at what they do. The problem is that we're programmed not to be competitive, to settle: "Everyone's a winner." That notion gets everyone involved at grass roots but it stunts people's desire to push on. In no aspect of life – not just sport – is it the case. If you've got 20 people going for a job, there's only ever one winner.'

There is one downside to risking everything in pursuit of victory: the pain that results when things don't work out. You could see the anguish on Rutherford's face as he had to settle for 'just' bronze at the 2016 Olympics, just as Thompson struggled when he missed out on the medals in 1988. It hurts to give it all and still come up short, but the greats calculate that the rewards outweigh any pain. In Daley's case failure didn't dim the brash self-confidence he earned the hard way – and wishes we could all share.

'The problem with most Olympic sports these days,

especially the decathlon, is that they're so hard,' sighs Thompson. 'Today's teenagers don't want to be told it will take seven years before you'll be really good. They don't want to go through the transition of being relatively good at the sprints but useless at the discus or pole vault; they'd rather be seen to be good at the other stuff. They don't seem to have the ability to think: "This is a process and I'm in it for the long haul." They want to make loads of money, get shoe contracts and go to the big events. That's the mentality of today's youngsters – and my own are exactly the same. If I asked my kids they'll say: "This afternoon I'm going to be World Rally Champion on the X-Box." It's a completely different outlook to 20 years ago but that's how it is – it's natural that things move on.

'Some people have more self-belief than others, but it could be very positive and useful for everybody to believe in themselves more. I was fortunate: most things went the way I wanted. When they didn't, I was quite prepared to go away, train some more, then come back and give it another go. Attitude is what stops people doing well at anything, whether it's sport or whatever else. When it comes to the mind most people are not actually interested in finding out the answer to the question "How good are you?" They'd probably rather not know. Me, that's all I want to know. I want to push to the point where it's a bit dodgy because I want to know if I'm as good as I say or I think I am. Most people never want to find that out.'

•

How good am I? How many of us truly want to know that answer? But this question has long fascinated Hungarian psychologist Mihály Csíkszentmihályi, who coined the term 'flow' in the 1970s to describe the state when we are engaged in any activity for its own sake, rather than for any external rewards. Now into his eighties, he has been researching and writing about the subject ever since – and he believes there is a happy balance between boredom and anxiety that comes into reach when we take the risk of pushing ourselves slightly beyond our limit.

'It is an interesting accident of evolution that humans tend to get an enjoyable experience out of doing something that's a little bit harder than what they did before,' he tells me. 'This constantly escalating challenge apparently produces endorphins in our brains and seems to be something we inherited from our ancestors. That helped us survive in circumstances where other species may have just enjoyed hunkering down and being comfortable. By contrast our ancestors felt better when they could go out of their comfort zone occasionally. That meant they learned new ways of surviving and exploiting their environment. Now we have inherited this potential to enjoy going beyond the comfort zone. That's not always a good thing as it may drive people to go too far: then they fall off the rock they are climbing, they lose their money at poker, or whatever. So we have to learn how to use this to our advantage.

'We did a study of 1,000 internet chess players from all over the world. After each game they rated their enjoyment, and we found they enjoyed it most when their opponent was about five per cent more accomplished than them. So the sweet spot seems to be a little bit above our own skill level: if you win you feel really good but it's fine if you lose against someone better. You also learn from that, and in the long run it's what makes you a good player. That's true not just in chess but in life as a whole.'

This is also the principle on which the entire videogame industry is founded. Games are designed to lead players by the hand until they master basic skills, before gradually upping the challenges, albeit always keeping it manageable enough to make consistent steps forward. In this way they are crafted to mirror learning any new 'real life' skill, but with a reward system forensically calculated to keep us chasing the next fix. It works too – and I've met plenty of gamers who have found the Zone. But there is a drawback to doing it all on a screen.

'At the beginning the availability of computers and the ability to communicate with people from around the world came as a huge liberation for children, particularly those living on the margins,' adds Csíkszentmihályi. 'So the internet and smartphones have huge potential. But they can also become addictive, to the extent that you don't notice what's happening around you, you don't know how to use your body and you can't make friends. So it's a constant struggle to find a balanced set of challenges and not to get addicted to virtual ones. These massive interactive war games are attractive and easy to get lost in. But if your whole life is based on virtual realities, eventually you'll end up feeling like an avatar in somebody else's game, not somebody who will live their own life and use their own body and mind.

'I know the lives of children have changed dramatically because of this, but we don't yet know what will happen to them when they become adults, so the jury's still out on the long-term effects. I have serious doubts about the implications of this new virtual environment that children grow up in.

But already, younger generations are not worried about it because they have negotiated and learned from it, writing their own code. That's very challenging, so the potential for good is there – but there is also the downside, which may be the one that will prevail. Consuming is always easier than producing and the majority will still be consumers. They will end up worse off than if they'd been playing football in their backyard, going fishing or whatever. We should also live in the physical reality that has been allotted to us.'

•

There are still adventures out there that don't involve sitting on a sofa playing games. The key to today's extreme 'action sports' – from BMX to surfing – is that they turn the world into a giant playground. Once considered alternative, these pursuits are now heading for the mainstream because they offer the skills of on-screen avatars plus the kind of freedom only money is supposed to be able to buy. Some don't even require a single piece of equipment, expensive or otherwise. You just run, jump, climb, vault and roll over anything you can find. A human body and mind are all you need.

'It's amazing something like the basics of movement has taken so long to have its own name or philosophy,' says founding athlete of the World Freerunning and Parkour Federation, Ryan Doyle. 'In freerunning and parkour you express yourself through movement, learning to use your body to its full potential and unlocking what it's capable of. Every sport has foundations in parkour. You learn how your body works then you go in any direction you want. When you put that into a creative environment you feel you're living life to the max. You were bound but now you've unlocked this freedom.

'You see what you used to be like and what other people are like and they're not being efficient. If the aim is to get over there, they could just go. But if there's a three-foot wall in the way, they've been conditioned to believe: "That's dangerous, I might break something." I do this to an extreme but getting over a three-foot wall is something the human body is easily capable of doing. If all the kids playing computer games and watching *Spiderman* put that many hours into their own bodies they could go out and be Spiderman. I don't do this to look good, I do it to make them look bad.'

When I meet Doyle, his passion is obvious as he busies himself teaching kids the art of using their whole bodies to play instead of just their thumbs on a keypad. He insists one of the main attractions of parkour (which focuses slightly more on speed than freerunning) is its inevitable steady progress, just like a videogame. He suggests a child can start developing aerial awareness with a basic cartwheel: upside-down, twisting sideways and using every muscle. What's more, any such progress in the real world instantly transfers into other areas of life.

'Parkour unlocks a new sense of freedom and completely changes the way you think,' he adds. 'It's self-rewarding. You're not getting a black belt at the end of the month, you're getting new skills at the end of the day. If you set yourself a challenge and regularly achieve it those rewards build up. Once you're in the habit of achieving goals and overcoming obstacles physically, your brain gets in the habit of connecting the dots on how to achieve goals mentally too. If you have money problems or some position you want to reach in your career, it teaches you if something goes wrong, do it differently. Do it again. Don't just mope about it for the next two days. If anything you should be celebrating because you now know how not to do it. It's that mindset. It's the people who fall and decide never to do it again that miss out.'

Hailing from the British city of Liverpool, as a teenager Doyle trained in the Korean martial art of Kuk Sool Won. He combined the techniques he learned with his own freerunning movements to develop his own style. A double winner of the sport's flagship Red Bull Art of Motion, Doyle illustrated the risks when he shattered his leg in the same event. But silverware has never been the real motivation in action sports. Instead it's about constantly striving for the next level.

'People consider freerunning a dangerous sport,' says Doyle. 'But if someone who hasn't had any parkour training and someone who has are on a roof, who do you trust more? We teach people how to be safe in unfamiliar situations. People do crazy things anyway. If you push limits and do something off the chain, as soon as it goes online it instantly becomes standard and everyone is doing it within a year. That's why the next generation is standing on the shoulders of giants. I'm in my thirties but there are 16-year-old kids smashing it. They grew up watching my tutorial.

'With so many new movements it's harder to be original these days. But once you've got the human body that dialled, the equipment is the environment – which is constantly changing. So you've got to think of a whole new set of skills that fits each location. You could have a set performance you just take everywhere, but that's just a memory game, not creativity. The challenge is to find movements that only work in that new environment. We go around the world with a camera crew to find a location and do something original that can only work there. That creativity is priceless.'

What if this creativity could even be our most precious gift? Doyle insists the denial of this simple idea is one of the main problems facing us as a society: 'People think only some of us are artists and some aren't, but everyone's got it,' he says. 'We lose it in childhood because the system forces people to conform to nine-to-five jobs. If you pay me money to move something over there, I'll do it. Manual labour. But if anyone says: "Paint a picture and I'll buy it," it's different. As soon as you start painting you think: "I love doing this. Give it away for that price? No, it's worth more." Because it's got your personal creativity inside it you can't get it anywhere else. Similarly, when you do that with your movement and paint a unique display, it feels like there can't be a price for that kind of performance.

'At the Art of Motion you see people from Brazil with a capoeira background, people from China with a martial arts background, and others with backgrounds in gymnastics or break dancing. When they perform you watch someone expressing their life's training for 90 seconds. This is not "art of motion"; it's their life in motion. It's funny: when you meet them and their parents and see the environment they grew up in you realise: "Ah, your style makes sense. I understand why you are the way you are and how you move." It's beautiful to watch someone paint a picture of their life on the course.'

There can be no more natural level of performance than expressing everything you are, especially in such an active way. It's no surprise that letting go and allowing your own self to flow out brings about some serious peaks.

'In a good set people zone out and they just freestyle,' adds Doyle. 'They're not thinking, "That was good" or "What can I do next?" They're just reacting, reacting, reacting. When they finish the performance they can't remember what they did. I've been there too. When you get to the end you have to watch the playback to see what just happened because you lost track of time. In that moment you're too busy in the present to notice. You are living on instincts like an animal.

'Break dancers do it as well. They don't know what they've just done or what they'll do next. It's all flip, movement, flip. They react to what the music tells them. In their head it's just the music and whatever emotion is driving that performance. If they've had a bit of a bad upbringing they'll use that to fuel the power for the dance moves. You see how they can bring out an emotion to fuel their performance.'

•

The fuel of emotion is versatile – and it can power wheels too. If there is something incongruous about a forty-something on a skateboard, one man can get away with it. Tony Hawk first skated when he was nine years old. Four decades on 'The Birdman' still averages two hours a day, having transcended what he considers 'an art form, a culture, a lifestyle' and etched it into global consciousness both via real-life action and the virtual arena of videogames.

'If you're going to do something, you have to do it with all your heart and all your energy,' he tells me. 'When you try a trick you can't think the trick is just going to happen on its own. You have to work it out, respect it, figure out how to do it and fully commit yourself. Skateboarding is the truest source of that but you can translate the challenges you get in skateboarding to any part of your life. My whole approach is that there's always something new to learn. You can always improve your skills and you can always push something further. That's what has kept me here skating so long. No matter how high you get you must practise, persevere and keep challenging yourself, because it's the only way you will ever become successful. If you practise and you're determined, you will succeed at it. Sometimes it just takes longer than you expect but eventually you get it. That's the best life lesson that skateboarding tells us.'

To 'try, try again' is a key part of competitive skateboarding. Hawk cemented his legendary status when he nailed the first ever 900 – two and a half turns in the air – at the 1999 X Games. But even that day Hawk didn't land the trick on his first go. It took him 11 often painful attempts in full view of the public. As he finally flew, he took his sport with him. Jamie Bestwick sums it up: 'When Tony unveiled the 900 it changed the face of skateboarding for ever and put action sports in a world we'd never seen. He'd been trying it for so long and he became the benchmark for others to chase.'

Hawk has now retired from professional competition but his schooldays aren't over: 'Skating keeps moving and every day there's a new trick,' he says. 'So there's stuff I still want to accomplish. But the level is tough: ten years ago people could only do certain tricks in videogames, now they're doing them live. The tricks are so technical that it takes dozens of tries, but it's worth it if you make that one trick. My approach was to go at it with pure confidence. I tell myself I've done it hundreds of times and this will be no different. If anything it will be better because I'll put a bit more effort in. If you approach competition with any sense of doubt, you've set yourself up for failure.'

This mentality is the essence of sport, particularly those where injury awaits unwitting disbelievers. Incredibly, despite skating without any protective equipment throughout his long career, Hawk has only ever broken three bones – ribs, elbow and pelvis. When things do go wrong he insists this mindset is crucial too: 'You've got to get out and keep trying to build your confidence up. That's the hard part but you have to believe you're still capable of doing it. When I came back from breaking my pelvis it taught me how much I truly love skateboarding; because it is such a trauma to your body, it showed me I was willing to do anything to get back out there.'

Skateboarding first developed in the 1950s when Californian surfers sought a land-based replacement for when there were no decent waves. The first skate parks appeared in the 1970s but now Hawk wants to spread the same love to as many young people as he can. His foundation has already financed hundreds of skate parks in deprived areas of the United States and he is proud of the sport's increasing presence in places from Cambodia to Afghanistan to Uganda. Just as he was inspired into skating as a 'little skinny kid' by the diminutive Steve Caballero – 'He showed me that you can be small and still go high so I wanted to fly like him…' – many more have since taken to the skies. Yet despite skateboarding's inclusion in the 2020 Olympics Hawk knows a certain stigma remains.

'In underprivileged communities, kids get into skate-boarding as much as any other sport but they don't have support,' he sighs. 'Either they don't have facilities or they're told not to do it. If they finally find something they love but they are then discouraged from doing it, what is that teaching about their self-confidence and self-esteem? I buy these facilities so they feel like they're looked after, that somebody believes in them. Those skate parks get used more than any other sports facility in their towns.

'Skating has given me a sense of self-confidence and identity. The fact I still get to do it for a living is something nobody predicted. I'm proud people trust me to be an ambassador, but when I started it was not popular at all so I didn't expect much. It was only when my videogames got released that I realised it was bigger than I ever imagined. The best part is the fact I still get to do it and travel the world at my age: to share something that was my passion as a child.'

Hawk wasn't alone. Brazil's Bob Burnquist turned pro at the age of 14, and in the quarter of a century since, his stunts have taken him beyond even Hawk as the first skater to land a 'fakie 900' (rotating the other way round to what's natural). His 30 X Games medals are another record, yet Burnquist took a real plunge into the unknown when he combined his skateboarding with BASE jumping and flew into the Grand Canyon in 2006. The first try went wrong as he missed his take-off rail and fell out of control before deploying his parachute. After adjusting the ramp he tried again – and nailed it.

'Skateboarding and skydiving require your full attention and force you to be in the moment,' says Burnquist. 'So it's almost a meditative force. If I've got something else on my mind I tend to slam or get hurt. If you start thinking, anxiety hits. So I just take six deep breaths, saying to myself: "I'm not going to suffer in advance, I'm going to do what I need to do. I can perform under pressure." When I go, I'm calm, which is crucial. To be in the Zone means you're living that particular moment right now. It's hard to be 100 per cent mindful all the time, so it's about getting yourself there when you need it; you've got one more run and the pressure's on...'

I doubt many will test out this theory by jumping off a cliff. For anyone with quieter ambitions, Burnquist insists it's not all about living life at extremes of speed. Indeed his foundation aims to educate schools about organic farming and gardening.

'We all have our own limits but it's good to push ourselves,' he says. 'A lot of people only live within their comfort zone. But progression and evolution comes from being outside that, so it's good to make yourself go there every now and again. I'm not constantly out of my limit either. People say, "He's crazy" but I just keep pushing my limit, testing to see where I can go. I know the human body is fragile so I'm not going to do something to kill myself. It might seem "he is out of his mind, he doesn't want to live..." Quite the contrary, I love life so much and I want to live it.

'Wherever life turns I feel I have to go with it – because when you fight it, life is hard. Not everyone has the chance to do what you love. That means we have to find value, whatever it is, so life is not boring. It could be the simplest thing, just getting away, taking time for yourself. We lose that because we've got phones and emails. So just stop. I do that a lot: I turn all notifications off. Otherwise we go crazy. If you're mindful of what's going on you can be in the Zone right this moment. It's about bringing you back to focusing on what you're doing.'

•

The quest for mindfulness began millennia ago in the East: it's a translation from the term 'sati', one of the factors leading to enlightenment in Buddhism. But the practice is now gaining popularity everywhere else as people seek an escape from a world that moves just too fast for us to compute without burning out all our processors. Sport is an active way of clearing out mental clutter, but we don't need a prize at stake to seek out this nirvana. While most sports have the tangible carrot of competition to spur us to ever greater heights, for some the heights themselves are incentive enough.

Robbie Maddison has carried the art of motocross riding beyond Evel Knievel via a series of stunts that have wowed crowds all round the world, along with legions of *YouTube* fans. The Australian set the record for the longest motorbike jump with a 360ft clearance of an American Football field. He leapt onto the ten-storey Las Vegas Arc de Triomphe – and down again – and backflipped over London's Tower Bridge. Hell, he's even found a way to ride his motorbike on water.

'You're putting yourself in that realm where you don't know what's going to happen next,' he tells me. 'Moments before a jump you think, "Are these the last few minutes I'll walk on this Earth? I'm about to find out." You're just waiting. You've practised, you believe in yourself, you're aware of what you've got to do to perform and be safe. Then you get to that point: "All right, now I'm going to do it."

'It's not about thinking, it's just doing, being and preparing to find this 100 per cent awareness and presence. Time definitely slows down, you just feel yourself and you're aware of what's going on. Sometimes you do get thoughts when you're doing a trick or a stunt. That's when it's time to just pull over because you're not in the moment. There's a right time to do things and a wrong time.'

Few have such a pressing need to be 'in the moment' as

Maddison, for whom perfection is the only option. His stunts are the final product of months of meticulous preparation, building elaborate sets to recreate the conditions he will face in as much detail as possible. He works to manage risk by raising the bar – both metaphorical and physical – as the event approaches. But he rarely has a chance to practise at the venue itself, so these really are leaps into the unknown. No wonder it can take him so long to calm his Monkey Mind: 'Try, try again' is not an option. For example when he saw the site of a jump over Greece's Corinth Canal – a gorge with a 300ft drop into water – his initial reaction was that it was just too crazy and not a risk even he wanted to take.

'With these jumps and everything I do, it's so important to believe in yourself, have confidence and not listen to the negative voice in your head,' he insists. 'Every day I deal with that. After months of chewing on the jump, one day it just popped into my head. I said, "You know what? It's just a jump. A mind game." I wanted to put myself through the pain of letting go of the fear, facing it and believing in myself.'

He calculated a 'point of no return' after which he'd either have to make the jump or it really was game over. That would be a costly time for a mechanical failure so he asked fellow extreme sports nut Travis Pastrana to borrow his BASE jumping parachute to wear as backup. But when Maddison opened up the parcel the day before the stunt, to his horror he saw the chute was red, his unlucky colour.

'We were there, the media were there, the jump was built, the testing had been done, we were a few hours away,' he remembers. 'I thought, "Well, this is how life is meant to go for me." I'm a firm believer that everything in life happens for a reason. The fact it was red was a signal for me from the universe that I wasn't meant to wear it. I thought if I wore the chute it might come open and something bad would happen so I didn't wear it and I was comfortable with that.

'I believe it happened for the right reasons and that it was a message for me to believe in myself. The whole reason I was doing the jump was because I believed in it and there was no reason for me to doubt myself and wear the chute. That was a lesson from which I got a beautiful message. It boosted my confidence again and allowed me to gain another level of knowledge. Now I'm going to face more fears.'

If any professional has the right to take superstition seriously, it is surely the daredevil. Maddison talks like a mystic, but as I chased him around Goodwood I soon started to understand this is because he is one of the most enlightened sportsmen I have had the pleasure to meet. As we walked towards the arena for motocross riders to show off their skills, he revealed he was a fan of books by spiritual gurus including Vietnam's Thich Nhat Hanh, India's Osho and German-born Eckhart Tolle. This all blends and manifests in an unquenchably creative approach, rooted firmly in the now.

'I work tirelessly to try to take the level of motocross higher,' adds Maddison. 'I consider myself an average Joe from a small town in Australia, so to have the big dreams I had as a kid really come true has been breathtaking. I've been blessed with a wonderful life, but these challenges are just me living my life, showing the expressions of the thoughts I have. I believe it is my destiny to do these jumps. I let life come at me, just trying to live spontaneously, let inspiration flow and stay present in the mind.

'That's why I'm happy to go and take the risks I take. People say, "Aren't you afraid of killing yourself?" but I say no. Dying is a beautiful thing. We're all going to die. It would be sad to go out in the wrong way by taking a risk, but we all do that by jumping in aeroplanes and cars so it can happen to us at any time. You've got to live loud and live dangerously to be happy, really. If you try and live your life by being safe, you're missing the whole point.'

Maddison was the son of a young surfer and he grew up with a half-pipe in his garden. His young family was known as the 'wild family' of the neighbourhood but Maddison insists his Dad was the perfect role model. Robbie was also the youngest of his group of friends so he was forever playing catch-up in the stunt stakes. At the age of six he raced a school bus down the hill on his BMX, overtaking it to the delight of the kids on board before ending in a giant skid. When his mum saw what he'd done, he was forced to wear a motorbike helmet on his push-bike. It made him a laughing stock but it probably ensured he lasted as long as he has – seeing as he racked up 30 broken bones, a string of concussions and knee problems even late into his career.

Make no mistake: for Maddison every failure hurts. Yet he considers each to be a lesson: 'Every time I fail it's important to stop, understand why you got injured and what you can do about it the next time.' But there's another level to the education he has received from life at the limit, which he describes as 'active meditation'. Since the age of 25, not least since he became a father, he has been on a different journey he is keen to share. Like Bob Burnquist, Maddison insists anyone can take a shortcut to similar heights via standard 'inactive' meditation. The fast track is to slow down.

'Everything is spiritual for me,' he says. 'There's this whole spiritual order out there that they don't teach you about at school. I only stumbled across it by taking the risks I take. It took facing all these fears to realise what achieving happiness and being successful in life is about. After acquiring material objects I used to dream about, I've realised they have no importance. Now I get a kick out of just breathing and smelling flowers and seeing nature. I've had to put myself through so much to find this out, but anyone can reach the same level without doing all that. A hundred per cent.

'We all have to work to earn money for food, electricity and bills. But once we realise a lot of the stuff we have isn't needed, we let go of the desire for materialistic objects. Yes, it's beautiful to have nice stuff, but we're not slaves. It's so important to enjoy life. People lose direction because they never shut down. If you get stressed out worrying, meditation is a simple way to make things more enjoyable. When you shut the mind off, slow everything down and stop thinking, you start to see life's illusions and feel the energetic world we live in. Everything becomes a spiritual journey.

'Once you're in that mindset, you're satisfied. The hunger for more and more peters out and you can really be satisfied just being. If everyone had the courage to live their dreams, that's when you acquire this way of thinking. If you wake up every day and do what you love and dream about, this understanding eventually dawns on you. You have to be like this to get success in your dreams.

'Now I have children I'm even more motivated to be even better. Family is such an important thing and to be a father is beautiful. But I'm not going to let go of my dreams or put my life on hold. It's not about being selfish, it's just about living life. I want to show my children that when you have dreams it's so important to follow them because you only get one shot at life. As a young child I dreamt of being like Evel Knievel. I followed my dreams. Now here I am.'

4

CONFIDENCE

As Novak Djokovic let rip with an unbridled scream of elation, somehow he found reserves of strength to rip his shirt apart and slam his chest too, rather like the Incredible Hulk. But he did not turn green. He just stood ten feet tall after converting a match point in the longest grand slam tennis final of all time.

The Serbian had just battled mano-a-mano with Spain's Rafael Nadal for five hours, 53 minutes – an hour longer than the old record – to win the 2012 Australian Open. Just two days after a similarly brutal five-hour semi-final win against Britain's Andy Murray, Djokovic had been expected to struggle. The final regularly seemed to swing out of his control too. In one of tennis's most relentless demonstrations of hard hitting, Nadal broke serve to lead 4-2 in the final set, yet Djokovic found even deeper reserves of energy to claw his way back for victory. A week after the win of his life, I grabbed my chance to ask him what sleight of mind he conjured up when things were starting to slip away.

'To be honest with you there are no tricks, there is just belief,' Djokovic told me. 'Just believe and you will find the mental push that you need to give yourself at that stage. In the fifth set of the Australian Open final there is no more thinking and there is no more physical strength you can rely on. It's just about will to win and that power that guides you to the end. It remains the most exciting match of my life. We went the distance over six hours and made history. Unfortunately there can be only one winner, but I think we were both very proud of what we did that night.'

It does indeed take two – and the fairytale ball sport, for fans at least, is one where more than one competitor finds the key to the Zone at the same time. But in a vintage era for men's tennis Djokovic had long been the unlucky number three, other than a brief party piece with his first Australian Open victory four years earlier. Grand slam semi-finals hardly count as failure but during that time he could find no way to break the stranglehold of Nadal and Roger Federer, who fought out several gruelling encounters of their own.

It was a defeat to unfancied Austrian Jürgen Melzer in the quarter-finals of the 2010 French Open – despite leading by two sets and a break – that finally prompted Djokovic to work harder to make the final step. After growing up in the family pizza parlour he cut all wheat products from his diet on the advice of Dr Igor Cetjevic. He overhauled his mental approach too, benefiting from an early confidence lift as he led Serbia to the Davis Cup. A major breakthrough followed at last in 2011 with another Australian Open win plus Wimbledon and US Open crowns, three out of four grand slams. The subsequent six-hour classic proved he was the new boss, hence the ripped shirt. Yet the leap up to number one was born not in his biceps but his brain.

'I'd been number three in the world for three or four years in a row,' he sighs. 'I was just behind the two most dominant players of the era and I wasn't managing to make that final step – apart from one win in Melbourne in 2008. It seems such a small step from semi-finals to winning but it's really a huge step. Then suddenly, bang! In 2011 I started winning. What changed for me was the mental stability, strength and experience from playing at the top level over the years. It was a matter of believing I can win against the biggest rivals in the latter stages of the major tournaments.

'So the last couple of years were a learning process. Everybody is different, especially in tennis which is an individual sport. So everybody has different paths, a different structure of their body and mind and a different mental set-up. You have to adjust to that and find the best possible way to benefit. Now I just have more belief in my abilities on the court than I had a couple of years ago. That's something you learn over the years and it makes the difference in winning the match.'

I'm tempted to shut my eyes now and 'believe' I'm Wimbledon champion too. Sadly for me this 'belief' only works in combination with the years of training needed to back it up with ability. But the top 100 players in the world already have those hours in the bank. As such it is still surprising how the difference between a great and a nearly man is apparently so straightforward.

If you do make it all the way to the peak, to stay there this belief has to embed itself even deeper. Shortly before Djokovic won the 2016 French Open to complete a career grand slam – even reporting a Senna-esque out-of-body experience during the final points – I asked how he had grown mentally since he first became number one: 'A lot has changed since then,' he told me. 'I've had the best time both in my career and my private life. I became a husband and father and that has brought a great sense of joy, happiness and a different dimension of love I never knew was inside me, which has positively impacted my tennis. I've become more serene and more balanced. I've tried to keep myself healthy and worked very hard with my team to perfect my game and take it to another level. In the last couple of years everything has come together. There's no one secret as to why I have achieved all this, just a holistic approach to the sport and life in general that has helped me get where I am now.

'That approach is crucial to me. I'm still very motivated and I try to extract the biggest energy and motivation from the source of my love and passion. It lets me stay humble with both feet on the ground, to keep in the present moment and keep wanting more. Of course my childhood dream was to win Wimbledon and become number one in the world. But I never saw achievements, trophies or success as the main source of drive and energy into what I do. Like any athlete, most of the time we spend on court is training and just ten per cent of the time competing. So you need something else to drive you: not just achievement but really to love and enjoy what you do, in my case hitting a tennis ball.'

This majestic career was all created by a young boy growing up in a war-torn nation, who once spent 78 straight nights in a bomb shelter as Serbia endured a NATO onslaught. But this little lad dreamt big and refused to give up on his vision.

When he turned up at his first tennis practice at the age of six he already had in his mind that he wanted to become the world number one. Indeed he pictured everything in such detail that the young Novak decided when (not if...) he won Wimbledon he would celebrate by eating some of the Centre Court grass – incorporating not just sight and sound but even taste into a grand vision he has brought to fruition three times so far.

'I come from a small but very beautiful country that has gone through a lot of troubles and war in the past 20 years and still remains very poor,' says Djokovic. 'So I didn't have great facilities and conditions to practise to develop into a great tennis player. But look: I dared to dream. I dared to dream about becoming the world's best tennis player. And now here I am. So I think everything is possible. I would hope that every kid around the world will dare to dream, and that they will use sport as the right example and the guiding star for the path they choose.'

•

Champions are not born free of the worries and inadequacies that plague the rest of us. The only difference is they find a way to block them when it really matters. Yet these doubts don't even stop at the top. It was South Africa's 1979 Formula 1 world champion Jody Scheckter who told me just how double-edged the pinnacle can be. It may be the goal for every youngster setting out in sport, but to fulfil a lifelong dream can have a surprisingly deflating effect: 'I'm motivated by the fear of losing,' he says. 'Even when you're world champion, though it sounds like you're on top of the world, you're not. When you're world champion you can only lose everything.

So the fun is coming up the ranks because you haven't got much to lose.'

This is a common refrain, though in a world that so values 'results', such an attitude can only be taken seriously from the few to have sampled both the climb and the summit. The problem for those who play on a global stage is that the inner heaven of the Zone can go entirely unnoticed if it doesn't translate into results. In terms of the purity of a performance this shouldn't matter. But for anyone in a competitive field it's a good idea to win occasionally – if nothing else to avoid the mental drain of life spent answering questions about what's going wrong.

This ascent took Andy Murray even longer than Djokovic, who was born just a week later. Despite being Britain's greatest tennis player for decades, the long-time 'number four' in the picture was hounded at home for his failure to convert any of his chances into a grand slam title – while his public image was not helped by his gruff on-court manner. When Murray was defeated by Federer in his first Wimbledon final in 2012, he could hold his poker face no longer and he burst into tears.

The result was instant and two-fold: it finally gave Murray a release from all the pressure he'd bottled up over long years as the chosen one – while the reaction of the fans showed how much sympathy and love they had been bottling up too. Murray duly defeated Federer on the same court a month later for Olympic gold before giving his nation its first grand slam winner for 76 years at the US Open. Proof the Scot had finally reached the top level came as he won Wimbledon months later.

Murray credited his new coach Ivan Lendl – who rarely allows himself any outward displays of emotion – with changing his mentality, finally stopping him getting carried away by frustration. That helped Murray keep his belief long enough to defeat Djokovic for both these breakthrough finals. But when he parted company with Lendl he failed to build on his new-found mental freedom, often letting his old demons back in at big moments. When the partnership finally resumed in 2016, so did the big wins: another Wimbledon and Olympic gold before displacing Djokovic for the number-one spot he had coveted for so long. Murray reckons the turnaround began in a Monte Carlo encounter with lower-ranked Frenchman Benoît Paire, who served for the match before the Scotsman prevailed, giving him a timely confidence boost.

'I don't mind failing,' Murray told the press after his second Wimbledon win a few weeks later. 'Failing's OK providing you've put everything into it. I've lost a lot of close ones, mostly against great players. After those losses a lot of questions were asked of me, but I put myself in a position to win. It's about not being afraid of failing and learning from my losses. That's what I've done through most of my career.'

No matter how long Murray and Djokovic stay at the top before 'failures' take over for good, both will take heart from Federer's nostalgic run to the 2017 Australian Open trophy at the age of 35 – after a five-setter against Nadal, no less. The veteran rivals ended up sharing out the 2017 grand slams. It seems belief can be as permanent as class: if you can find the Zone once, it's then a mere matter of finding the way back. The only pity is that everyone else is chasing the very same magic. So you need hunger because, to quote Murray before his cathartic Wimbledon tears: 'It's not going to be easy…'

•

Peak performance really starts with 'beginner's luck'. If there's nothing to compare ourselves with, we can forget all about results and just enjoy ourselves, like children. Even if we have only minimal technical ability, to use all of it unhindered can work better than having the skill but a blockage in how to access it. The jams begin as we improve and build up expectations, both our own and those we perceive in others.

Golf is a classic example of how a little knowledge can be a dangerous thing: when I first picked up a club my only exposure had been from watching the greats on television. Something of their expertise had wedged itself into my head and my swing was initially easy, the ball regularly sailing straight down the middle. What was all the fuss about? Then I had a few lessons – but not enough – and started thinking about grip and stance, inhibiting whatever natural flow I'd had. It was downhill all the way. After a literal low point where I could no longer get the ball off the ground, I gave up.

I'm not alone. A world champion from another sport put it beautifully: 'I'd go round in 100 shots, of which 99 were crap and one was good. If 99 pints tasted awful and one tasted good you wouldn't drink, would you?' With perseverance I may have broken through to the other side – until the next stumble. Everyone endures such lows but the stars find the inner resources to force their way beyond all the moments when their ability seems to plateau or, worse, dip. No matter what, they never, ever quit.

For the perfect storyline, Hollywood might recommend a sportsman should save their day of days for the very end of their career, preferably a stunning victory out of nowhere on the day they retire. But that overlooks one minor plot detail:

a couple of decades of torment as the universal acceptance that your chance has gone reaches a point where even friends and family look upon your continued efforts with the kind of bemused pity normally reserved for a caged animal determined to gnaw their way out.

As Northern Ireland's Darren Clarke limbered up for his 20th attempt to win golf's Open Championship in 2011 he was about to surprise his doubters. In atrocious weather, the 150-1 outsider walked calmly through the storms. He led into the final day and while others faltered he sauntered to glory by three shots – at the age of 42.

'I still don't know how I managed to do it,' Clarke tells me. 'But that week I was very calm and collected. For that final round it was as if it was my time. I played well but also got a couple of good bounces and breaks. I'd served my apprenticeship and it was given to me. That's the way sport goes, isn't it? You need to get the breaks to win. But it's not as if I came out of the blue. I'd won 20 times around the world including a tournament in Arizona two months earlier. It's been a long road and it was great to be able to plough through, persevere, persevere, persevere... and I got here in the end. The support and love the people showed me walking down the 18th was even more special. It wasn't just the roar, it was the compassion.'

Clarke had indeed been through way more than the average sportsman, having lost his wife Heather to breast cancer five years earlier. Hitting a ball into a hole pales into irrelevance by comparison. Nonetheless he'd already earned one early moment of redemption just six weeks later as he won all three of his matches in the Ryder Cup at the K Club. After that Clarke's form disintegrated again and before his Open triumph he hadn't finished in the top ten at a major for ten years. Even then his self-confidence never deserted him. It helped that top golf psychologist Bob Rotella kept reminding Clarke about what he terms 'unconscious putting'. The key is to create a clear picture of the desired outcome, then let all fear of failure go and trust the natural skills honed over the years of practice. Don't think, don't fret, don't try, just do. Sound familiar?

'In my heart of hearts did I think I was good enough? Yes, of course I did,' he adds. 'I had no doubt in my mind and I knew 100 per cent I had the game to win. Did I know I was going to win? No, but that's slightly different. Still, I do scratch my head sometimes at how it has all turned out. The K Club was wonderful and the Open even more so. I've had a difficult time in my personal life but the world of sport gives and it takes. It's taken from me in many different ways and it's given me an awful lot back as well. I've got to be grateful for what the game has given me.

'Challenges are in front of everybody, whatever walk of life they're in. If you give in that's not the way forward. You've got to battle on and sometimes good comes out of bad. I'm a good example of that. You have to get through the bad times to get to the good times. Certainly I went through the bad and eventually came to an awful lot of good that's coming to me now.'

•

Believe it or not. These four words make up a choice that is a critical factor separating out those who make it from those who don't – in any field. It may sound like a simple 50-50 with an equally obvious answer, but picking heads over tails is far from easy. Even in elite sport, where the difference between best and rest comes down to control of the mind, precious few have this perfect mentality from the start. The greats either learn it through the lessons of life at the limit or they seek specialist mind coaches. To have any chance of facing up to those who really know how to 'believe', many need a complete overhaul of their internal computer first.

Say the word 'hypnotist' and the first image might be a man with a beard and purple cloak swaying a watch on a chain, or a stage entertainer humiliating his subjects for laughs. It's not always like this. On the outskirts of the British city of Bath, Don MacPherson (aka 'the Mindbender') routinely hosts young hopefuls in sports ranging from rugby to snooker – including champions in everything from F1 to Wimbledon. There's no watch but there is a reclining chair where he puts on soothing music and sets out to put their subconscious minds back on track. Rather than implanting sinister ways of thinking into vulnerable heads, MacPherson insists hypnotherapists tend to be called upon to rectify the effects of a life of hypnosis from another source entirely.

'Ask my wife Jane to play tennis and she will politely but firmly decline,' says MacPherson. 'She'll say: "I can't play tennis! I don't have an eye for the ball or any hand-eye coordination." She is so certain of her complete inability to hit a ball over a net, most people don't even bother to challenge her. But if you gently pry as to why she holds such a view, she'll say it must be true because: "Everybody has always told me I am hopeless at tennis."

'If you dare to go any further you might enquire who this "everybody" is. You may know a few: mothers, fathers, grandparents, friends, teachers, vicars, politicians, policemen, lawyers, doctors. They are Jane's "everybody" and probably yours: all are "hypnotists" who were in action from her first attempt to hit a ball. No doubt she missed or mishit the ball, at which point I doubt she received much encouragement, more like "Oh dear, it doesn't look like little Jane has much of an eye for the ball, shame..." from a well-meaning parent who didn't realise the effect their negative comments can have on a young child hanging onto and believing their every word. The "can't do" opinion was maintained by the next authority, her school teacher who probably said she didn't have much hand-eye co-ordination either.

'Who was next? Other family members and friends, all hypnotists joining in, compounding and confirming Jane is no good at tennis. Unless somebody interrupts this hypnotic trance, she is well on the way to believing it. Finally, whenever tennis is brought up, you will hear her unequivocally state: "I am hopeless at tennis". This is as close as you can get to self-hypnosis, but she has already been a victim of "accidental hypnosis". It is now so deeply rooted in her subconscious that to shift it she would need a mind expert to try to reprogram her into "can do" Jane. She may not have become a champion but she could have been competent because her coordination and hand-eye skills are fine in many other ways – so why not tennis?'

I'm sure we all have a similar example of a pursuit we long ago abandoned as far beyond our capabilities – whether it's sport, art, music, languages, maths or anything else. If we were to work our way back through time there would no doubt be a similar cast list of hypnotists. But few of them are likely to realise they were ever in our lives at all, just as we live in blissful ignorance of the similar effects we've had on countless, faceless others. We now live lives so complex in terms of interactions – from good old face-to-face contact to television, internet and social media – we face a daily onslaught of more swaying watches than Switzerland in an earthquake.

Some situations can make people especially vulnerable to hypnosis, according to MacPherson, notably every child in Santa's grotto or the classroom, or the England football team facing a penalty shoot-out in the firm belief they always lose. This can even affect a matter of life and death: 'You are in your doctor's surgery, about to hear the results of some tests,' he adds. 'Your conscious mind freezes whenever something important, emotional, exciting or scary is happening to you. At this point your GP is a full-blown hypnotist because they now have direct access to your subconscious mind, the real you. So they had better be very careful what they say... because you're about to become another victim of accidental hypnosis.

'If it's bad news your first question is likely to be: "How long have I got?" If the reply is "six months" it is uncanny how accurate this forecast turns out to be. Have the patients been hypnotised, their brains programmed to believe it must be so without question? If the GP clicked his fingers just before giving the results would the patient suddenly cluck like a chicken or sing an Elvis song if they suggested it?'

Before we start blaming anyone else on our end credits we have to remember that there is only one true leading light in our production: ourselves. No matter what the minor characters say it is only when our subconscious minds choose to believe it that the plot twist is written in stone. To quote parents everywhere: 'If we ignore it, it will go away.'

The only problem is that our deepest selves are not easy to control, no matter if we're trying to ascertain whether or not to believe a news story, whether or not to believe we can hit a tennis ball over a net, or even whether or not to believe we will live to see another Christmas.

•

Away from the couch, Don MacPherson has a range of tricks elite sportsmen can use to regain control ahead of crucial events – not least 'Zen Breathing', which slows the heart rate with a simple deep breath, exhaling for longer than you inhale. His charges also do meditation and visualisation; indeed he insists hypnosis is meditation too, simply a guided form that encourages the inner critic to take a back seat when the rest of you is anything but relaxed. The aim is always to clear out lingering mental clutter and thoughts of past and future to focus on the all-important now.

Andrew Jordan went to the three-race Brands Hatch finale of the 2013 British Touring Car Championship with a big lead as he chased his first title. Things didn't go according to plan. After Jordan crashed out of race two he needed a charge from the back of the field in the final race to make the top ten, which would secure him the crown. In the wet. Cue a phone call to the Mindbender.

'I spoke to Don a couple of times between the races,' smiles Jordan. 'The first two races were very intense but Don's the sort of guy who calms you down if you're feeling bad about yourself. I had a bizarre feeling before race three. I felt calmer than I'd ever felt: I knew we'd do whatever it took and get where we needed to. There was no doubt we would win. We had a goal and it was: "Let's go and do it." Normally you think about what might happen, but amazingly, even though a lot of people were watching, I wasn't even nervous. That's something I don't understand to this day. I was genuinely looking forward to going racing. I wish every race would be as relaxed as that.'

The bliss didn't quite continue to the end. Once Jordan had done the hard part of passing cars, he had to preserve both his race position and his focus while driving a couple of seconds off his usual pace. During the last couple of laps every little noise echoed round his head but both he and his car held together to the chequered flag and the title. Now he appreciates just how much we tend to under-use the mind.

'If Usain Bolt goes into a race he will 100 per cent think he's going to win,' he adds. 'It's not being cocky; it's just having belief you're capable of it. If you head into qualifying thinking "I could go off at that corner", it will probably happen. The mind is a huge part of racing, yet people overlook it. They think if you see a mind coach or a sports psychologist it's because you're weak in the head. It's absolutely not. Everyone trains physically – and you get more out of the gym with a personal trainer than going by yourself – so why not mentally? Top Formula 1 drivers do it even if they don't admit it in public. Working with Don makes my head, mindset and focus better. More people should do it and I don't get why they don't – but that suits me...'

Double Formula 1 world champion Mika Häkkinen recently revealed the impact on his career of McLaren's team doctor and performance coach Aki Hintsa. Originally a trauma surgeon, Hintsa decided success is built on a foundation of holistic well-being after spending time observing Haile

Gebrselassie and other elite Ethiopian distance runners. He helped many F1 drivers including Lewis Hamilton and Sebastian Vettel, going on to run a human performance centre until he succumbed to cancer in 2016.

'If someone wants to be better in sport, there has to be science behind their progress,' Häkkinen tells me. 'It's like developing a racing car: it has to be calculated, with tests to analyse how to make it better. A human being is the same. Formula 1 has physical demands but it is a mind game. Every lap, you need maximum concentration. You need to focus 100 per cent so everything influencing your life must be in the right place and there can be nothing disturbing your mind. If you have stress, don't keep it inside. You need the right people who you can talk about it with. Whatever problem you have, find a solution. That is an important part of success. Aki understood what drivers need to reach their peak at every test, every qualifying session, every race. He helped me become a better racing driver: one of the key points I learned was that if you know exactly what you're doing, you will win.'

Nonetheless the mind is a curious beast, strangely vulnerable for a source of such immeasurable power. Even the few who beat off caution to follow a dream can be stopped by a stray word – as World Touring Car Champion Rob Huff knows.

'What transformed me from a good driver to a top one was when I met a chap called Will Holden who got me to go deep and change my inner subconscious,' says Huff. 'When someone brakes in front of you on the motorway, you don't think: "Oh God I need to brake", you do it instinctively. That is your subconscious working for you. Will gave me the key to reprogram my subconscious to believe what I wanted rather than what influential people had told me as a junior.

'A key one was my early coach at Silverstone. I could never qualify well but no matter where I was on the grid I'd come through to the podium. Once I started 18th and still won it. When I got out of the car he said: "Huffy, you're a hell of a racer but you can't qualify." That stuck with me and I believed it because he was the guy I looked up to: my "God". That was why I didn't qualify well from then on. Will helped me go back to that and completely transformed it. It's stayed with me and it always will.

'Now in qualifying, when I sit there I know I'm going to do the perfect lap. I know I will extract everything that is physically possible to get out of that car because I've programmed my subconscious to believe I can do it. There's so much more you can do if you believe it. This works in any field, but there are limitations. If I tell you to jump off a 300-foot cliff onto rocks you ain't going to survive and you can't teach yourself to believe that. But with anything that is physically possible in reality, there is no limit. If you can believe you'll do it, you'll do it.'

•

Keeping up this belief is the real trick, but it's not easy even for true greats. Such was pole vaulter Sergey Bubka's supremacy in the 1980s–1990s, he could earn a living from bonuses as he raised his world record centimetre by centimetre. His definitive mark of 6.15m stood for 21 years until it was finally surpassed by Renaud Lavillenie in 2014 – again by a single centimetre. On the physical side, Bubka's secret was fast approach speed and strength that allowed him to use a heavier pole and hold it higher for extra leverage. But it may now come as no surprise that his physical strength was directly linked to his mind. As he stood on the runway his subconscious was also coiled up, ready to spring.

'When you are preparing, you need to use visualisation,' Bubka tells me. 'That is how to send signals from your brain to your body and your muscles to do well. This is a special mental feeling: especially when one area is crucial or you suffer from a particular problem, it helps you concentrate better on how you should do it. You visualise both before and during competition but it's important to compete in the stadium, not before.

'The mental and psychological side has big value for athletes. You can have all the technique and ability in the world but if you cannot control the stress and you cannot control yourself and your movements, you cannot achieve. You should be focused in training but as an event gets closer you start thinking, which creates stress. So it's also important to be yourself and to feel like you're competing at home, when you are the best. During the event itself you have breaks you can use to prepare. You need that to be ready for the moment you go before the world.'

Bubka took a record six consecutive world championships between 1983 and 1997, first for the Soviet Union then his home nation Ukraine. Yet he had one major psychological blind spot: the Olympic Games. Having been denied his first chance by the Eastern Bloc boycott of Los Angeles in 1984, Bubka travelled to Seoul four years later, only to find himself jittery. After two unexpected failures at 5.90m he realised his mental computer needed an urgent overhaul.

'That is the only competition in my life when I sent instructions to my body but my body didn't listen,' says Bubka.

'I was over-tense because the Olympics are so important for me, so emotional, and I'd missed the previous Games because of the decision by the Politburo of the Communist Party to stage a boycott. That was an incredible punishment for the athletes. The statistics say only 15 per cent of athletes manage to participate in a second Olympics, so normally you only get one chance in your life. This was my dream. And my dream was stolen from me by politicians.

'That's why I wanted to win so badly in 1988, but such pressure gets you into trouble. When you push so hard and think so much, you can block yourself. At those Games my muscles did not follow me. You are prepared, fit and ready to jump well but tension is the danger. It was only before my last attempt at 5.90m that I tried to release tension and feel more relaxed. Luckily I managed that and I cleared it. I had some good jumps in my career but that win was unique, given what I was feeling.'

It was indeed 'lucky' that Bubka relaxed, because circumstances conspired to ensure he never won another gold despite the ability to be an all-time great Olympian: 'I'm very happy to have won an Olympic gold medal,' he says. 'That is a dream come true and really helped me. Of course I dreamed of winning more and had the potential but I achieved what I achieved. The greats get more but maybe I didn't deserve it. We all have obstacles to overcome in our lives – I had many too – but I was responsible for every competition I entered. If I got injured, like Atlanta in 1996, it was my and my coach's responsibility. When I didn't handle the stress, like Barcelona in 1992, it was because I dreamed of setting the world record in a big official event to prove I was jumping because I love sport. I didn't achieve this goal and it's my fault.

'But the 1984 boycott is even more painful for me today than at the time. Then I was only 20 and I was still positive: I looked forward and focused on the next one. I felt we could do nothing about it as we didn't have any rights. They didn't care about our thoughts or the pain we felt. Luckily four years later I won gold, but how many of my friends lost their dream? They felt the same pain, especially the older athletes who missed their last chance. They had worked all their lives for this moment, to stand on the podium and enjoy the unique feeling. Now they'll never know if their dream could have come true. It was a competition between political systems and we paid the price. What for? My medal was stolen. Today the countries don't even exist any more…'

Dare to dream, yes, yet sometimes we forget how many dreams can be snuffed out by external matters. But all things being equal, Bubka reckons there is no end to our true promise: 'Human nature means when someone breaks your record it pushes you to look for the next step, but I had to chase records on my own. The highest pole vault I ever did was at the 1997 World Championship in Athens. The bar was at 6.01m but the replays show I went over 6.40m. That shows how much human potential there really is in the pole vault. To do it you have to forget that limits exist…'

•

With so much to gain and so much to lose, it's no wonder sports psychology is going through a boom. The English Institute of Sport's Lead Psychologist Dr Ben Chell has worked in everything from table tennis to speed skating, golf, sailing and football. He knows how things can go wrong even for elite sportspeople, having researched a PhD on what causes athletes to 'choke' in big events when the culmination of their lifelong dream is finally in sight.

'Because the Olympics only comes once every four years, the importance of performing well increases, putting athletes under high levels of pressure and stress,' he says. 'When we see athletes choking, they start to become preoccupied with their own feelings and thoughts, internalising and overanalysing things. That leads to what we call "conscious control of movement". In essence they're using the wrong part of the brain, which is very limited in its capacity to process information to control their skills. In extreme cases, that's when we see athletes reverting from being experts in "autopilot" mode to novices, unable to get the ball over the net or to do the basic skills they've been rehearsing and reinforcing for 20 years.

'My role is to condition the mind to execute the right skills at the right time under high levels of competitive stress. So we start by identifying an athlete's psychological strengths and weaknesses, evaluating their needs. We educate them about how the brain operates and how their particular brain is wired, then work on mental skills that play to their strengths.

'Performance psychology helps bridge the gap between technique and skill. Technique is being able to do a manoeuvre under low pressure, but skill is when you can do it no matter what – like walking across a plank 100 feet up instead of on the floor. That's what differentiates between good and great. It's ensuring the correct part of the brain is driving skills and decision-making. This is primarily the parietal lobe or what's sometimes called the "computer", which works 20 times as fast as any other part of the brain. It's where our "autopilot" resides; that's where we need our athletes to be in order to consistently perform to their best.'

Chell was mentored by sports psychiatrist Steve Peters, author of *The Chimp Paradox,* who has worked with everyone from Liverpool FC footballers to snooker's Ronnie O'Sullivan. But Peters made his name in cycling by helping some of Team GB's most decorated Olympians including Chris Hoy and Victoria Pendleton, who was far from your typical athlete oozing self-belief. Instead she used Peters' insights to get her head straight when it mattered en route to gold in two successive Olympics.

'One of the keys to getting in the Zone is to have mental preparation as much as physical preparation leading up to a race,' Pendleton tells me. 'You have a mental warm-up strategy in place, something you go through regularly, that becomes almost automatic when you reach competition and your thoughts start flying everywhere: "Have I done enough?", "Oh my gosh, they look really fast", and all the other doubts that are very hard to avoid under pressure. Steve Peters helps us as individuals to find strategies that really address our own personal mental insecurities or weaknesses. For me it was about reassuring myself with facts about the training I'd done. For example, I knew I'd done every session that was planned to the best of my ability and I couldn't have done any more if I'd tried. It's about positive reinforcement.'

Since their retirement from cycling after the peak of London 2012, both Hoy and Pendleton have made belated switches to other sports – motor racing at Le Mans for him, and just one 'horse power' for her in National Hunt racing. The mental skills they have acquired are directly transferable but a mighty challenge awaits to overcome the years of physical experience they lack. Pendleton's choice has a drawback according to Liz Halliday, one of few to have excelled both in cars (six class wins in American Le Mans) and on horseback – in her case eventing.

'In motor racing you have times when you can bang in the same lap time over and over again without consciously needing to think about it,' says Halliday. 'It's fast but doesn't feel fast, just a really good flow. On a horse you also have days where everything is working and you think: "This is awesome." But it's not quite the same: because you're on a living animal you have to think too much. So much is happening: you've got the other brain involved, so the horse needs to have a good day too. You're sometimes having a better day than the other half…'

When you start multiplying monkeys by ponies it might earn you a fortune in cockney rhyming slang but it's not quite so prosperous for mind control in the heat of competition. Pendleton has described her bid to race in the Cheltenham Festival as the hardest thing she has ever done, insisting just making it round felt as good as winning the Olympics. But if she ever finds herself yearning for a nice compliant, brain-dead machine she will just have to focus on keeping her own mind in gear.

'It's a lifelong process, just as physical training is,' adds Pendleton. 'It becomes a lot easier, the more you practise it. It's something some people have naturally. They have a level of confidence within themselves which is always there and never falters. Then there are other people who do have slight insecurities. I'm one of those people. So it's something I personally had to work hard on to realise my own performance. It's about eliminating negativity to focus on the task in hand without any doubts or distractions.'

If you can rid yourself of the negative, confidence sweeps in to replace it like air rushing into a vacuum – and the benefits can be taken anywhere. When I meet Hoy it is back in London's Olympic Stadium where he carried the flag for Team GB in 2012. This time he is wearing a crash helmet and racing overalls, preparing to face a field of Formula 1 greats in the 2015 Race Of Champions. Talk about 'in at the deep end'. Thankfully, Hoy is adamant he is still benefiting from his old vocation.

'The work I did with Steve Peters is transferable to your whole life; it's not just about sport,' insists Hoy. 'It's about getting perspective, dealing with pressure or perceiving it as not being pressure. Some people would think this is pressure because I'm going out to race the world's best drivers tonight. But I'm thinking the opposite. Compared to when I was in this stadium three years ago, this is a luxurious situation. I know I'm never going to be as quick as these guys: they're professionals, this is what they do. So people won't expect me to be quick, they'll expect me to be slowest of all. That means I've got nothing to lose. If I come second last, that's a victory for me. Even if I do come last, it's fine as long as I come out with a smile on my face having given everything and been the very best I can be.'

This is not to say Hoy is just happy to make up the numbers in his new sport. The Scotsman partnered pro racer Charlie Robertson to the title in the 2015 European Le Mans Series. Even if he knows he'll never catch up on the practice his rivals collected over the decades while he was providing the power to his own wheels, he can sit safe in the knowledge that few can match his level of mental training and discipline.

'The main thing I can carry over from my cycling is the ability to block out distractions,' says Hoy. 'You have however many people watching and you're sitting on the start line with Sebastian Vettel next to you. If you think: "What the hell am I doing here?" or "If I stick it in the wall here I'm going to look a right idiot" you're not going to be able to perform. If you let any such thoughts into your head, either you will do exactly that or you'll go really slow. What I've carried over from my cycling is to focus on what I have control over and what I need to do to be the best I can be.'

The repetition of 'be the best I can be' in the above two quotes is telling. This is what it's about for the likes of Hoy. It's never just 'winning gold' or any other end target, but reaching the peak of your own performance on any given day. In cycling, the long years of graft armed Hoy with thighs the size of many waists, helping ensure his best was ahead of the rest: when he hit the Zone at the velodrome he could expect to leave with heavy metal. In motor racing the challenge is greater against others with far more experience but this true confidence is already helping Hoy to similar highs.

'It's all relative but I would say I have reached the Zone – for my level,' Hoy tells me. 'Being in the Zone for me means you're flowing, you're not thinking about the mechanics of driving the car or about braking and turn-in points or all the things your instructor's trying to tell you. You're just doing it instinctively. You can finish a stint without actively thinking about anything from that race. It's not easy and it depends on the car, the circuit, what's happening around me. At the moment I'm still so far off the pace of the professional drivers, it's more about chasing and trying to be mindful of the data, realising there's a tenth in this corner and two tenths in that one.

'I'm still thinking about that because I'm still chasing the times. I'm not at the stage where I can just let it flow and knock out a fast lap without even thinking about it. But when I did get to that level for the first time it felt so much better. I didn't have the fear or any thought of all the consequences. I was still a couple of seconds off the really quick guys, but that was the closest I've been to being able to let it flow, just do it naturally and not be having to consciously think about anything. I was just driving.'

Perhaps the fundamental difference between Hoy's new life and his old one is that the original chance came to him in a relatively haphazard way. Throughout his cycling career, Hoy was in the army of top athletes who keep a meticulous record of their goals, having once read that putting pen to paper makes you 'nine times more likely to do it'. In his teens Hoy wrote he wanted to become the Olympic champion in 2004 – then still 13 years away. It worked, but only via a mix of short, medium and long-term goals crafted with painstaking care as stepping stones to turn the dream into reality. By contrast...

'Motor sport was never really a dream,' smiles Hoy. 'Or rather it was exactly that: it was a dream, never a goal because I never thought I'd ever get a chance to do what I'm doing now. Really it's thanks to (Scottish world rally champion) Colin McRae because he's the person who really inspired me to take an interest. It was his driving style, his commitment and his unique driving ability that caught my attention. That was what got me hooked. Then when I did a documentary about Colin's life I was offered a chance to race in the SR1 Cup with Radical. That was the start of the journey. Nissan have since given me this amazing chance to do British GT and the Le Mans 24 Hours.'

There are doubtless many young racing hopefuls looking at that accelerated career path with envious eyes. Motor sport is notoriously dependent on funding and Hoy has skipped the queue. But it wasn't just pure 'luck' that took him into his new life on four wheels. He may not have planned it in the same intricate detail as his first sporting obsession, but his focus on getting all the way to Le Mans was absolute. Hoy knows from experience what it takes to make any dream happen. You don't just wave a magic wand, you keep plugging on day after day. That's how he has made it so far along the road – not only competing but completing the epic race in 2016. I'd wager there's a piece of paper floating around in his files with that precise target on it too.

Of course not everyone has the luxury of years of backup from the likes of the British Olympic cycling team. Yet finding this ultimate level of self-belief is no secret and Hoy is desperate to help get us all moving in whatever field we choose.

'In general we all underestimate what we're capable of,' insists Hoy. 'A lot of people look at Olympic or world champions and think they're born to be a champion, a different breed. But when I was small I wasn't one of these kids you'd have thought would have gone on to become Olympic champion. I didn't stand out from the crowd. What I learned over the years was that if you work at something, if you're committed and you focus on one thing to the expense of everything else you can surprise yourself with how far you can go. It's the same for anyone. Everybody can surprise themselves with what they're capable of doing.'

5

ATTITUDE

It's impossible to quantify the expectation on Cathy Freeman's shoulders as she lined up for the Olympic 400m final at Sydney in 2000.

The definitive dream for any aspiring athlete must be to romp to Olympic gold in front of your adoring home crowd. But the lucky few to whom timing presents the chance to be the 'face' of an Olympic host nation soon learn the real meaning of pressure. As an indigenous Australian athlete, in Freeman's case there wasn't just national pride at stake but centuries of national guilt too. This fever spread far and wide, and the entire globe has rarely shared such emotional investment in the outcome of a running race. Thankfully the face of Sydney, who lit the Olympic flame to start the Games, wasn't running for the faceless billions watching. She wasn't running for her race either, no matter how many headlines her story had generated. She was running, as she always had, for the pure fun of it.

'When I realised Sydney was going to have the Olympics, my initial feeling for about half a second was a little bit of fear,' smiles Freeman. 'But then it changed into excitement and joy. Oddly enough I'm not the most competitive person, but as a runner I found such pure happiness. When you watch the Brazil football team, their play expresses joy for every single second. It's amazing, and it's the same for me in my running. For me sport means joy.

'Even as a child I enjoyed running in front of my family and friends – not to show off but to share my expression of excitement and my passion with people. It's a funny relationship you have with spectators: some athletes like being watched, others don't like it or don't care. I fall into all three brackets but because I ran predominantly for myself and I wanted to win a gold medal predominantly for myself; it was a sheer bonus that I got to achieve my dream in front of my whole country. I guess it was just going to be part of my destiny, for which I'll always be grateful.'

Freeman's Sydney bodysuit radiated attitude, yet when I first meet her in Rio de Janeiro she speaks with the easy charm and enthusiasm of someone whose destiny never involved a trip to the top of the world. But the Australian's gentle nature belies the drive and determination required to make it that high. Freeman had come close to victory at the 1996 Atlanta Olympics before settling for silver. The final step is hard enough even without the extra demands of being an entire nation's focus of attention. What won through was her hard-won ability to focus her own attention.

'It was my third Olympics and I wanted to be an Olympic champion 17 years prior to the Sydney Olympics,' adds Freeman. 'So I was very clear in my heart and in my mind that this was my moment, this was my time. There wasn't anything that was going to happen to take my opportunity away.

'It's important to make sure that you are very clear with your goals, that there is no questioning your commitment or your desire. That also means being fair on your team, your coach and the people around you like your doctor or your physiotherapist. You have to make sure you're all united and determined to do the best you can to get to that goal – whether that's a personal best, making the national team or winning an Olympic gold medal.'

Freeman now reckons her body was ready to win in 1996 but her mind wasn't: she didn't really believe she could do it. She told her coach she would win silver and duly did. That is an impressive feat of prediction, not to mention self-knowledge. But our subconscious minds tend to act out our requests blindly and follow suggestions to the letter – whether positive, negative or anywhere in between.

The performance did, though, boost her desire and conviction that she could win eventually. Four years and two world championship gold medals later, so positive was her attitude heading into 2000 that at no point did she allow the notion of defeat even to cross her mind. Instead she reinforced her belief by mentally running through the final over and over again. By the time Freeman walked out in front of the 110,000 delirious fans packing the Olympic Stadium she was at peace and on 'autopilot', both classic components of ultimate sporting performance.

So immersed was Freeman in the Zone that at the finish line she didn't go wild in celebration, or even crack a smile. Amid the delirium she was an oasis of implacable calm, sitting on the track and staring blankly for a full minute as the realisation of what she had done started to sink in. It would take a lot longer than that. I had the privilege of speaking to Freeman twice for this book. If I thought she would have her description of the Zone nailed down by our second meeting, in Berlin in 2016, I was wrong…

'I've had so many years to think about it but it's really hard to put it in words,' she tells me. 'The first word that comes to mind is sacredness. It's holding your own space, the sheer freedom and sheer bliss. For me it was always about a personal joy, and bringing to the surface in a physical sense anything that's ever meant anything to me. It's a unity of sheer, pure joy. But that's the first time I've actually articulated it and I'm freaking out… where did that come from?

'There's absolutely no doubt that it was the process that brought the joy, more than the end product. It's a journey, it's each moment, it's a whole lifetime. For me it was 17 years but because of my connection to those before me – my ancestors – that's where I gained a lot of strength and inspiration. There's always something in my heart and mind thinking about the future too. So it's the connection of past and future. Each athlete's different, but that higher purpose was always really important to me.

'That's how people who may describe it in broadly the same way can cope so effectively with everything going on around them and to them. It serves as a kind of resilience and internal stabilising mechanism that helps ground you and not lose your focus. It's a stillness mechanism. I still go for runs – obviously not like I used to – but there's a touchstone there and I always find it running. Just yesterday I went for some "strides" on a grass patch and I still feel that's where

I find a bit of a meditative space. Some people pray, some might go for walks, sing or play music. For me that's where it is a spiritual feeling. It's almost profound…'

That's what happens when you meet a master practitioner. It's not about a single moment, it's an entire lifetime. In Freeman's case it starts even earlier in the history of her ancestors. Having first raced at the age of five, her journey to finding the Zone in Sydney began in earnest at ten, when she first decided she wanted to win Olympic gold. If such an idea ever seemed unrealistic she drew encouragement from the feats of indigenous Wimbledon champion Evonne Goolagong Cawley and grit from elder sister Anne-Marie, who suffered from cerebral palsy and played a part in Cathy's original support network much closer to home.

'My first inspiration came from my parents,' says Freeman. 'Because of their support, the fact I wanted to win an Olympic gold medal didn't overwhelm me. I felt at ease with being different to the other kids in the neighbourhood. Not everybody is fortunate enough to have support like that – whether it's your parents, a neighbour, a coach, an aunt or a friend's mother, but I was really supported in my goal at home.

'That's why it can sometimes be tricky to communicate this message to kids: especially if you are at Palm Island (the community for indigenous children now run by the Cathy Freeman Foundation in her mother's birthplace), it's such a struggle just to wake up in the morning and it's a battle just to go to school. So I have to pick and choose what kind of language I use and how forthright I can be because people simply don't have the self-esteem or self-belief, let alone the self-love.

'Generally speaking if I'm in the boardroom with high-performing corporate executives or over-achieving university students of course I'll change the language somewhat. But hopefully everyone wants to learn, even children. They ask questions and they want to investigate and dig a little bit deeper into what makes my mind tick, where my story is different and where are we similar.'

Through her foundation, Freeman now devotes much of her time to inspiring the next generation to dream big too. When I ask her if a human being is capable of more than we generally give it credit for, she laughs as she replies: 'Absolutely'. It's amazing how a little early external love can boost the internal self-love needed to aim high. If so Freeman struck gold with her own family, not least as they guided her towards the 'Belief' required to jump from 'C' for Conceive all the way to 'A' for Achieve.

'My parents were big believers in mental rehearsal and visualisation when I was a little girl,' adds Freeman. 'Once you've planted that seed of belief in your mind you need the courage to go out of your comfort zone and actually visualise, close your eyes and imagine trying to face your greatest fear. That included writing your goal on paper so you became comfortable with it and it felt manageable. They encouraged me to write down and say out loud, or even to my own mind: "I am the world's greatest athlete" of all things, which I'm clearly not… I might have a bit of an ego but it's not that big! Of course I wasn't and I never really claimed to want to be. But you know that saying: "Always aim for the moon – even if you miss you'll land among the stars…"'

•

'I am the world's greatest athlete': as declarations go, this one sounds at best fanciful, trite even. But this phrase is a classic example of a mantra. It's one thing to daydream positive thoughts about a goal, but it works much better if you write it down or say it out loud as the young Freeman did in her training. This apparently simple move turns it into a rock-solid ambition for the subconscious mind to pursue. The final step, if a chance presents itself, is to say it out loud while the whole world is watching.

This technique is used against us relentlessly in all areas of life – indeed it is the basis of the tidal wave we face every day from all types of mass propaganda. It's simple: say something loud enough, proud enough and often enough and it becomes accepted as truth, no matter how false it may be. The overriding emotion this aims to inspire is fear: 'Only WE have the power to save Little You.' No matter how media savvy we are, few have mental flood defences watertight enough to stop these claims seeping in and making us all feel small. A mantra is one way of strapping an outboard engine onto 'Little Me' to fight back.

The most famous exponent of the sporting mantra was Muhammad Ali with 'I am the Greatest'. He was proved unequivocally right, but ahead of his first world title fight with apparently invincible slugger Sonny Liston he had no way of knowing if it was true. Still Ali rightly reckoned 'will' is more important than 'skill', and the mantra was his way of drowning out any kind of self-doubt.

Of course the reason Ali is so revered is not just because he converted his will into skill inside the boxing ring; it's because he used it to fight a bigger foe outside of it. By refusing the Vietnam War draft he sacrificed the peak years of his boxing career to stand in the name of love against the all-encompassing political maxim that 'might is right'. This is what the wider world owes 'the Greatest'.

For dreamers, this is the final step: to help give everyone a chance to live the dream too. Few have the self-belief and courage to risk everything and peek above the parapet: we remember the 'black power' salute by Tommie Smith and John Carlos at the Mexico Olympics in 1968, and Zimbabwe cricket's Andy Flower and Henry Olonga's black armbands representing the death of democracy under Robert Mugabe in 2003 because such stands are so rare.

'Andy and I took a stance because our conscience wouldn't let us take the field in that environment,' Olonga told me in *Overdrive*. 'But it's one thing for that thought to enter your mind. To follow through and transfer it into action was the hard part. I watched *Gladiator* with Russell Crowe looking macho, challenging the emperor. It looks good in the movies but in real life it's a different story. Still, that emboldened me and gave me the impulse to think: "I can do this." Somewhere in each man is a desire to stand up against tyranny. It helped that I wasn't doing it alone, of course...'

Already a pioneer as Zimbabwe's first black international cricketer, Olonga indeed had the backup not only of Flower but his own faith. It was a combination of God and *Gladiator* that saw him through the dangers of the stunt and the career halt and international exile that inevitably followed.

You don't make a mark without having to overcome these insecurities on the biggest stage. In sport the battle usually remains an internal one with their own minds, yet some don't just have to face their own inner demons but those of an entire culture. When Morocco's Nawal El Moutawakel won the inaugural women's 400m hurdles at the 1984 Olympics she became the first woman from a Muslim country ever to win a gold medal. Her success disproved the notion that women of Arabic background did not have what it takes to succeed in athletics, and beat a path for others to follow.

It can't be underestimated just what a burden it is to be a pioneer, particularly when that involves standing up to centuries of politics and prejudice. When I asked El Moutawakel what extra hurdles she faced to get to the right mental state to race to the limit, her reply unsurprisingly bore many similarities to Freeman's: 'When I speak to kids I always say that everything you do in life is 99 per cent hard work and one per cent chance. Nothing is dropped from the sky. You have to earn it; and to earn it you have to learn it. You have to work on your mental side and you always have to have PMA: Positive Mental Attitude.

'I remember during my competing days, my coaches always asked me to say I was the best, that I was number one and that I have to win because I must win. I was always embarrassed to say it but I was forced to because it played on my mental side. I had to rehearse it and say it out loud: "I am number one. I am the best. I have to win because I must win."'

Something must have paid off: El Moutawakel's upward momentum did not stop with her Olympic gold. A member of the International Olympic Committee since 1998, she was president of the evaluation commissions that selected London and Rio de Janeiro as the host cities in 2012 and 2016. Just like Freeman, she now works to spread the message of this not-so-mysterious secret further afield.

'By affirming it you turn it into a self-fulfilling prophecy,' she adds. 'I still use it today. The mental side is very important to any project in life and this still helps me after my career in athletics. I visit high schools, jails and orphanages – and wherever I go I say: "You can do it. You must do it because you're number one. You will do it one day." Kids come out with a totally different attitude. They say, "You looked at us and you made me feel better just from saying it." I think this is my role now.'

The good news is that a Positive Mental Attitude doesn't have to be all about getting in people's faces. It can even be infectious – indeed when you meet some of its finest exponents you are either lifted or dragged up a step on the happiness ladder. Swimmer Missy Franklin was 17 when she took four gold medals at the 2012 London Olympics, yet this ever-charming American is proof that we don't have to be outwardly brash to develop the inner strength to silence Little Me and make it all the way. Here's what she told me about what it feels like to swim in the Zone.

'What I've learned from swimming is that I can flip a switch. I can be really bubbly and happy, then when it's time to race I know it. I hone in on the event coming up. It's that moment right before a race, when you know you've put in the work, you get up behind the block and you're just ready. You can't wait to get out there and show yourself and everyone else what you can do. There's no better feeling; it's incredible. That's why I always love to smile before I race, just to remind myself to have fun and remember why I'm doing it.

'There's a big difference in difficulty between doing something with a positive attitude compared to a negative one. When I attack a practice or meet, if I go in with a negative attitude it will be a hundred times harder. Even if I don't do as well as I want there's no point in wasting energy being negative about it, especially if I have another event coming up. You use those races to grow: each year I want to be a better version of myself. It's about keeping that positive outlook and staying happy all the time.'

Franklin managed to retain this happy-go-lucky attitude even after a deflating Olympic return in Rio, when she took 'just' one more gold for her race in a relay heat. She admits such a comeuppance was hard to take after her four long years of training, alongside studying at the University of California. But if anyone can find a silver lining, this smiling American can. Franklin makes such a fine advert for the power of positive thinking that I had to ask how much of a head start an Olympic champion gets on her fellow psychology undergraduates in understanding the workings of the mind.

'Sport gives a wonderful insight into how we function and how when we get knocked down we get back up again,' she says. 'So I'm grateful for the life lessons it has taught me. I try to be positive all the time: that relates to every aspect of life and it will stay with me for ever, when I have my first job or a family. I race because I love having a chance to get better at what I love. I am very in the present, and in swimming I focus on goals that are weeks or months ahead, not years. But I think about life after swimming all the time. I have many dreams, and one is to be a mum some day. I love kids more than anything and my dream job would be a kindergarten teacher. So after swimming is over I'll still set goals in my life.'

•

History has now all but forgotten that American swimmer Mark Spitz won two relay gold medals at the 1968 Olympics.

Not bad by anyone's standards – except his. Then just 18, Spitz had travelled to Mexico expecting plenty of individual glory too, and he told the world about his bid for six golds. Such was his mortification at missing out, he embarked on four years of pure punishment ahead of the Munich Games in 1972. This time he was going to make sure he would stick in history's memory.

Sporting the bronzed, moustachioed looks of a leading man, Spitz displayed the kind of unerring self-confidence indistinguishable from arrogance. This isn't even all about finding the Zone for yourself. There are also ways of getting into the heads of your rivals to make them fall out of it at the same time. It doesn't have to be active gamesmanship, it's just attitude: exuding an air of total belief.

What is most remarkable about Spitz's Munich blitz is the effect it had on his challengers. He kicked off with gold in the 200m butterfly, in which he'd finished last in 1968. Then, despite his increasing fatigue as his golden treasure trove mounted up, a curious thing started to happen. Spitz found the more he won, the more he deflated the hopes of his rivals too, even if they had entered fewer races and were thus fresher.

'I had a lot of different events – one every day,' Spitz tells me. 'So for me the idea was not to confuse one day's activities with another day. I wasn't thinking about what I had to do tomorrow, I had to stay focused. I also used the fact I was successful from yesterday to encourage me for today. That worked in my best interests because my competitors were saying, "Wow this guy is definitely in shape, he's rested and he has a positive attitude. He's definitely on his game and prepared to win again. What am I going to do about it?" So the fact I had so many events actually helped me.

'I was in the Zone, definitely. Of course being in the Zone means you can also get out of the Zone immediately, because from one day to the next there can be quite a difference in one's ability mentally and also physically. As every day happened and it was one fewer thing to worry about, which lightened my load, it was also one more day I had to compete and I was getting tired. I remember the last stroke I took in the relay on the last day: I don't think I could have taken one more stroke. I put in 100 or even 120 per cent energy the whole time I competed, all the way to the last stroke. Then I ran out of gas. That's exactly what you want. You want to run out of gas at the finish line, not before. So I was thankful it happened right then and not a moment before.'

It was Spitz's control of his mind that allowed him to overlook the increasing discomfort in his muscles until the very second it no longer mattered. He went home with seven gold medals, the greatest haul the Olympics had ever seen. Along the way he set seven world records, each a further dagger into the minds of anyone imagining they had a hope of stopping his run to legendary status. Spitz also calculated he had left himself no more room to go any higher and he retired from the sport immediately. Perfect Hollywood.

Of course not everyone has the swagger which marks out the classic image of a champion that Spitz personifies. Early in life most of us learn not to be cocky as we work out that modesty is generally a better way to make and keep friends. Such humility is admired into adulthood, with good reason. But this kind of self-effacement – whether genuine or not – doesn't actually help any of us, let alone the potential competitor.

If we start believing the hype behind that sentiment, little do we know how far the attitude of 'Little Me' works its way into our subconscious and eats into the actual ability we believe we have. When such thoughts are allowed to creep in, the chance of even setting out in pursuit of a dream – let alone getting anywhere near achieving it – diminishes accordingly. This deflating habit can crop up when it seriously matters too: the dream job interview, chatting up your dream partner. Trouble. If we don't believe we can do something, no one else will either. It begs the question of why we aren't all routinely taught that talking the talk really can help walking the walk.

•

Giant performances invariably leave a generation of dreamers in their wake, some of whom later turn into giants themselves. Britain's Steve Redgrave was ten years old as he avidly watched Mark Spitz's feats on the television. He would go on to break new ground on water too, albeit with the help of a boat, becoming the first Olympian in a power sport to win gold in five consecutive Games from 1984 to 2000.

'As a kid, most of us dream about achieving great things,' Redgrave tells me. 'Sport is such a visual thing and for me it was Mark Spitz who sparked the feeling of "Wouldn't it be nice to compete at the Olympics?" But it was four years before I even found my sport of rowing. Then if you get reasonable success early in your career as a raw youngster, you get this inner belief you can do it. This sounds very arrogant, but I always felt I was going to be an Olympic gold medallist. I did think I was only going to do it once, not five times, but in hindsight as a more "whole" person, I now wonder where did that desire and inner belief actually come from?

'But there was something in me – and the mind is very much part of that. The power of the mind, the experiences you have and belief make the difference in sport. In some of the tennis matches in recent years at five hours plus, even if it's not going their way, the players keep that belief, thinking: "He's on a hot streak at the moment, it can't last for ever. It will change." You just hang in there – and it's the same in a race.

'In rowing we do physical training involving a lot of hard work. The saying is "miles make champions": the more miles you do ploughing up and down water, the greater your chance of winning. But the mind is the real strong place. If you have any doubt in your mind you will probably fall down somewhere on the path. If you reach an Olympic final your competitors have the same ability and they've done the same sort of training. So what makes some win and some lose? It's partly physical, but it's more the mental side of knowing you can do it and you will do it.'

This belief took Redgrave on a run of Olympic glory unmatched in endurance sport. But the initial breakthrough still wasn't easy in an unglamorous activity which was undergoing a slump at home: 'Success breeds success so it's easier to follow than start it,' he adds. 'In the UK we weren't performing on the international stage so there wasn't a winning culture. I changed that, coming in with a gung-ho attitude of: "Sod you all, I'm going to show you whatever…" My coach Mike Spracklen got us training with the other men's teams. We weren't far behind. Then the belief came: "We can't beat them but there are 14 Olympic events. If we can get close we've got a chance."

'I was fortunate to compete at a high level very young. We

did a coxed four at my first Games: that was a bunch of misfits. I carried on with Andy Holmes and we were recognised as two of the best athletes in the world at the time. Then along came Matthew Pinsent, who became the best oarsman of his era. To have the skill for the early part of my career, then to be able to row with people with the skill at the end of it, there was a lot of luck involved. But it was hard work too.'

That hard work included mental training, led by Team GB head coach Jürgen Grobler. One of few with an Olympic record that tops even Redgrave's, Grobler has led crews to gold in every Games since 1972, bar 1984 when the Eastern Bloc boycott precluded his native East Germany from competing. It's no coincidence that the night before every big event he gathers his crews for a detailed row-through on dry land.

'It's about 240 strokes and they run through every one, so they send signals to their muscles and know exactly how everything should be,' says Grobler. 'You can't predict everything so you have to prepare the guys on what our strengths are and what we can expect from each other. This mental preparation is important and always gives them goosebumps. Before a big race they are tense. But it's about having no fear, just going out and executing what they've done in training. It's about how far can you go, how you can focus and concentrate to execute your plan. You need that killer instinct too. That sounds hard in a sport like rowing where we don't touch each other, but what separates out the best is in the mind. The strongest people find that little bit extra.'

Pinsent, whose own collection of golds in successive Olympic Games reached 'only' four, confirms: 'We would go through the race and talk about what we wanted to happen. We did very intricate planning – and yes, in my experience it works.' This was a technique Redgrave used throughout his career, first casually then in a formal setting with Andy Holmes's doctor brother Simon, who even used hypnosis to put the pair in a trance. In the four years leading to his final Olympics in 2000, even when he was diagnosed with Type 2 diabetes and forced to monitor his insulin levels ten times a day, Redgrave would picture his race every day too.

'The more you think about things, the more you look at "what if" situations,' says Redgrave. 'If you're the favourite, what you don't want is surprises – because surprises normally mean failure. In rowing finals it's about trying to go from A to B as fast as you possibly can, hopefully fast enough to beat everyone else. But there are five other boats seeing you as favourites, thinking: "If we do this, this and this, we can beat you." So you've got to be ready with the answers for every situation that arises.

'We only race internationally three times a year. That's not a lot of experience of what can happen in different races. The race itself happens so quickly: six minutes. It's either happening for you or not – and if it's going dreadfully wrong there's very little you can do. So visualisation is crucial. I used to ask myself: "Who will be in the final? What if the Australians do this?" Mentally, you put yourself in thousands of situations so when one arises something deep inside says: "Right, we're going to do that" instead of thinking "Oh no, what are we going to do?" If you think that, it's over.'

Despite four years of countless mental permutations, it doesn't stop the jitters on the big day. That is when 'Little Me' syndrome kicks in even for a sporting giant like

Steve Redgrave – who can smile about it now: 'The worst time is the two or three hours of mental hell beforehand,' he says. 'I'd sit in the warm-up area thinking: "Why am I doing this? This is the worst..." Then you remember all your training and think: "You've done all that, don't waste it. Go out there, win, lose or draw, give it your best shot. Then you can walk away from it."

'But you need that adrenalin boost. Something Matt and I were really good at was that the bigger the race, the better we performed. That taught us we needed that world stage, that horrible position to be in. Different people react differently. Where Matt focused on the positive and would always think how well things were going, I was a slightly negative-minded athlete. I'd respond to doom and gloom: "This could happen, wouldn't that be a disaster? I can't allow that to happen..."'

Olympic greats have such supreme ability they ought to be impervious to such negativity. But they only get one chance every four years, when their every move will be dissected by a crowd of thousands and a television audience of millions.

In 2000 Katherine Grainger became one of the first British women to win an Olympic rowing medal, taking silver in the quadruple sculls. A great achievement – but of course it left a tantalising final step. Rowing is a punishing sport involving four years of early mornings and putting your body through hell but it was worth it for Grainger, who returned in the coxless pair in 2004. Another mighty performance, another silver. Olympians love heavy metal but silverware is a bit tiresome. Four more years of pain down the line, would it be third time lucky in Beijing? Nope. Silver again, back in the quadruple sculls. And the tears that flowed on the podium were anything but joyful.

ATTITUDE

The mental strength required even to contemplate embarking on years 13 to 16 of such an apparently doomed quest is immeasurable. But the thought of ending up with just one colour of precious metal in her collection – coupled with the knowledge that 2012 would be at home in London – somehow pushed Grainger into yet another cycle of exertion. When I met her at the pre-Olympic training camp I expected to see someone being inexorably swallowed up by what lay ahead. Wrong. Grainger exuded the easy-going confidence of the British team's natural figurehead. When I asked how she found her way to the Zone when it matters, she initially stated: 'I don't think you create it, you don't find it, it finds you.' Then she detailed exactly how she and double sculls partner Anna Watkins made sure it had a Sat Nav…

'The Olympic final is the hardest thing to prepare for because nothing can compare to it,' she says. 'Even the final of the World Championship or World Cup comes nowhere near it mentally because of the nerves, the expectation and desire to produce the result. It's hard to create and it's almost hard to imagine. So what we've done with our big events is put pressure on ourselves to get nervous, to make sure it's uncomfortable and edgy and not enjoyable. The Olympics are very special. But once you've experienced it, you know you can come through and perform. Then when the alarm goes off on the big morning – even though you're usually awake already – you know it. You don't need to get in the Zone. You're in the Zone.'

When Grainger duly struck gold just weeks later after decades of painstaking silver mining, her Hollywood ending came as no surprise to me. But so much for the movies; just like Michael Phelps and Jessica Ennis-Hill she returned to

Rio four years later, offering the fates yet another chance to ruin her big finale. Grainger and partner Victoria Thornley had been racing so poorly earlier in 2016 that they were initially left out of the team altogether. Then, after a late reprieve, they recovered to race all the way to the Rio final, taking an unlikely, glorious silver. This one was every bit as welcome to Grainger as her first. As was this final, magical trip to the Zone.

•

It was at the 1992 USA Olympic trials that sprinter Michael Johnson first discovered what he terms the 'Danger Zone'. After running his 200m heat into a strong headwind his slow time left him drawn in the (worst possible) outside lane for the final against a field featuring the likes of Carl Lewis. It should have been curtains but a mix of anger and determination to rub everyone's faces in it revved Johnson up. He took the field apart in the world's fastest time for four years. The intense sensation of focus came as a revelation to Johnson that there was another gear to be found out there. This became the archetype for the mental state he tried to recreate.

Fast forward four years and Johnson was the undisputed home superstar of the Atlanta Olympics. As if that pressure wasn't enough, he made an extra statement of intent, upping the fashion stakes to the max. He later summed it up: 'How could you look more stupid than to be the guy accepting a bronze medal in gold shoes?'

Such humiliation was far from implausible. The American had suffered food poisoning just before the 1992 Barcelona Olympics and failed even to reach the final, belying his status as clear favourite. That meant he went into 1996 knowing he could end his career without the crowning golden glory his ability merited. Yet during the build-up, such doubts were far away. Johnson didn't have just one medal on his mind; he was aiming to make history as the first man to win both 200m and 400m. A gold for each shoe. He even had to plead with the organisers to accommodate his bid with a change of schedule, leaving him with a daunting run of eight races in a week.

As he settled into the blocks, Johnson saw his gold shoes glimmering away at him. Were they taunting him to picture the mortification that lay ahead if he failed? Hardly. Like a physical manifestation of 'I am the Greatest' they were the final kick in the backside of 'Little Me' syndrome, booting it clean out of the stadium. He duly escaped such indignity, winning the 400m and his second gold by smashing the 200m record in 19.32 seconds, four tenths faster than anyone before and since beaten only by Usain Bolt. It remains one of sport's most memorable moments.

Later asked how it felt to run so fast, the closest experiences Johnson could conjure up were his boyhood rides in a go-kart built by his father. The American remains a Formula 1 fan who enjoys thrashing fast cars around tracks. As such I couldn't resist asking how Johnson's 'Danger Zone' compared to Ayrton Senna's day of days around Monaco.

'People often ask what you think about while you're running, but when you're competing at that level I don't know if the average person could understand it,' smiles Johnson. 'I wouldn't describe it as an out-of-body experience as much as... for me it was just this hyper-focus and awareness. Nothing else matters – what's happening in the next lane or in the stadium, none of that. I didn't hear the crowd. I couldn't hear them because you're so hyper-focused on what you're doing and every little element, it gets to a level where it was about going inward to where it's only what's happening right here. I could really feel and sense everything that was happening with my body, and how I was executing things. That's probably the equivalent to what Ayrton Senna described, but that's the way it was for me.'

Even after he ripped up the Atlanta track, Johnson couldn't shake the memory of a stumble on his third step – imperceptible to most but a critical blemish to an artist for whom the track was his canvas. That prompted a change in his approach that took him on a quest for even greater masterpieces.

'The Danger Zone took on a different complex,' he tells me. 'Up until 1996 I literally wanted to be putting my training kit back on before the other guys crossed the finish line. I wanted to beat them as bad as I possibly could and I took great pride in that. But the second half of my career was more about my own personal goals. I focused on times, records, making history and doing things that were unprecedented in the sport.

'On the blocks the intensity went up another level. Early in my career in those final moments when I was visualising how to execute the race, it very much depended on the other athletes. That was a help because all I've got to do is beat them. But later I wasn't relying on the competitors any more. I had to beat them but I also had goals that had absolutely nothing to do with them: I've got to execute this race effectively – and it rarely happens that the race is executed 100 per cent to the point you set.'

This obsessive chase for perfection is the preserve of sport's elite. Winning a gold medal or a world championship is a mighty achievement, but the next level only comes into sight when you are clear of all rivals and the battle begins with yourself. This is the step from great to legend. Soon Johnson's real chase was for what would ultimately prove an elusive goal: the perfect race.

'Athletes have to be motivated and inspired to go out there and do everything they possibly can,' insists Johnson. 'The great athletes are obsessive about finding the most effective training methods, obsessive about competition and trying to achieve the perfect execution of a race and they are very, very critical of themselves. When you are in pursuit of excellence you're constantly thinking about the things you don't do well.

'It got to a point where some of the guys I raced, who are now my friends but not at the time, say: "One thing we never liked about Michael was that he acted like we weren't there." That was because I was so far ahead, the others were still crossing the line while I was already thinking about what I didn't do right. That's the mind of a champion and a high achiever. My coach (Clyde Hart) is a high achiever too – he was also a very good sprinter – and he had the same mentality: there's more and better that we can accomplish, so that's what we've got to focus on.'

While perfection may remain tantalisingly out of bounds, the fun is in the hunt and the payback just for getting close is out of this world. Yet even these moments of glorious vindication are not what Johnson treasures most.

'Crossing the finish line when it has all worked out is a tremendous feeling,' adds Johnson. 'It's the feeling of accomplishment, all that work you've put in – but honestly that's not what I miss. What I miss most, really and truly, is that time about 45 minutes before the race in the call room. You're with the other athletes and it's just intense pressure. I miss that part. I adored the pressure, I thrived on pressure. That's why all my world records were in big championships. I always knew my best chance for records would be when there was a lot on the line because I responded well. I went into every championship knowing exactly what condition I was in, how well prepared I was and what I was capable of. That doesn't necessarily mean you will deliver on the day because you still have to go out and execute correctly. At every race I knew I could win but I didn't know if I would win.'

Both Johnson and the rest of the field could have had a pretty good guess: at one point he won 58 one-lap races on the trot. This supremacy came about because he was a meticulous planner with his training regime, a trait he credits to his father who insisted on such an approach with everything from family life to holidays. Johnson Jr thus didn't just have airy plans in his head; he wrote them down, keeping a training log of everything he did on track. He also wrote specific plans plus daily and yearly goals as he plotted his path to gold.

'Even with all those wins, I had losses as well,' adds Johnson. 'Athletes learn as children how to respond to being knocked down and how to get back up. Whoever you are, that lesson can help young people for the rest of their lives – because we all get knocked down from time to time. What I've found with the legends of sport I've met is a real sense of self, understanding who they are. That gives you a tremendous amount of confidence. If you set out to do something great and you do it, it boosts that confidence even more. Once you've achieved at the highest level there's nothing else to prove. So the idea that you have to try and show somebody you're better? You've already gone out and shown the world you're one of the best there ever was…'

•

If belief breeds success and success breeds belief, like chickens and eggs it begs the question of which comes first? If you're in the vast majority without a golden history, the surest way to break into the cycle is to act as if you do. This attitude serves simply as a reminder that there is nothing Little about Me. If you really want to make it big, you'd better believe it. Suddenly it makes perfect sense for a young girl to repeat 'I am the world's greatest athlete', a boxer without a belt to declare 'I am the Greatest' or an Olympic hopeful with no medals to wear gold shoes.

Even if you do convince yourself all the way to the top, the next question isn't far behind: now what? For decades a champion's entire focus can laser in on a single moment in the future. When it finally passes, those who succeed get to bathe in some well-earned fame and adulation. We might consider this the ideal time to go stew on a desert island. But big achievers aren't made that way. No matter how hard it seems at the time, the process trumps the result. The other rewards glory brings generally seem pitiful compared to the joy of throwing yourself heart and soul into your dream.

With such peaks at their disposal it is not surprising so few sports stars find the 'right' time to retire when they've spent their lives building towards the same end and often know nothing else. If every day of their training counts as a single brick, it can be heartbreaking to abandon the palace they've crafted, even if advancing years mean the paintwork is worn and the foundations are starting to subside. It takes rare insight to recognise when the moment has come, which is one reason why apparently ill-judged comebacks are so widespread. One who did get it right is Johnson, who quit athletics at 32 after four years of typically painstaking planning for it. He then forged successful careers in broadcasting, business and charity work but admits his decision was made easier by his 'fortune' at having completed everything he set out to achieve.

'Some end up making comebacks because they feel there's still something else to accomplish,' he says. 'They miss that intensity and the atmosphere or they haven't found anything to focus on. With the athletes who stay too long, much of it is hearing the crowds roar and people screaming your name. Some people identify with that and can't imagine their lives without it. But I never identified myself as an athlete. I was very fortunate to be one but it's not who I am.

'Many athletes also make the mistake of thinking they will be able to replace it with something. I can tell you nothing in life will ever feel like that and I don't expect anything to, ever. It's an indescribable feeling. It is that special. When I have success in business it's phenomenal but it's not going to feel like that. Preserve it, have great memories of it but to look for something to equal it would be stupid.'

Some highs may be impossible to reproduce but there's good news for anyone who has ever chased a dream: all that bricklaying does not go to waste. Regardless of the outcome, just setting out to stack the blocks marked Conceive, Believe and Achieve turns into a habit and makes us more likely to take on another build. And no matter how all-encompassing a dream has been, there is always a new one waiting when it reaches its natural conclusion. Moreover, all the knowledge of what went right – and especially what went wrong – instantly converts into the first floor of the next dream.

Nonetheless, Johnson is acutely aware that for much of the world's population the notion of chasing a dream is still out of reach anyway: the obstacles blocking mere survival take priority over those shielding Olympic gold. Sport is a rare field that can even claim to be a real meritocracy. Elsewhere the success or otherwise of the world's dreamers is much harder to measure, not least because for many the query 'How good am I?' will never stretch beyond bringing home the bacon.

Johnson was touched by the planet's problems during his travels as an athlete but his career didn't grant him spare time to act. Getting to the top in any competitive field requires a commitment that inherently renders it a selfish activity. Thankfully the attitude he built up over so many years of success is directly transferable. The highest level of self-belief brings a realisation that you have no need to prove anything about yourself; instead your expertise is best used to help others. Now Johnson is devoted to giving everyone else the attitude to start believing too, no matter where they start out. Today he uses his celebrity to give back, most notably via the Laureus Sport for Good Foundation, which has helped millions of kids to date.

'The projects Laureus supports give kids a chance to play and find something they love,' he says. 'As athletes we have the ability to inspire young people with our presence, to help them understand someone cares and that they are important enough for us to travel to – even if some are so young they don't know who I am. We try to help kids in tough situations who need all the support they can get. For a lot of people, if they could just wake up without having to overcome a tremendous amount of really high hurdles, that's a win for them. So we're trying to get them a win.'

Whatever challenges we face in life, it seems nothing is insurmountable with real attitude and belief. Of course far too many people need basic physical resources first before they can even dream of making full use of their mental capacity, but I can vouch for one thing: those who truly believe in themselves to the level of Michael Johnson ooze charisma. If you are lucky enough to meet an achiever of this calibre you walk away with your head held that little bit higher – and you soon find yourself investigating how to make best use of whatever opportunities you do have.

Still, pushy parents should take note: Johnson is refreshingly reluctant to usher anyone down his chosen road. Today's sporting hopefuls are forced into ever younger starts but it always has to come from within: 'As adults, coaches and media we have to stop picking a kid who's ten years old to aim for the top,' he insists. 'It's really not helpful to tell young kids to aspire to something that's ten or 20 years away. We have to let kids choose their own path. If there's something they want to do, let them find their way and pursue it slowly. Focus on the right now, being the best you can be and believing in yourself – whether it's sport, music, academic or whatever. Everyone has their special situation, so you have to find your own way and what works for you.'

That's how we can all find our own private paths, following CBA all the way. Once we've conceived our dream and we truly, honestly believe in it, there's really only one step left.

ACHIEVE

6

FOCUS

This level of expertise – and its peaks – is not limited to sport. When Captain Chesley 'Sully' Sullenberger's Airbus struck a flock of Canada geese shortly after take-off, he made the apparently snap decision to land on New York's Hudson River. He later told CBS he'd spent 42 years making small deposits in a bank of experience; that day his balance was sufficient to make a 'very large withdrawal'. Nadia Comăneci's 'bag' (as discussed in the Introduction) yet again… and it led Sully straight to the Zone when it mattered, saving 155 lives.

No one is born able to fly an aeroplane, just as no one is born driving a car. To get good at either requires long hours as the brain gradually learns how to interpret the sensations sent in from all over the body as the vehicle rolls and yaws, converting this mass of data into instructions to send back to the limbs perched on the controls. This eventually crafts an ability to complete even the hardest tasks without thinking. Still, the proficiency of a lifetime of practice will be no use if you can't access it on the one day, the one second, when it *really* matters. If you ever suddenly find yourself having to think about what you're doing, it's a one-way street to remembering in vivid detail how staggeringly complex your skills were in the first place.

Some professionals have an even bigger bank to draw on. British Airways 747 captain Paul Bonhomme doubles as a triple world champion in the Red Bull Air Race, where single-seater planes twist, spin and loop just metres above land and sea. Pilots are invited to compete only after proving they are among the world's finest aerobatics aces. Bonhomme's 19 career wins leave him clear as the best of the best.

'Whatever you're flying, you have to be in the right mood,' says Bonhomme, who retired from racing after his third title in 2015. 'It varies if it's an air race, an aerobatic display or just a flight from A to B. You're supposed to fly a jumbo jet so far within safety levels that it should be relaxing. But then, depending on how extremely you're operating an aeroplane, you have to be in a better mood or, yes, "in the Zone".

'You could fly round an air race course without much aerobatics experience but the challenge is getting out of a tricky situation. For that you need years of tumbling, flicking, stalling, spinning and all that wacky stuff we've spent 20 years doing. That once saved my bacon in an air race and I know others who had similar situations. You need a heap of aerobatics experience before you go air racing, just as you would want the best stick-and-rudder pilot flying an airliner. Ironically, in both cases if you've got the experience then hopefully you won't need it.

'Air racing is extraordinary because everything else in aviation is super-safe whereas this requires motor racing skills. So there are two fears: the fear of not doing very well and the fear of frightening yourself or worse. You need to get the mix in clear proportion. The fear of frightening yourself should be a massive bubble compared to the fear of failure, but often it works the other way round. That's why you have to be really careful. It doesn't really matter if you come fifth instead of first but it really does matter if you're not around at the next race…'

When Brazil's Adilson Kindlemann crashed into the water at 200mph in Perth, Australia in 2010, he somehow swam away with no more than a scratched neck. But it prompted race organisers to pull the plug for a few years until the series returned with stricter safety rules. Bonhomme is himself the veteran of a 1994 crash in a plane that suffered a mechanical fault and flipped. Two seconds later he hit the ground, enough time to utter just a single expletive. He also escaped with minor injuries.

No wonder the Briton admits to getting ratty before air races, avoiding crowds to cope with what he terms 'healthy anxiousness' as he aimed to find the crucial calm to perform. He would even nap to split his day up so he could wake up with only one thought: 'Just empty your mind and go and fly.' This clutter-free mind is crucial for all sport, hence the chase for techniques to clear our inner selves out and create a vacuum to suck all those years of practice back in. But really there's nothing new about this hunt. 'Zen' Buddhism derives from the Indian Sanskrit 'dhanya', meaning meditative concentration – and Japan's 2017 Red Bull Air Race world champion Yoshihide Muroya is a good example of how it still pays off as a practitioner of 'zazen', which translates as 'sitting meditation'.

'Meditation helps me because it's mental training,' says Muroya. 'At a race I do it every morning. I use it to focus on myself, just to calm down and take away the extraneous thoughts that have been going through my head. In racing there's no time to think so you need to be focused and automatic. Directly before the flight when we need a high mental state – not overheating, a good temperature – meditation would cool me down too much so I just sit down instead. But meditation is good for flying and it's a big help for life too. Everyone can benefit from it. We all have so much going round our brains all the time and we're normally looking outside so it's quite difficult to look deep inside. But it's really good to calm down, and looking inside helps make life easier for anyone.'

Once pilots are in their cockpit, their canopy offers a perfect cocoon from the outside world. Racing is a fast track to total focus, as Britain's 2014 world champion Nigel Lamb explains: 'I come back to the hangar and people say I must have heard the crowd. But I can't hear the crowd. Once you're in the air you see pylons and trees. The rest is not even there.' Germany's 2016 world champion Matthias Dolderer agrees: 'You are so focused and concentrated that there is nothing else that can or should distract you. So you don't even have to think about it, there is nothing. You don't have time and you are fully 100 per cent concentrated on what you're doing. Whatever happened before this is just gone, it's not there at the moment when you fly. Actually to fly in the racetrack is the best way to get rid of all distractions.'

There is a proviso: once the distractions are cleared, what fills the gap should be alertness. Bonhomme even admits during one race he remembered he'd forgotten to hand in his washing at the hotel: 'When you're pulling 4G and wondering about laundry it's a bit odd. I had to say, "Are you going to be a klutz all your life? Just for the next minute concentrate on this." It's wrong. If you have that much spare capacity, you should be using it to find the extra tenth of a second.'

The Briton did nail together all his experience and ability for what he rates as his best performance in New York during his second championship. Due to the city's unhappy aviation history the pilots were given strict instructions not to take risks, so Bonhomme chose to focus on consistency. Over three separate 7km flights he clocked 1 minute 10.09 seconds, 1 minute 10.07 seconds and 1 minute 10.03 seconds, just six hundredths apart. 'Whether you can think like that at the last race of the championship is another matter,' Bonhomme tells me. 'Say you're a point off your rival. Do you have it within you to say: "I'm not going to try too hard. It doesn't matter whether I win or lose." You need an "I don't need to win" pill...'

Australian ace Matt Hall tasted that pill during a 2010 air race in Canada when he skimmed the water with his wingtips. He has since become a big player by learning to manage his self-belief to be ready to peak: 'It's all about being consistent in your thought process and confidence level,' he tells me. 'Until you fly the track you're not sure how it will go, so you've got to be confident you'll make it work. As the weekend progresses, your confidence in your ability to fly the track cleanly should increase with track time. Where you can start to get nervous and have to work really hard on the sports psychology side is if you make a mistake. This is also common in Formula 1: if someone hits a wall in qualifying or practice they think: "Holy crap, I hope I don't do that again!" It's the same in air racing if you hit a pylon (resulting in a time penalty). But if you have clean training sessions you go into race day feeling confident in the track and thinking: "I can probably even go a bit faster now."

'I have set times for visualising the track, otherwise you end up over-preparing and you become stale. So in the hours leading up to the race, on the hour I spend five minutes just thinking about it. Then with one hour to go I'm in a formal routine where everything is planned by the minute so I'm not distracted and I'm in zero stress. The stress only comes when you start looking too far ahead.'

Hall approaches his mental groundwork with the rigour you might expect of a former Wing Commander in the Royal Australian Air Force. His countdown increases in rigidity as take-off time approaches, starting with a stretch first thing and a walk to clear his mind. Media interviews fit into the morning before the daily pilots' briefing. Within the final hour he lies down in his hangar for precisely 21 minutes, with music building to a crescendo to wake him up with half an hour left. Then comes another set of mind flying, a last look at notes and video before he gets 'suited and booted' to be in his plane with 20 minutes left – all with an ongoing soundtrack until he swaps his headphones for his helmet six minutes before take-off.

'I know music works for me and in recent years I always listen to the same set of songs in a row,' says Hall. 'Every song represents something to me. There's a song to pump me up when I'm getting dressed, then more relaxing songs as I'm visualising the track. When I'm strapped into the plane it's rock music – not hard rock but happy rock – and I'm thinking:

"I'm happy to be doing this, my life's not depending on it, I'm just here having fun and racing planes." That's the last thing I do before I start the engine, so when I go to the track I know I've done everything I can, I'm confident and I'm really happy to be here. Then it should all go well. If you're too pumped up you're just going to wreck it. If you go out hoping you don't make a mistake it won't work because you won't fly aggressively enough or you'll be really tentative. You've got to go in saying "How good is this? I can win this race, let's have a crack at it..."

'On the best runs you don't think about two gates' time, you're thinking about this gate coming up right now and the feel of the aircraft. That's all you're thinking. That's when I know I'm on a really good run because there's not a single thought of doubt in my mind and not a single thought of the future in my mind. They talk about being "in the Zone" in sport and when I have a good run, I definitely know. It's a euphoric feeling. When I'm in the track I can't hear the engine any more, I'm just a passenger in the aircraft, just riding this magic carpet through the track.'

•

This level of total focus has a welcome side-effect: when the brain is entirely engaged in what it's doing, our inner critic has no option but to shut up. That's why it is crucial in extreme activities with life and death at stake. Indeed mindfulness isn't just about sitting cross-legged in meditation: its aim is to bring our attention back to the present moment no matter where we are.

'Whatever challenge we face in sport or life the ability to concentrate – longer, harder, deeper – is the way to better performance,' says mind coach Don MacPherson. 'Eastern martial arts disciples have long known that, and the first step is to recognise that concentration is a deliberate action. It is under your control and at its best when you are calm and confident. To find the Zone we must be in subconscious mode. This is where the highest level of concentration is based, where things happen automatically and without thinking. Pure concentration comes when both past and future fade away. The great performers – in sport, music and elsewhere – live entirely in the now.'

Margins are so tight at the top of world sport that techniques to find this extreme level of focus are increasingly common as everyone seeks an edge. NBA basketball teams have been known to meditate before big games, while Nico Rosberg credited it with maintaining his concentration during his 2016 run to the Formula 1 title. Then there's Spanish motorcyclist Jorge Lorenzo, a triple MotoGP world champion.

'When you feel nervous ahead of a race you can do meditation,' says Lorenzo. 'In my case this is about relaxing: if you don't have any thoughts you can relax more to be ready. If you are nervous you are more tired and you cannot be at the same level. With every year of experience you can be calmer. Before, if I was heading for a crisis, I would crash or do some something stupid. Now, in a tough situation I'm not agitated but more relaxed and calm so I can think more and find a solution.'

It seems a motorbike is a surprisingly effective vehicle to inner peace. Dougie Lampkin won 12 world titles in trials riding, where you go over a series of obstacles without letting your feet touch the ground. His focus took on a new level as his brain would block out any irrelevant sensory information.

'It's a strange feeling when you're 100 per cent concentrated on the job,' says Lampkin. 'Ten thousand people can all be screaming within 50 metres of you but you don't hear anything. In our sport you have a "minder" on the back wheel to make sure you're in the best position to leap off for the next gap. What's amazing is you hear your minder crystal-clear but everything else is a complete blank. You're so focused on the moment that nothing can get in the way if it tried.'

It sounds fanciful to suddenly develop super-sensitive hearing but this is what can happen at moments of intense concentration. We all have the ability to hone in on a specific conversation in a crowded room; it is a phenomenon termed the 'cocktail party effect' by psychologist Colin Cherry. When nothing else matters the brain can cut out anything superfluous. As British swimmer Adam Peaty smashed the world record twice to win the 2016 Olympic 100m breaststroke he found similar focus, telling me: 'It's just tunnel vision, isn't it?' This sensation is regularly reported by accident survivors and I've met racing drivers who have found themselves harnessing it at big moments: one even claimed to start seeing only in black and white. Other senses can raise their intensity too. Ayrton Senna could smell the state of his brakes and knew if anyone had spun ahead of him from the aroma of grass.

Motor sport is one of the noisiest activities there is, yet if you attain such focus it may as well be a Tibetan mountaintop. Alexander Rossi, who won the Indianapolis 500 as a rookie in 2016, confirms: 'It's very peaceful, actually... At such high speed if you operate solely on a conscious level you'd be too slow to react. So you no longer think about driving, until it becomes second nature. That's when you perform at your best.' This unlikely state of rest was also the key for triple Indy 500 winner Johnny Rutherford: 'I've had my crew tell me to slow down because I was in front, so I'd get comfortable. A couple of laps later they came back: "We told you to slow down!" I'd go faster because I'd relaxed.' Scotland's Dario Franchitti, another three-time winner, insists: 'When you are operating to your highest level you almost dismiss it because it comes quite easily. You're processing so much, focused on extracting everything out of yourself and the car, there's no room left for: "This is great." That happens later...'

This state of extreme focus can make even apparently huge challenges seem easy, especially when we know we have the skill and we let ourselves get on with it. There are endless alternative routes to this apparently blissful peace in circumstances that may seem the diametric opposite – not least in the natural world.

'There is no better demonstration of relaxed concentration than a cat stalking a mouse,' adds Don MacPherson. 'He is here, now, trying without trying, perfect balance, effortlessly alert, relaxed and focused only on the mouse. Not a single thought crosses his mind about missing his target: there's no thinking at all, he's involved only in the process. Nothing else exists. Suddenly the mouse makes a bid for freedom and in the same moment the cat leaps. Thoughtless action, perfectly executed. Game over.

'Here's how you too can be catlike. Find an object, anything will do. A candle is easy on the eye but a mark on the wall will do. Now become fascinated with all its detail. See how long you can go without looking away. As soon as you get distracted, bring yourself back. Gradually build up the time you can stay focused. Nobody can concentrate all the time but the more you practise, the closer you'll get. As you raise your skills you block out distractions and zero in like a laser beam on a single activity. It will now be easier to keep focused on a tennis ball, even under extreme pressure, as will entering your Zone. When you master the art you'll start to feel things happening automatically – or as if somebody else is doing it. Meanwhile you're going with the flow, not thinking just doing.'

•

Sometimes sport isn't even about winning at all. Mike Atherton captained England in 54 Test matches yet he modestly describes himself as a 'decent' rather than 'great' cricketer. That all changed under the Johannesburg sun in 1995 when Atherton's team faced an unlikely total of 479 to win in their second innings. With victory out of sight England aimed to draw by batting through five two-hour sessions to finish the final day's play with wickets intact. That's when Atherton came into his own, frustrating the South African attack for nearly 11 hours for an unbeaten total of 185 runs. Far from the free-flowing joy typifying Zone experiences, this was a grind – requiring patience not flair. But this 27-year-old built up such intense concentration he gradually worked himself into the archetypal trancelike state of total control.

'The only time I've ever been in the Zone was during that innings,' Atherton tells me. 'It was bizarre, but for the last three hours I knew they wouldn't get me out. It's a particular feeling which came from time spent at the crease. You can't just feel you're there after three balls. It was seven hours of batting before it came, and in my case I had to go through that process to get that feeling. It's difficult to explain but it felt great. I wish you could bottle it but I don't think you can. Still, I'd guess the best players have it often.'

If we think this state of total concentration is when the brain is working at full capacity, apparently we'd be wrong. Science will readily admit it is a long way from unravelling the deepest mysteries of this three-pound lump of grey matter, but its hunt is gathering pace. Using technology such as EEG (electroencephalogram) and SPECT (single-photon emission computed tomography), everyone from meditating Tibetan monks to improvising jazz musicians have been studied to ascertain what's happening in their brains. Since the expansion of functional magnetic resonance imaging (fMRI) over the last 20 years, it has been possible to measure activity in different areas by detecting changes in blood flow. A map is gradually being drawn up – albeit in very low resolution, limited by what this fledgling technology can see.

When neuroscientist Arne Dietrich studied the 'flow' state of the Zone, he focused on the prefrontal cortex, a region associated with problem solving, detailed analysis, data collection and future planning: the basis of the intelligence that sets us apart from other animals. We might think this should go into overdrive when we're performing at the limit but Dietrich has theorised that parts of this region instead shut down, in a process he terms 'transient hypofrontality' (meaning a temporary slowing down of activity in this area). In effect we are thinking not more but less, losing our thinking selves and honing in on the here and now. But Dietrich has a head start in the field, having found the Zone for himself as a triathlete.

One of sport's most brutal challenges, the triathlon features a 1.5km swim, a 40km bike ride and a 10km run. That was clearly far too much of a trifling 'sprint' for Germany's 2008 Olympic champion Jan Frodeno, who later stepped up to the even more insane 'Ironman'. Unimaginable for most, it features a 3.8km swim, a 180km bike ride and a full 42.2km marathon. Frodeno somehow completed all that in 7 hours 35 minutes 39 seconds for a new world record in 2016, adding to his victories in the 2015 and 2016 Ironman world championship at Hawaii's Kona. Make no mistake, this is one mighty fit human being. Yet the German is adamant that even in this ultimate physical field, the secret is not in his muscles but in his head.

'It's much harder on the mind than the body,' insists Frodeno. 'Of course you have to be fit – but all the competitors are fit, they've all got great VO$_2$ maxes (which measures a body's rate of oxygen consumption) and all that. But it's in the mind that victory is won or lost. It's less about strength than concentration. Moving up from the triathlon to the Ironman, the main change is in attitude and mental strength. It changes from competitors playing mind games, to you against yourself and the elements. No one can hold focus for eight hours – unless you're the Dalai Lama. With fatigue you go through so many ups and downs and find yourself dipping in and out, so it's a fine art to get back to that focus. You outweigh negative thoughts with positive thoughts, using self-talk to control your emotions and let them control your muscles. For weeks after an Ironman I find myself hearing voices because I'm mentally so exhausted.'

Few of us can even compute the level of physical exhaustion we'd experience after an Ironman but we all know what mental exhaustion feels like – even if it is just the result of a long day sat at a desk or a late night of fun. Endurance athletes need to control any urge to give up to have any chance of keeping competitors at bay.

'I've learned it is an ongoing process, all the time,' he adds. 'I do my mental training while I'm out doing the physical training. Of course when I'm sitting reading a book, it all helps. I worked with sports psychologists, read a lot of books, did yoga, all the classic things. In the end it made me realise the best psychologist is myself. I train a lot on my own and once you know how to be honest with yourself, no one can analyse your mind quite like you can.

'When you're doing hard training sessions you have to talk yourself through it, thinking: "How am I approaching this?" You engulf yourself in conversation and it becomes an inner circle. It starts way earlier because what you expect from a session decides the outcome as well. If you think it will be easy, your level of expectation is totally different compared to going into it thinking it's going to be the hardest session of your life. Funnily enough it always turns out to be the opposite… and your mind becomes a wonderfully powerful thing to turn pain into nothing.'

Born in Cologne, Frodeno grew up in South Africa and began his sporting life as a swimmer before returning to Germany to start a competitive triathlon career. He wasn't the Olympic favourite heading to Beijing in 2008, but on the day after his 27th birthday he took gold in a sprint finish. Even so he rates his 6th place in London four years later – behind British winner Alistair Brownlee – as the greater feat as he was returning from injury. The payback is increasingly familiar.

'I like to call it floating,' he smiles. 'Really it's an empty state of nothingness. I'm not thinking of five seconds before or what's happening in the afternoon, I'm just thinking of that very moment. That's what I call being "in the Zone". It's the old trick of staring at a candle, but when you do it during movement it's wonderful because you are just absorbing everything around you in that moment. It's where I try to get but to be honest I can't hold it too long because everything has to be perfect in that moment too. I've had it at the Olympics and for very brief moments in an Ironman. I might get it once a month when everything comes together. But it's what I look for every day and in every session and I'll keep searching for it.'

•

This ultimate focus seems the holy grail of sport, but finding it is a complex process. Emerson Fittipaldi's 1972 and 1974 world titles set Brazil on the road to Formula 1 domination by inspiring a host of young racers including Nelson Piquet and Ayrton Senna. When I asked Fittipaldi about the mind of a champion four decades later, he surprised me by reaching for my notepad, something none of my interviewees had ever done before. He promptly drew three circles linked together in a triangle. Each contained a single word: 'mind', 'body' and 'spirit'.

'Everything comes from motivation of the mind: the desire to win, the passion for the sport,' says Fittipaldi. 'But the mind, the body and the spirit – the soul – have to be in total coordination. The three circles have to have the same proportions too. To achieve the highest mental and bodily level of performance you have to work on each separately, then put them together with the spirit. For any sportsperson it is the same. If you have all the ingredients together you can perform at 100 per cent. But if one of them is not in complete harmony, you aren't at your peak. You can have the strongest body, but if you aren't at a high level mentally or spiritually the body will not perform. Even if you are in a good physical state and you have a very powerful mind but your spirit's not there, it's not going to work.

'The reverse is different. With mentality and spirit you can overcome a weak body because then you can put the body through extreme stress, like I've done twice [Fittipaldi broke his back racing in 1996 then again in a light plane crash a year later]. This doesn't just apply to sport, but any business or just to have a good life. It is very similar in any field. Anybody wanting to perform to their maximum should try to find this balance and to feel good in mind, body and spirit.'

If the whole secret to life boils down to just three words, how hard can it be? It's a shame that as words go, they're biggies – and in reality most of us lesser mortals struggle to get even one out of the three into any real working order. Intriguingly, even Fittipaldi admits he didn't understand enough about this balance to find his true peak in Formula 1 – despite finishing in the championship top two four years in a row. He only completed his mental education, for example, when he moved to IndyCar in the 1990s and was taught visualisation, a technique he didn't know about in F1.

'This knowledge comes from life experience,' adds Fittipaldi. 'By the time I was racing in America I was more together with the three factors – mind, body and spirit – than I had been in Formula 1, because I was too young. If I'd had that in F1 I could have reached an even higher level. The mind was always there: I had a strong mind – very focused and very concentrated –

and I never made a lot of mistakes at any time of my career. What I was missing were body, spirit and motivation.

'There are questions for the next generation about how to improve mentally, spiritually and bodily, how much the mind can do and the power of our consciousness. It doesn't matter how well you are performing, you always have ground to improve. When you think you are the best you start losing. In any sport, you always have so much more to learn. That's what takes you to the next level of performance. You can always go one level more, one level more, one level more. We can develop and develop and develop. There is no limit.'

If that is eerily reminiscent of Ayrton Senna, stick around. The parallels come thick and fast as we go through Fittipaldi's tips for improving the other two corners of the triangle: 'The body has to be extremely sensitive to work together with the mind and spirit,' says Fittipaldi. 'The human body is so complicated, so sophisticated – such an incredible machine. If we put the wrong fuel into a high-compression car it won't work. You need good food with no toxins. But there is so much junk in what we eat, it pollutes your body. I've been on a special diet for years and in all my life I've never been so sensitive. A good diet helps to put the right energy in the right places. If we eat properly, we learn to get the maximum out of ourselves. When the body is completely cleansed, we're better receivers to the spiritual life. That's why fasting is sacred in many religions.'

Fittipaldi's beliefs are based on the Christian faith of his homeland. Yet there is another element to his third circle, 'spirit', which has nothing to do with religion but comes from sheer enjoyment. Whatever path we choose, he insists it is crucial never to lose sight of what made you love it in the first place. This is how the elder Brazilian reckons Senna overstepped the mark.

'When I say spirit that means the faith and energy you have in yourself and God; they go together,' says Fittipaldi. 'First it has to be internal; you have to have this high spiritual energy within you. Then you can help others by knowing there's a creator who creates everything. But Ayrton was over-demanding of himself. He was too intense to a level where he sometimes didn't enjoy the sport. I was here to enjoy it first, then be a professional second. This comes under the "spirit" banner. I recall my best experience in Indianapolis was in 1994 when I had a Mercedes engine, more than 1000hp and very little downforce. I lapped at an average of 238mph: that's fast. And whenever I was able to qualify on that first flying lap and get pole, I was just so happy…'

•

Joyful or otherwise, by combining mind, body and spirit these Brazilian greats both attained the highest levels of concentration – and their peaks also share another eerie similarity. When I brought up Senna's day of days at Monaco, Fittipaldi revealed his compatriot was not the only one to find an unsettling viewpoint as he drove.

'I sometimes had a situation where I knew exactly what was happening at the side of the car without looking,' says Fittipaldi. 'That's because you have perception at a high level, you have sensitivity. You have the sense of feeling what's going on around you without looking. This comes from the highest level of purpose. When an athlete has that in their career, when you're at your top performance, you sometimes know what's going to happen before it happens. You know what the other guys are going to do before they do it. And you know there is a car on your left trying to pass on your inside without looking in the mirror.'

Fittipaldi and Senna aren't even the only ones to experience this extreme focus in a racing car. Fellow Formula 1 world champion Nigel Mansell agrees: 'You need to reach a level of total understanding. When you're at that level it's a wonderful feeling. You're very connected and you know things are going to happen before they happen.' Senna once wistfully recalled his 'pure racing' against karting rival Terry Fullerton, who reached these highs too: 'You do go into a different Zone,' the Briton tells me. 'If the kart is handling brilliantly you get this invincible feeling. It's hard to explain, but it feels strangely magical – that's the right word.'

Heading to Japan's Suzuka circuit for the penultimate race of the 1994 season, the year of Senna's death, the Brazilian's final team-mate Damon Hill needed to beat German rival Michael Schumacher to keep his slim title hopes alive. Rain interrupted the race, favouring Schumacher, who was renowned for his car control in the wet. Yet it was Hill who prevailed with a performance he treasures more than any other.

'In that wet 1994 race I drove out of my skin,' Hill said years later. 'I regard that as the most performance I ever extracted from myself. It was very intense but at the same time it was peculiar. I felt like I wasn't even in the car – it was someone else doing it. It was a really strange, special experience that I never got close to before or since. It was amazing. It was like I said, "OK, you drive." And to actually win... to cross the line and come out triumphant after all that was fantastic. Suzuka is a tough track – and a fast one. It demands more concentration but it gives more satisfaction, that strange contradiction we have to understand about F1. And I let something else drive the car. I don't know what was driving the car.'

Derek Warwick made his F1 debut in 1981 in a Toleman known as the 'Flying Pig' that was 20 seconds off the pace. Thankfully that wasn't the last time he flew. 'Sometimes when you drive a racing car it's like you're sat on the roll bar looking in,' he tells me. 'That's how bizarre it is. I've had that. I remember qualifying on the third row at Monaco in 1989 in the Arrows. It was a brilliant car, designed by Ross Brawn, and it was just easy. This may be inexplicable to people who haven't experienced it, but that's because people don't push to the absolute limit. That ultimate limit creates that Zone. When you get there it's a beautiful feeling.'

There are exceptions when someone gets a glimpse of the Zone without a lifetime of practice. When I spoke to Warwick it was only a week after his daughter's wedding – and the father-of-the-bride was still buzzing: 'This can happen to normal people in general walks of life as well,' he beams. 'We were driving to the church when she said, "Dad, I'm having an out-of-body experience. I feel that I'm looking at myself sat here with you." I'm going all tingly thinking about it…'

This phenomenon is surprisingly widespread in everyday life; one in ten of us has gone through some kind of out-of-body experience. The very word 'ecstasy' even derives from ancient Greek, meaning 'to stand outside'. It can be induced chemically using drugs such as ketamine but such interventions are far from the only 'way out'. Danger is not a prerequisite to finding yourself outside looking in but intense focus does seem to help, so this very natural ecstasy reaches epidemic levels among those who push boundaries as they perform. The sensation is rarely considered the target in itself but it has surprised everyone from actors to musicians, often when they're producing their finest work. You don't have to go out of your body to find this extreme version of the Zone but it really can help if you go out of your mind.

Nigeria-born concert pianist Glen Inanga tells me: 'You do a lot of preparation but then when it comes to it you have to let go and allow things to happen in a natural way. You always have to try to avoid interfering. I've had out-of-body experiences as well. It tends to happen in performances rather than practice. There's something about the excitement of performing: the nerves, the adrenalin. What happens is you see this stuff happening in front of you and you don't really believe it's you. Things just happen: your fingers have this capability and you let them get on with it.

'I don't get into this state all the time – perhaps about one performance in ten – but I know it when it happens. It can last all night and it always coincides with the good nights. When it happens I feel very humble and I enjoy listening to those performances again. As I listen it's as if I'm listening to someone else, not me. You don't even believe you're the one doing it. I don't know how I did it, it just happened, but that was amazing, just how things should be.'

•

The out-of-body experience is not always so idyllic or comforting; indeed it can also be brought on by extremes of stress. The sensation is widely recognised as a chronic problem for epilepsy sufferers, for whom it can be anything but pleasant. Of course it is most commonly linked to the near-death experience: patients looking down on their hospital beds as they undergo lifesaving interventions. Similar stories abound from all over the globe throughout recorded history.

Formula 1 great Jackie Stewart once held his hand above his head to show me the point from where he found himself gazing down on his car during a crash at South Africa's Kyalami circuit. Just as Stewart has no rational explanation, many scientists are sceptical, dismissing it as a trick of the mind under duress. But research continues into the phenomenon, recently focusing on the brain's temporoparietal junction (TPJ), damage to which is believed to bring it on.

Meanwhile, the anecdotal evidence continues to flood in. I was at a lecture detailing the latest scientific research on the subject when I met a British man with a clearer view than most. In the 1990s he joined the legions of bronzed young things taking to the Australian surf. Two weeks after his first lesson he paid his first visit to Sydney's Manly Beach. But when a wipeout sent him tumbling to the seabed he found himself stuck on a rock 12 feet down. He was a strong swimmer and reckons he could hold his breath for two minutes, even more in an emergency. It wasn't enough.

'I can remember the water turning red, then I got dizzy,' he says. 'After that there was an overwhelming sense of peace and happiness. I told myself, "This isn't so bad." Then I had the classic flashback, all the way back to day one. I think my brain was looking to find that crucial memory of what I did last time that could help. There wasn't one. Then I opened my mouth.

'Suddenly I was outside. I was 50 feet above the surface and I could see the whole of Manly Beach. Because my leg rope and the board were each about five feet long there was just a tiny bit of the board sticking up above the water. Someone must have seen it and raised the alarm. I could see the lifeguards going in wearing their red costumes and red-and-yellow quarter caps. A big guy got there first – and as he dived in I saw him cut his leg on an obstacle. Then I watched him rescue me. He got me out, dragged me up the beach and gave me emergency CPR. I was still up there watching. I knew I was dead. Then while he was doing it I saw all this stuff was coming out of my mouth. Then BOOM. I was sucked back in.'

He woke up in hospital in a bath of iodine to treat infections from all his torn skin. Weeks later he visited Manly Beach's South Steyne lifesaving club to thank the big Australian who had saved his life – despite admitting to feeling 'utterly pissed off' during the moment itself, as he was robbed of the bliss he was experiencing and dumped back in a very painful body. When he saw the pictures of the lifesavers on the wall he recognised his man instantly – despite having no vision and no hearing during his ordeal as he was all but clinically dead.

'I've hardly ever told anyone this story because people think you're deluded,' he sighs. 'No one wants to talk about this kind of stuff. Lots of people go down the religious route. I went down the tunnel towards the white light too, but I'm not saying God was at the end of that. I just think it's what happens when you die. But it was the best thing to happen to me. Now I'm not scared of dying.'

That message, so often repeated by those who have come closest, should be a source of comfort. Of course it's far from easy to keep thinking that way, whether we are contemplating our own eventual demise or, even more so, those of our loved ones. Australian surfer Mick Fanning is no stranger to tragedy either. By his mid-thirties, he had already lost two of his three big brothers: his idol Sean died in a car accident aged 20, then eldest brother Peter died in his sleep at the age of 43 in 2015. Even so, Mick knows there are two sides to luck. The flipside is that he considers himself 'lucky' to grow up on the coast of South Australia, learning to surf when he was five. This lifetime of education on the water has let him earn a living from what he loves most. Now known as 'White Lightning', he has been crowned world surfing champion three times.

In a series of famous experiments dating back half a century, scientists tested expert chess players on their ability to recall a board they had only seen for a few seconds. When the set-up came from a genuine match, the experts could accurately place most of the pieces, managing the task much better than inexperienced players. But when they were just scattered randomly, the masters fared little better than the novices. The conclusion was that chess masters are busy 'chunking' the individual pieces into recognisable patterns they remember from previous games. It seems the same effect can apply anywhere, no matter how cerebral the pursuit. This is how master surfers learn to read the patterns of the sea from their boards too.

'The ocean is forever changing so you never know what it will dish up each day,' says Fanning. 'You can have the same charts but every wave is totally different. Like anything, with experience you see the different shape of the wave or a different movement in the ocean and think: "I remember that back then…" It becomes a sixth sense for some people. There are surfers who always find themselves in the perfect place in the line-up but that's just from experience and reading the ocean.'

There are limits. Fanning was competing at South Africa's Jeffreys Bay in 2015 when every movie lover's worst seaside nightmare suddenly got real. He felt a presence behind him, then heard a splash. The fin that duly appeared next to him was not a dream, it belonged to a 12-foot-long great white shark. The Australian's instant reaction, captured on live TV and since viewed 24 million times on YouTube, was to hit out and wedge his surfboard between himself and his aquatic acquaintance, which bit off his leash. A response team eventually picked Fanning up, by which time he'd saved himself from turning into a main course for one reason: he was in the Zone.

'Throughout that whole day I felt amazing,' Fanning tells me. 'If you can get in that Zone and not think, it just becomes autopilot. That's when you're in your best form, and it's what we focus on as athletes. So it was probably a blessing in disguise that this happened during an actual event and I was so centred at the time. If I wasn't in that place maybe something else could have happened and I wouldn't have reacted that quickly. To be totally honest when I got back to land and saw the footage, I was sitting there wondering: "When did I make this decision? Or that one?" To me it went on a lot longer than what the footage showed. It felt like a good five minutes when it was really just ten seconds. But I guess that's how fast the mind works.'

This is another classic component of life at the limit – in car crashes and other near-death experiences. When we are scrabbling for a way out of trouble, the brain is awoken from its everyday 'tick-over' slumber mode by a sudden influx of adrenalin and speeds up accordingly. Survivors consistently report the outside world – such as the shards of glass shattering on the windscreen – going into slow-motion. This 'fight-or-flight' mode doesn't let us move our limbs any faster but our decision-making does accelerate, as long as we don't go into panic mode and freeze. At our highest peak of total concentration it seems we can not only bend space, we can bend time too.

Fanning was already at such an extreme of focus, he could slip straight into the right state, fitting 300 seconds' worth of critical life-saving calculations into ten. Even more mind-blowing is the fact Fanning was back surfing within a week. He admits to feeling jittery when he heard splashes near him, yet he found a way over it: a year later he returned to Jeffreys Bay and won the event.

'It was one of those moments that sticks out, that's for sure,' he deadpans. 'It put me off a bit from getting back in the water but the more time I took away from the ocean was going to make it even harder. So I just felt I needed to get back in and get on with life. We have to deal with different adversity through life: you can either be crippled by it or you can move forward. I always try to take a step forward. I've been lucky to be in the ocean my whole life so to have one incident… I put it in the same perspective as when you're walking across the street and almost get hit by a car. That happens to people every day and others have been hit. So I consider myself extremely lucky.'

7

RESILIENCE

The champions in this book are living proof of how it is possible to tailor the future to fit our perfect vision. But what are we supposed to do when we fall off whatever wave we've been riding, we get knocked off our course or our plan just plain falls apart?

As a young athlete, Derek Redmond is one of many who dreamed of creating an iconic Olympic moment. In one of the best illustrations of how we should be very careful about what we wish for, he went on to achieve exactly that – albeit not in the way he had imagined. When his hamstring gave way early in the 400m semi-final at Barcelona in 1992, the Briton's dreams ended in searing pain. Yet he forced himself back up onto his one working leg to finish his race. Seeing his son in such agony, his father Jim ran onto the track, swatting officials out of the way to help him across the line. It prompted a flood of tears from Redmond junior, plus the thousands standing to applaud in the stadium and the watching millions who could see this was the Olympic spirit encapsulated. Faster? No. Higher and stronger? Definitely.

'Things don't always go the way you want in life,' sighs Redmond. 'Life has a way of throwing hurdles into your way. I refer to them as challenges. You have to rise to those challenges and take them on. Sometimes you've got to be creative: we end up doing things we didn't expect, that weren't written in the form book. Sometimes you have time to think or ask others for help to get around it. At other times you have to deal with it there and then. If there's a traffic accident on the way to work you take a different route. You have to think on your feet – take a left here, miss the problem and you're back on course. If a dog runs out you don't think "mirror, signal…" You just get round it. People think: "Blimey how did I do that?" But they've just reacted and been creative and it's become the natural way.'

Redmond faced rather more hurdles than seems fair for a flat runner. He endured a total of 13 operations during his career yet kept bouncing back, enjoying a highlight with Great Britain's world championship 4x400m relay gold medal in 1991.

'To be a good champion, sometimes you need to experience the lows in order to get the highs,' he insists. 'That makes the victory all the sweeter. It also keeps you grounded and level-headed. The downs are as good for you as bad in one respect. But you have to stay strong and have faith, whatever you do. When you do have a downer you need to know: "I'm going to come back from this and get back to where I was." You also need the utmost belief in whatever you're going to do.

'I'm not a good loser but I'm a gracious loser. I don't want to lose at anything but if you are beaten you've got to be gracious about it. It doesn't mean you have to be happy within yourself. If you are a true champion you won't be happy because you didn't do what you were supposed to do. But if you've given 100 per cent, you've got nothing left in the tank and you were still beaten, tip your hat and say: "Good on you, that's what I'm striving for." Then go away and work to raise your game.'

Two years after Barcelona, a doctor told Redmond he'd never represent his country again. But he defied the odds, going on to play for England at basketball and even having trials for the rugby sevens side. He later started his own motorbike racing team, took up kickboxing and still works as a motivational speaker.

'There's always good to come out of anything, even if it's not something you plan,' adds Redmond. 'I'm unbelievably surprised at the reaction to Barcelona. I can't believe how me pulling a muscle in a race has inspired people who have lost limbs in battle, had major illnesses or other serious issues in their lives. But I'm glad it helped them, because it means something good is coming out of something that was bad for me. I do believe everything happens for a reason.'

•

The fifteenth of September 2001 started well for Italian racing driver Alex Zanardi as he headed for his first win in years at Germany's Lausitzring. Then he put a wheel in some oil and found himself sideways with 20 other machines bearing down on him at 150mph. One of them tore off the front of his car, cutting off his legs at the knee. An hour's helicopter ride and three cardiac arrests later Zanardi arrived at a hospital in Berlin with just two pints of blood left in his body.

Zanardi woke from a medically induced coma a week later to find he was not all there. He then turned his rehabilitation into what he knew best: a race. First on the list was to carry son Niccolò on his shoulders. Within three months he began walking on prosthetic legs – a process that can take years. After two years he made his racing return in the European Touring Car Championship. Reduce it all to a few lines and we can fast-forward through the long, hard days of recuperation when Zanardi had to take everything step by painful step. Crucially, he never doubted he could race again.

'Before my accident, if I'd been asked what I'd do if I lost my legs I'd have said it would be better to kill myself,' Zanardi admits to me in *Overdrive*. 'I never think like that now. Things can look one way but when you have to live through them they are very different. Sometimes we forget what we have. I know only one guy out of a thousand could have gone home alive after my accident and I'm that one. But you can't call me Superman. That's sending out the wrong message as people might think it's not possible to achieve what I have unless they are special.

'Frankly I don't think the accident made me a better person. What was there before is exactly the same, but my knowledge has been extended and I feel richer because I've seen the other side of the coin. That makes me less afraid of what lies ahead because life brings fantastic things but also bad things. That's what makes it marvellous. If it was all good or all bad, it would be boring.'

This attitude mirrors Redmond's. They're right but most of us would settle for a bit of boredom to steer clear of such extremes – at least until they're forced on us. Yet even if none of us would volunteer to test this out for ourselves, if Zanardi is as typical as he claims, it is reassuring to know just how much we might be able to draw on if we ever have to face the unthinkable.

'I've experienced how great it is to be alive and how strong a man can be,' he adds. 'Every time we think, "That's it, it's over," we surprise ourselves and find inner resources in our heart. This is a sign of hope I have witnessed in my own skin. Now I see the human being is an incredible machine, totally undiscovered in many ways. Every one of us has a hidden tank of energy that just comes out when it is needed.'

Sure enough Zanardi was soon moving on to his next adventure, hand-cycling, and promptly fell in love with the sport. Never one to do things by halves, he started chasing Paralympic gold at the age of 45. He was given an early psychological boost when he heard the venue selected for his event at the London Paralympics in 2012 would be one he knew well: motor racing circuit Brands Hatch. He then set about meticulous testing on the ideal materials for his bike. With just months left he was still playing catch-up on his more experienced competitors, but he finalised his choices just in time. It was starting to look like this could be his week.

There was also the considerable matter of a mind tuned over years at the limit in another kind of vehicle. Zanardi insists there was no difference between his mental preparation for motor racing and hand-cycling, only the speed difference that allows you more chance to rectify a mistake in the latter. He thus went into the Games with a major head start over the rest of the field.

I was thrilled to be at the start line to see Zanardi take on a gruelling 40-mile road race, which involved several laps that ended on the Brands Hatch home straight. The Italian was forced into a change of strategy when a tactical breakaway did not go according to plan. He was still down in sixth with a few corners left, yet he prevailed in a sprint down the straight where he'd once raced rather faster machinery. Over the years I've been privileged to witness many top sporting moments first-hand but I will gladly admit I've never found myself screaming so hard for pure joy.

Zanardi then had a further sublime moment of his own when he kissed the hot asphalt and felt electricity flood through him 'like touching uncovered wire'. Like the life flashback often reported in a near-death experience, his mind raced through the highlights that had led him to London – from his first laps in a go-kart, his first wins, the harder times, his pole position on the same Brands Hatch tarmac 21 years earlier, his brief career in Formula 1, his success in America, his accident and his recovery. It all came flooding back to the Italian in an 'incredible, intense' two seconds.

Marvelling at the irony of the ideal outcome at such an ideal venue, Zanardi reckons the plot must have come from 'up there' because it was just 'too perfect to be human'. Yet he remains reluctant to place too much emphasis on the final result.

'Everybody knows I won, but I knew that already because I knew what I had to do just to be in London,' Zanardi tells psychotherapist and sports mind coach Linda Keen. 'In this new adventure I've met fantastic people who are life winners – because to be at that level in Paralympic sport means everything that can happen to you is well behind you, otherwise you wouldn't be there. If someone is still spending half their day wondering why this happened to me, how I'm going to live with no legs or whatever, this attitude won't serve you well at any level and especially in a sport like paracycling where the level of competition is incredibly high. They may not have the same exposure as me but all the guys I have met in this sport have personal stories that are at least as good as Alex Zanardi's.'

Four years on Zanardi collected even more gold in Rio, amazingly at another venue where he previously raced cars. Anyone might think someone somewhere was trying to offer him some payback: 'I'm a very optimistic guy, who's always tried to see the glass half-full rather than half-empty,' Zanardi adds in typical understatement. 'Following my accident I said, "Let's see what I can get out of it." Everything I now do is related to my new condition and I have a great life. So you'd have to say losing my legs was one of the greatest opportunities of my life.'

•

On Zanardi's big day at Brands Hatch I was honoured to meet Leon Gaisli, a Haitian racing in another hand-cycling class, whose house collapsed in the 2010 earthquake that devastated his home island. Gaisli suffered a spinal injury, losing the use of his legs, and he was trapped in the rubble for three days. When he regained consciousness he was told he had lost his wife and his entire family of eight children. Unimaginable for most, Gaisli's reaction was to treat his new life as 'coming back from the dead', handing it over to God in a bid to change attitudes to Haitian disabled people, often regarded as surplus to requirements. The human spirit sure takes some beating.

What Zanardi and Gaisli have gone through must have drained all but the very final drop out of their glass. To see it as 'half-full' seems to take optimism to a level bordering on self-delusion. Yet they insist there is nothing special about themselves, other than the undesirable hand they were dealt. If so, we should all be grateful: at its best, human mental strength clearly has no bounds and can take any of us to the level of the champion when we most need it. The key is to accentuate the positive even in the face of what seems the worst life can throw at us.

'To be "positive" is easier said than done if you have just received some news to challenge every last drop of your positivity,' says mind coach Don MacPherson. 'It is only natural to have negative thoughts: it's the brain's way of keeping us safe, our number one priority. When a caveman was about to go out to be confronted by wild animals his brain would have been in ultra-cautious mode – with good reason. Today we face other dangers so the Monkey Mind will keep bringing us negative words of caution: some are helpful but many are not.

'Most of us are unaware of our internal dialogue and its effect on how we feel and perform – especially under pressure – and most are surprised at just how negative the Monkey Mind is. Words have energy, so it is wise to be vigilant about what your Monkey is saying, especially if you are preparing to enter the Zone. What you allow it to say will direct your focus and confidence levels, therefore your ability to be at your best. Whatever challenge you face, negative thoughts lead to negative feelings, greatly increasing the chance of a negative outcome.'

No wonder we fail with such predictable regularity. Yet

if Zanardi and Gaisli can turn negatives into positives, we all have this ability. It's not easy but MacPherson insists we can take control of our inner dialogue with the energy of a few well-chosen words. Where the negative thought is: 'I can't handle the pressure' the positive thinker says: 'Pressure is a privilege.' Errors become opportunities for learning, struggles turn into a great lifelong dance. The mistake last time doesn't exist, there's only this time, the now. That way 'poor me' soon turns into 'this is my lucky day'.

'Negative words are as disempowering as Kryptonite is to Superman,' insists MacPherson. 'Some are obvious: "I don't think I'm good enough to win" or "I've never been any good at this", but others are subtler. Whenever I was facing a challenge I noticed my inner voice saying: "I'll try". It sounds alright, but when you think about it "trying" fails. If you invited me to the pub at 8pm and I replied, "I'll try", would you really expect me to turn up? So when I caught my Monkey saying, "I'll try" I replaced it with, "I'll do my very best" or, "I'll give it a go". Better still, just do it.

'This was harder than I thought. I kept slipping back and was surprised how often "try" was my default word even though I knew it was not positive enough. But I persevered and in the end I persuaded my Monkey Mind the word was no longer part of my language. Changing your words into something more positive is a mental skill and, like all skills, the more you practise the better you become. It is vital to recognise when your "Kryptonite" is present, and release the antidote immediately: positive words. It's not about a complete removal of all negativity, just rebalancing in favour of the positive. Negative thoughts tend to be stronger than positives so the more you let them roam freely in your mind, the stronger they become. Don't suppress or deny them, just zap them with a more positive word, like changing the channel when you don't like what's on TV. Control your words or they will control you.

'This is what winners do even though they might not be aware they are doing it. This "progressive language" lets you be a more positive – and therefore confident – person. When you are more confident you're automatically more competent whatever the challenge. You perform how you think you will perform.'

•

Anger is far from a positive force for most sports stars: rile them up and even the best can fall apart. That's why sports psychology is primarily aimed at inducing states of calm under pressure. But there are exceptions: instead of accentuating the positive, a few draw on harsher ways to psych themselves up. British sailing legend Ben Ainslie is one sportsman who thrives on getting mad and usually even.

Sailing seems genteel to the uninitiated, but at the top level it is rarely about just getting as quickly as possible from A to B by sea. In the Olympic regatta sailors amass points in a series of races over several days and it often boils down to tactical battles. You can legitimately pick on your competitors too. In the deciding race of his 1996 Olympic debut, Ainslie was herded to the back of the fleet by Brazil's Robert Scheidt. It's fair to say it riled up the young Briton. He started flying as he seethed, gaining 15 places but falling just short of gold. Ainslie displayed his utter contempt for silverware with his revenge on his nemesis four years later in Sydney.

'A lot of people talk about the 2000 Olympics,' says

Ainslie. 'I had a massive rivalry with Robert Scheidt and I took him out in a race. People were outraged by that, especially in Brazil. But they forget that four years earlier he did a similar thing to me when I was only 19. So for me from then on the gloves were off. If that's the way you want to play then that's fine...'

The move earned Ainslie death threats and a protection offer from Australia's secret police. In Scheidt's home town of São Paulo, residents took to the streets to burn effigies of the Briton. Even then, Ainslie wasn't tempted by anger-management classes. When he slumped to 24th in the 2004 Olympic regatta after falling foul of a protest, it prompted a run of three wins in four races. He duly won another gold before repeating the feat in 2008.

You'd think Denmark's Jonas Høgh-Christensen would have known about all that. By 2012, Ainslie was chasing a record fourth straight sailing gold in front of his British fans but it was going wrong: Høgh-Christensen had beaten him in each of the first six races – and he seemed on course for a dominant victory. Then the Dane had a moment of madness of his own, ganging up on Ainslie with Dutchman Pieter-Jan Postma as they claimed to spot an infringement. Big mistake. This forced Ainslie into a penalty turn, otherwise he risked disqualification if he lost the argument later.

Back on shore Ainslie famously gave the Dane a reminder of the revision he should have done with his David Bruce Banner-esque avowal: 'They've made me angry and you don't want to make me angry.' He promptly embarked on another stunning run of results for gold, retiring as sailing's greatest ever Olympian. Perhaps Høgh-Christensen should have listened to my chat with the Briton a month earlier...

'There are pros and cons to being the guy everyone's trying to beat,' Ainslie tells me. 'I'd rather be favourite than not but sometimes it's not easy. Once or twice I've found people make life hard for you, especially at the Olympics. That's because they know the only way they can beat you is to catch you out with something like a disqualification. Experience tells you to look out for that. Normally when I'm under pressure or I get angered by something, it seems to bring out the best in me. I don't necessarily know why that is. But it's a good trait to have because that's what often happens when you're racing. For some people, if they get put off their natural stride it really doesn't go well and they just fall apart. But anger works as a trigger for me. It just makes me want to do better or try harder and normally that's the case.'

It's one challenge to find the Zone in a race where all you have to do is go hell for leather, but with so many variables at play sailing is a different proposition. Yet it seems even this game of maritime chess doesn't stop the magic kicking in.

'That peak performance comes when absolutely everything comes together at the same time, when you're really at one with the boat, the conditions and yourself,' adds Ainslie. 'It doesn't happen often but when it does it's a great feeling. The hard thing is replicating that. Of course you always try to get to that level, but it takes one tiny thing to be not quite right and you don't get there. That's the challenge in sport. No one ever sails a perfect race. It's about the person who makes the least mistakes.

'It's definitely possible to get in the Zone in a tactical battle. That's when the training comes in. At that point you're sailing the boat on autopilot because your mind is so focused on the tactical ramifications of what you need to do next. You might not sail at 100 per cent but you can be at a very high level even without thinking about it.'

Ainslie played a major role in one of sport's all-time great comebacks at the 2013 America's Cup as replacement tactician for Oracle Team USA, who sealed the last eight races in a row to win 9-8. Never one to shirk a challenge, the next target for his unique blend of Jekyll and Hyde was to beat his old team-mates by helming the first British crew to win the oldest trophy in international sport.

'When I was younger I was a bit of a hothead on the water but on land I was so shy I wouldn't speak to anyone and I was no good in public,' he smiles. 'That was partly because of the problems I had at school, where I was bullied. That had quite a marked effect on me. I really felt I needed to prove myself and it made me fiercely determined to be successful. As I've got older the two personalities have merged. I'm more confident on land now so I guess that develops naturally. I'm also calmer on the water, which helps me enjoy my sailing more than before.

'But hurdles come along all the time. A friend once said: "Nothing ever seems to be easy for you." I agreed, "No, but it's not easy for anyone." It might look easy for the best Formula 1 drivers but it clearly isn't: they have issues as we all do. You go through periods where everything you touch is perfect and it's easy, then times where it's not rolling your way and you have to fight through everything. But that's life...'

Negativity, hurdles, doubts, even bullying? We don't always hear how much mental baggage the world's champions are carrying, but there are similar back stories behind many who go on to greatness – from Lewis Hamilton to Michael Phelps. No one would prescribe a dose of bullying for a prospective sportsman (or anyone else) as many have crumbled under similar onslaughts. But mental pain – or avoiding it – can be a powerful motivating factor. Talk about a crash course in grit.

'The truly great athletes have two main ingredients,' says sports psychologist Dr Ben Chell, who spent a decade with Team GB's sailors. 'First they're incredibly resilient and mentally tough and can deliver performances time and time again when it really matters. Second, they have a huge fascination for the process. Their attention to detail and professionalism is second to none. Throw in a bit of talent and expertise and you've got a gold medallist on your hands.

'I use the metaphor of our brain being like a library. You have to pick the right book for a given scenario. The more experience you have, the bigger the library. That doesn't mean younger athletes can't perform too; they've trained for years and would not be in the team unless they have those skills to an automatic level. But it's about accessing them and delivering at the right time. It's also about recognising when you need to take a risk. In sailing you need consistent results throughout a series, but in the "double points" last race you might have to do something different. That might mean taking another boat out, like Ben did in Sydney with Robert Scheidt, or going all out to win and taking a big risk to get a good start. All that is about priming the brain for what you want it to do and being aware of what your tactics are.

'People mix up "dreams" and "goals". The dream is to win Olympic gold. But if you focus on that, it won't be helpful for the day-to-day processes you need for the best chance of winning that medal. The goal is to go out and consistently do your best in each leg of the race. In sailing, for example, you have to put a great series together. To perform well every day, it's important to choose to send blood to that "automatic" part of the brain. But when we mix the goal with the dream we engage the emotional brain, which can negatively affect performance. I'm not saying emotions are bad, just that athletes need to know how to channel them in a positive way. Again, that is very individualistic. It's a skill – and it takes time to learn.'

As he spent his life mastering the motions of the English Channel, Ben Ainslie also became a master of channelling emotion – thanks in part to the bullying he faced on dry land. It turned him into an unstoppable force on the water. Ainslie knows how big a role psychology plays in sport – but after all he's been through he claims it now happens 'naturally' for him. As such he's one of the lucky ones.

Of course none of this is limited to sport. Chell also works with businesses and he doesn't understand why you have to be an Olympian to learn the secrets: 'Why basic human function is not taught in schools beats me. Often there is stigma attached to psychology but that shouldn't be the case. It's a performance-enhancing process, like other disciplines of sports science and medicine, and can be applied to anything. Nine out of ten people run on their emotional brain, which is powerful but primitive. If they could learn they have a choice in what they engage in, it would be a massive help – not least in terms of behaviour in school. At least give people the choice…'

•

Modern schooling's standard route to success is to be good, do good work, get good exam results, get into a good university then get a good job to guarantee you can buy yourself the good life. Yet even the good pupils who follow that plan to the letter do not always rate the result as good as the hype would have it. Roz Savage stuck to this path until the age of 34, by which time she was an Oxford graduate and a high-flying management consultant. She had all the established trappings including a nice house in London and a fast car. It was just on the inside that everything was falling apart.

'Towards the end of my time working in the City my self-esteem was really going down the pan,' she tells me. 'I wasn't thriving in that environment at all. It felt like my soul was being eroded. I had to get out of there. But I just didn't have much confidence or faith in my own abilities. So this really was do-or-die. I needed to find some way to rebuild myself.'

The epiphany came when Roz sat down to write her own obituary. Twice. One was the version she was heading for: all very comfortable and safe, but dull. Next she wrote a fantasy version, full of adventure. The attraction was such that to the alarm of her family and friends she made the first big independent decision of her life: she quit her job. Still she had no vision of what to do instead – indeed it took years of casual work and drifting until lightning struck. To earn herself a platform to speak out on her passion for the environment, she would row single-handed across the Atlantic Ocean. Cue a thunderstorm in her emotional mind…

'As I'm signing up I can imagine my little observer saying, "What the hell is she thinking? HQ we have a problem, she's lost it,"' smiles Savage. 'But when you behave courageously it thinks, "OK, let's see how this goes…" Then it is constantly re-evaluating when it sees that it makes you feel better about yourself. When I began my voyage, people posted nice comments on my blogs, saying they admired my courage and resourcefulness. At first I didn't own those words. Courageous? Not me. Then I thought: "Why not me?" I had a whiteboard in front of my rowing seat where I wrote the words, then I'd deliberately embody courage and resourcefulness as I went about my day. I made some significant progress with that.

'Early on I became so overwhelmed with the 3,000-mile figure that I did start skipping rowing shifts. I fell into this fallacious thinking that I could make up for it later on, but you really can't. You've got to consistently show up. And my self-esteem was getting even worse because I was being lazy. It was important to my sense of self-worth that I show up. That was partly from a practical perspective of getting to the other side but it was also to ask: "Who am I? Am I the lazy cow sitting in her bunk or the professional adventurer?" I could still have gone either way but eventually I figured it out.'

According to Savage, resilience isn't something we either have or we don't; it's a character trait we learn along the way once we've made a big decision. To cross the Atlantic she had to row for 12 hours every day for over 100 days. She faced up to 30-foot waves with only herself for company, above all when she lost her only contact with the outside world, her satellite phone. Having seen *Jaws*, she admits to terror any time she had to leave her boat to clean barnacles off the hull, not least when she once had to cut away her sea anchor after it got stuck and started dragging her in the wrong direction. 'That might sound trivial, but to me it was a big deal,' she recalls. 'I took a video in case I didn't make it back, but by the end I'm beaming. I felt proud of myself that I did something that really scared me. It takes a lot to scare me now, and it's not a showstopper to be scared of something.'

Savage went on to become the only woman to row single-handed across the world's three main oceans. Along the way she has taken five million rowing strokes, each a crucial step towards building up enough grit for her to take on the entire world. The adventures have now given her an inner steel she could never dream of during her chase for conventional success – and an even deeper understanding of the flaws in the ambitions that are supposed to be vital for happiness.

'We are not taught really important life skills in school, especially things like finding a purpose and having resilience,' she adds. 'Today's kids will go through such uncertain times – and now communities are more fragmented, so they are often not as exposed to grandparents or great aunts and uncles who might have educated them on what really matters in life. Personal development gurus are stepping into that vacuum, but they're supplying what should be in the core curriculum. In my teaching at Yale I see many wonderful undergraduates selling out and going for the money. So we need a fundamental change in our definition of what success looks like in the 21st century, away from the materialistic model that, to paraphrase Gandhi, serves our greed rather than our need. It's time to craft a new narrative about what makes a successful human being, closer to the values and integrity of Atticus Finch in *To Kill A Mockingbird*. We need a new definition of success where we admire character, courage and taking action for a cause that you believe in.'

•

Some of us have no choice about whether or not to learn resilience. As a child, Tanni Grey-Thompson wanted to play rugby for Wales. When she was told it would never happen she asked: 'Is it because I'm a woman?' The answer: 'No, it's because you're in a wheelchair.' That's a fair assessment for a girl born with spina bifida. But when the 12-year-old Tanni watched wheelchair racing, she was instantly smitten. She went on to win 11 Paralympic gold medals plus six London Marathons.

'I'm just really stubborn, and really stroppy, and really focused, obsessive actually,' she smiles. 'To be successful as an athlete you just go: "Do you know what? I'm going to keep going." You get to that point in a marathon 21 miles in where you think "Euurrgghh", but you don't spend all that time and effort to stop at 21 miles. It's hard to articulate where the reserves come from, but you can force your body through that if you want. You can push your body to the limit. You know you've just got to get to the finish line. You can only think about stopping when you're there.'

This approach is widespread in elite sport but especially among Paralympians, who are often used to pushing limits every day just to get by. Tatyana McFadden was born in 1989 in Leningrad (now St Petersburg) paralysed from the waist down due to spina bifida. She was given up by her birth mother and grew up in an orphanage that couldn't afford a wheelchair. So she taught herself to walk on her hands. The young Tatyana had been propelling herself like that for six years when visiting American health official Deborah McFadden adopted her and took her to live in Baltimore.

Only then did Tatyana try sport, eventually falling in love with wheelchair racing. By her teens she told her teacher she wanted to be a Paralympic athlete to find out what it would take. Whether thanks to the physiology developed in her unconventional early means of movement or the extra mental strength it brought – or both – she made her Paralympic debut at 15. Her haul of medals stands at 17 including four 2016 golds in Rio, plus a long unbeaten run at the world's four major marathons.

When I asked McFadden about Ayrton Senna's attitude to pushing the limits, this is what she said: 'In racing it's always about giving that little bit more, to the point when you cross the line when you shouldn't really have anything left. I definitely felt that way at the 2015 Boston Marathon. There was a strong headwind and conditions were so tough that a lot of athletes got sick afterwards because of how we were pushing our bodies. That's what this sport is about: everyone's getting faster each year so it's about how can I do a bit more? But once you're in the Zone you shut everything else out – or you can choose to take in the support from the crowd. It's just about focusing on yourself, your goals and where you want to be in the race.'

As the Paralympics have grown, so has the standard of the competition – with professional athletes at the top. The equipment required just to make the startline has become correspondingly expensive as technology has improved. Racing wheelchairs cost thousands of dollars, plus hundreds more for each pair of tyres. Given McFadden once blew out six in a single week she appreciates her fortune at having strong home support, notably at the USA national training base at the University of Illinois. When harsh winters make it impractical to go outside she trains on rollers that can simulate hills. When I met McFadden she was finishing a book of her own to inspire kids on what happens when you ignore limits.

'It's important to share my story,' she says. 'I've been adopted, living life with a disability but also travelling the world, being a student yet at the same time living a normal life. It has always been a dream of mine to write a book: it's called "Ya sama" which means "I can do it" in Russian. It has always been my attitude as a young child: whenever it looked like I wanted help with something, I didn't want help. If someone came up and tried to push or something, I said "No, no, ya sama, I can do it." I have always been very independent, especially at a really young age.'

●

These extreme challenges can clearly arrive at any time of life. Tim Prendergast was an eight-year-old in Wellington, New Zealand when his eyesight started to go. It got progressively worse until, by the age of 13, he'd lost 95 per cent of his vision.

'It wasn't a sustained void or black hole every day but there were some really tough moments,' he says. 'I recall feeling isolated in terms of being different – and as a teenager you didn't want to be different. I couldn't look a person in the eye so I was really shy. Finding athletics was a way for me to find confidence away from this guy who was never going to be able to drive a car or look people in the eye. This gave me an identity away from all that. As they'd say: "It's character-building, mate…" That's putting an insensitive face on it but knowing the person I am now, it was largely that way. Coming to terms with the sight loss was tough at the time but it taught me many lessons about life and determination. If you come out the other side of something like that it equips you for other challenges.'

Prendergast went on to take gold in the 800m at the 2004 Paralympics, then set a personal best at London in 2012 but missed the medals. He now lives in the UK, keeping up his running – not least regular appearances at the London Marathon – as he embarks on family life. It begs the question of how far overcoming such massive adversity helps the mind overcome the minor adversities we all face every day.

'I often get asked if I hadn't lost my sight, would I have gone to the Olympics as an able-bodied runner,' he says. 'I don't know because through that you learn about determination, things not coming as easily to you and taking things for granted. In that respect it helps, though sometimes it is still hard to get out of bed to train. It's a cliché but a key message I pass on to kids is about being the best you can be. I talk about the gold medal but also the 5th and 6th places in London and how satisfied I am with that performance because it was everything I had that night. Of course I went in aiming for gold, but that was the best I could be. Hopefully through my stories young people can have inspiration for whatever they're pursuing, whether in sport or elsewhere.

'If you have that mentality about being the best you can be, that's going to be transferable to other areas – no matter if Plan A doesn't work. When I go into schools and I ask about all the different dreams, I often hear: "I'm going to be a professional footballer when I grow up." The reality is that not all those young people are going to be professional footballers. But even if you don't, all those skills you've learned along the way – learning how to work hard, being committed and working as a team – that effort will hold you in good stead for other aspects of life. In one school they talked about "growth mindset". If you have that, things are going to happen. That mentality hopefully becomes habitual, just as a self-fulfilling prophecy of doom and gloom and "I'm rubbish at everything" goes the same way.'

Psychologist Carol Dweck's 'growth mindset' stresses that ability stems from effort instead of natural talent – the foundation of the move to praise kids for work not results. Crucially success or otherwise is seen to be controlled by the individual rather than external forces such as genetics or circumstance. This mindset sets us up to cope better with the setbacks that inevitably come our way. It doesn't halt the drama but it overhauls our reaction to it, which has a big impact on resilience. It is slowly being picked up by schools but Prendergast is as frustrated as many parents at the enduring focus on statistics like 'A to C grade' percentages instead of well-rounded kids.

'We definitely underestimate our potential,' declares Prendergast. 'Sometimes when we get into tricky situations we feel locked in by it. Often we don't think about the solution: how would I want to behave in this situation or act with that person? One approach is to put things in perspective. If you have a disagreement, think how this is going to feel in a month's time. I'd have forgotten about it. So what's the point of me investing this time in being negative and getting stressed about it?

'All this doesn't diminish how competitive I was on the startline but I did have the perspective to say: "After this race, having given everything I can, the sun is still going to rise tomorrow." It takes a lot of practice to be able to take stock under stress in the heat of the moment but this solution-based thinking can help. Things happen in life that are very hard to deal with, but others might have dealt with similar things and worked through them. If one human is capable of something, with the same resources why shouldn't it be possible for someone else?'

•

Esther Vergeer was also eight years old when she found out how low a day can sink. She had been born with a birth defect around her spinal cord, eventually requiring back surgery. Unfortunately, during the procedure the blood transportation to her nerves was damaged. When the young Dutch girl woke up she'd lost the use of her legs.

'At first I didn't really realise I'd be paralysed for the rest of my life,' recalls Vergeer. 'I was little, I was in pain, I was in hospital, so all together it made me think it would just last a while – and when I didn't have pain any more I'd be able to walk again. Then when I got back home and I had to go back to my own school and play with my friends, I eventually realised it was taking a long time. This was not working out and it was not going to be easy. Then it dawned on me it would be for the rest of my life.

'In the beginning it was hard of course because I compared everything with how it was before. It had been easier and more fun when I could walk. But the people around me made me realise the world doesn't end. I focused on what I could do rather than what I couldn't. Today I don't see myself as a disabled person because I'm living an amazing life and I can do all the things that other people of my age do.'

Vergeer does rather more than most, actually. After

meticulously relearning the basics like getting dressed, the young Dutch girl discovered an outlet. Before she was paralysed she hadn't been remotely sporty, apart from the odd swim. Then as she recuperated in her wheelchair she picked up a tennis racquet for the first time. Not a bad choice. She would become a genuine sporting phenomenon, the perfect example of a competitor who won't settle for just a single day in the sun.

When I met Vergeer she was at number 444 of a ten-year run of singles wins dating from 2003 to her third and final Paralympic gold at London in 2012, when she retired on an unbeaten 470. But while her opponents scrabbled around for the chink in her armour Esther ensured she stayed a moving target.

'The secret to staying at the top is to constantly find new ways to improve,' says Vergeer. 'Each year I add and take away stuff and improve so much that I am basically a different player. With the help of my coaches I find tactical, physical and equipment improvements but also mental improvements. I wouldn't be able to do that if it was just me by myself. But having a team around me makes me see even a small change can have a huge impact on the court. I see improvement on so many levels, but there's still much to learn. My main motivation comes from inside me. I just love the game, I love playing, I love training. But I also see I can improve in so many ways.'

Such words struck fear into her many challengers, who became increasingly desperate as the years passed. Forget Paralympic gold, the big crown was to become 'the one who beat Esther'. The last title-holder was Daniela di Toro, who can scarcely have believed what was about to kick off when she dared beat the Dutchwoman early in 2003. Vergeer was already world number one but arrived jetlagged in the Sydney heat from Amsterdam's winter. Apparently she learned her lesson. Her next big scare came five years later in the Paralympic final when opponent Korie Homan even dared make it as far as match point. But no further, due to the mental strength lurking on the opposite side of the court; Vergeer even won the rally with a drop shot. On the rare occasions Vergeer lost a set (just 18 in 470 matches) or found herself approaching similar trouble, she used a master mind trick to force herself back into the Zone.

'During the run there have been great days but also days when I get out of bed and I think, "Oh my God, this is not going to be a good day",' insists Vergeer. 'When things start going wrong on court I focus to get the feeling back from a match when I felt in total control, at the first round of one US Open. Grand slams are special so my preparation and mental alertness were a bit higher that day than a regular tournament. Having so many spectators watching makes me more energetic and eager, so when I got on court I knew I could win it. It gave me such a kick and such a rush that for the whole match I didn't know what plan I had any more, it was just mental "flow". That was a good feeling and every time I'm nervous I try to think back to that match. When I get that mode back, I get a sort of calmness over me.'

Vergeer's off-court work rate is renowned but this mental trick was surely the key to her dazzling winning streak. She was effectively going back to 'her day' and recreating it every day. This is a sure-fire way to dismiss the negativity that happily occupies the mind – which, remember, remains in control of the limbs that are hitting the tennis ball. It works in any area of life but it is especially effective within the time constraints of sport where you must find the ability to perform straightaway.

This is an example of what Neuro-Linguistic Programming calls a 'trigger', a way of re-setting the mind on your own terms. Such tricks come in particularly handy in tennis because no matter how close you get to victory you can't simply coast home; you always still have to convert the winning point. That has caused many a meltdown. In these all-important moments Vergeer's inner tranquillity was in marked contrast to her opponents, who would start to read tomorrow's headlines when they got close to becoming the one to depose the queen.

'They don't talk to me when I'm about to play them,' admits Vergeer. 'But there are times when I see my opponents raising their confidence and then I just do a couple of things. There are these tactical games and if I'm a little bit nervous or close to losing a match or a set I switch back to that safe tactical mode. I just make myself stay 100 per cent controlled and I guess I make the right decisions on the right points.

'I can also give my opponents less confidence by playing to their weaknesses. Then I can turn myself around, gain more self-confidence and just raise my game up again. Meanwhile I see them going down: with their lack of confidence they swear at themselves. They seem desperate, like: "What do I have to do?" Even after the match they're the same. So yeah I'm curious what they think exactly.'

When we met, Vergeer was resigned to the fact her run would come to an end. Indeed she claimed to look forward to it so she could get up in the morning without the relentless pressure of wondering if this would be the day. Yet that day never came. Her winning streak led to fame in the Netherlands, though she admits it was not quite universal because she hears from other women in wheelchairs who get mistaken for 'Esther'. Now the real Esther wants to give back, having started her own foundation aimed at getting disabled children to follow her path, which she even reckons 'saved her life'.

'Sport can do so much for kids to work together and raise their confidence,' she says. 'For kids with disabilities it's even more important. It's not just about being independent, seeing what you can do physically and ways to improve; they need the material support of a chair or crutches just to get around in everyday life too. What's most important is for kids to feel they're still kids, part of their group of friends, part of society. So the people around them should know and treat them that way. I grew up in an environment where people respected me for who I was. So I never got excluded. I never got sworn at. I was still Esther, just in a wheelchair.'

8

TEAMWORK

'**K**a mate! Ka mate! Ka ora! Ka ora!'
These words – Maori for 'It is death! It is death! It is life! It is life!' – mark the start of the most traditional version of the haka, the ritual challenge laid down to their opposition before matches by New Zealand's rugby union team, the All Blacks. To face 15 large men puffing out their chests, slapping their thighs, stamping their feet, sticking out their tongues and shouting at you is hardly ideal preparation to get in the Zone – unless, that is, you're one of them.

'It's a pretty powerful way to start work,' smiles Sean Fitzpatrick, winner of the inaugural 1987 World Cup and long-serving team captain in the 1990s. 'But it's not for the impact it has on opponents. Sure, it's about throwing down a challenge to the other team, but it's more about us coming together as a group. It's the power and unity that it generates. It's for our country, our friends, our family and the players who have been before us. The haka is about us feeling good.'

No wonder the All Blacks are the greatest team in the history of rugby union. Yes, it is their national sport, but the impact of such a public declaration of collective force just before kick-off is immense.

The chance for a team to remind both themselves and everyone else they mean business when it matters is rare in sport. The closest equivalent is the national anthem, but shouting at the top of your lungs trumps a piped brass band playing a dirge. There are exceptions – notably Wales's 'Land of my Fathers', always rousing enough to lift any roof. That's why the Welsh Rugby Football Union took a brave step at Cardiff in 2006, insisting the All Blacks could only do the haka before their anthem, not after.

'I'm thinking, "Hey, that's perfect",' recalls Fitzpatrick, by then long retired. 'If I was the Welsh I'd be saying that. Why should we get the advantage of doing the haka one minute before we play when their haka is effectively their national anthem? So they wouldn't let the All Blacks do it. And [captain] Richie McCaw said, "OK, we won't do it." They did it in the changing room instead. We had to watch the haka on the big screen, which was disappointing as everyone loves watching it. But Richie later said: "That was the most powerful haka we've ever done. We did it directly to each other and the passion it developed was phenomenal." Then they beat the Welsh 45-10. After that they said you can do the haka whenever you want…'

The haka is such a spectacle that it is held in sacred status in the rugby world and its long-term future is guaranteed. The best anyone else can now do is to come up with ever more novel ways of facing up to it. It took until 1989 for Ireland to pioneer standing directly in front of the haka – and while Fitzpatrick insists such tactics make no difference he admits he was briefly taken aback, thinking 'What's going on here? This is our space...' before normal service was resumed. A France team bedecked in 'all white' memorably moved up the pitch in arrow formation before the 2011 World Cup Final – but it was not quite enough to unsettle the favourites who won in front of their home crowd at Auckland by a single point.

Richie McCaw became the only man to lead teams to two straight World Cups when they repeated the feat in 2015, just before his retirement. Put it in one sentence and it all sounds easy, but to stay on top of a global sport that long is a rare feat – and McCaw recognises the team ethic that makes the All Blacks such a dominant force.

'The great thing about our set-up is that we always say the team is bigger than any individual,' says McCaw. 'We all buy into that. It sounds simple but that helped us for all the years I've been there. After 2011 we were determined to keep raising our standards to stay the world's number one team for the four years leading to 2015. We had a great group of guys who had been through a lot together and shared a desire to be the best. That's the drive you need to find the margins that make a difference.'

McCaw is the most capped player in rugby history, captaining the All Blacks for 110 of his world record 148 test matches. When I asked him to recall 'the day the haka never was' in Wales it brought out a big smile: 'There were a few games played at boardroom level so we thought we had to make a stand. It sorted it out. But while people think the haka is a way of intimidating, we really don't do it to try and wind up the opposition. It's more of a symbol of who you are and where you come from, a bit like the anthem. We do it with passion and pride because it's a symbol of who we are as Kiwis. So we want to do it properly so people enjoy it and are proud of it.

'Our main inspiration comes from the All Black teams that have gone before. They set the standard. One of the great things about rugby is that you go hard at each other for 80 minutes but there is a respect above what happens on the field. We play as well as we can, then after the game we meet the opposition and keep those values. That's a big part of keeping feet on the ground. When you lose you're gracious about it, but when you win you're also humble. That's important to us.'

•

Humility might not seem the most important component of success at the top of world sport. I hope we have now established the importance of confidence and self-belief to success in any venture. But when you have these in abundance the next step kicks in and you realise that no matter what apparent magic you can produce, you're never the only conjuror out there. That insight is especially important in a team sport where no one can win anything on their own. The best teams are built on respect – not just for team-mates but for the opposition, the crowds watching and the entire sport that has given them their platform to perform.

'There's a huge history of New Zealand rugby,' admits victorious 2015 head coach Steve Hansen. 'So there's a real understanding of what our responsibilities are. Over time that legacy has grown so now there's an expectation that we win every test match – playing well, in a style acceptable to the team. That has raised the bar.

'It's about being grateful for the opportunity to be an All Black. You're there because you have extraordinary skills but that doesn't make you a superhuman. So it doesn't give you the right to be arrogant. If you've been given those skills you've got to use them. Rather than be frightened by that, we've embraced it. Whether we coach or play we say: "I'm only here for a short time, I don't own the jersey, so what do I want to achieve to enhance that legacy and make it better than when I arrived?" If people do that over a long period, it has to get better and better.

'The secret to team culture is living it every day – from the top down. There's alignment from the coach to the baggage man to the captain to the new guy. We live like a family. Your family is made up of different individuals but you're tight. There are times when you may not like their behaviour – and when that happens there have to be consequences – but you still love them. You're still a family.'

You'd have to be a brave man to cross Hansen, who first joined this family as assistant coach to Graham Henry in 2004, before inheriting the top job after the 2011 World Cup win. Starting a new role is daunting, let alone when the only way is down. That's where confidence really pays off. In this case the All Blacks embarked on a run that defied even their own high standards, losing just four test matches in five years.

The Zone is usually an individual phenomenon, a private sensation within the head of an expert doing what they love. Yet a group sometimes gels so perfectly they produce a performance seemingly greater than the sum of their parts.

The All Blacks are one of few teams who always seem to have this ultimate sporting alchemy within reach. Even so Hansen admits such perfection is rare.

'For me "in the Zone" is like driving a car without having to think about it,' he says. 'You get from A to B but have you thought about changing the gears, braking or putting on the indicators? No, it just happened. To do that in sport you have to remove all the things that could take you out of it. If someone does something stupid in a car, you're suddenly threatened by that. Your focus narrows right up and you're not in the Zone any more. So in rugby it's making sure preparation includes things that could go wrong. It doesn't mean you won't come in and out of the Zone but you'll get back in the Zone quicker, see things and do them without having to second-guess yourself.

'I don't think you'll ever get everybody totally in the Zone. Players come and go within the game and momentum has a lot to do with that. The opposition have to have their turn... unfortunately... but that's sport. It's how you deal with the good or bad luck you get. We try to win the momentum moments – particularly the big, most important ones. Success gives you confidence and confidence gives you belief. Being successful allows you to believe a little stronger than others. When you get into that tough situation, it's believing you can get out, saying: "We don't give up." Not just one person but en masse. It's all about your belief.'

South African winger Bryan Habana, who equalled the late Jonah Lomu's all-time record with his 15th World Cup try in 2015, reveals how much effort goes into helping teams peak both individually and collectively in this professional era.

'As an athlete you know the techniques you need to get

into the Zone,' he tells me. 'A lot of work is done off the field with mental "gurus" to get to that point but it's different for every person. Some guys work on it the day before, maybe with music or something to flick that mental switch. It's about making sure your body knows what's coming and the physicality you're about to face. It's crucial to understand what gets you in the Zone so you can refer back to those trigger points going into the big games.

'Belief plays an important part in creating and maintaining success, not just in rugby but in every business or team context. They say any team is only as strong as its weakest link, so it's harder to keep that belief in a team set-up. A good leader takes on responsibility but they need the same responsibility from the players. No matter what happens you must continue believing in yourself, your team-mates and the structure. That's where the All Blacks are a step ahead of the rest. Whereas with other teams there's sometimes a bit of doubt whether or not they can do it, they have that belief – no matter whether they're ahead or behind – that they're going to win the game.'

Still, if New Zealand's last-minute group therapy session aims to get 15 heads collectively into the right place, Hansen insists it can go too far: 'Sometimes the haka is a disadvantage because you're too pumped up. It doesn't make you too confident, but over-aroused. You need to take a breath and come back to Planet Earth…'

Even in the ultimate team environment it helps if you can call on individuals with the class to steady the ship when needed. In the 2015 World Cup Final the All Blacks lost a player to the sin bin before Dan Carter's drop goal saw off an Australian fightback, decisively swinging the momentum.

When Richie McCaw later lifted the Webb Ellis trophy it was the culmination of his lifelong dream, albeit one shared by his entire nation: 'Most kids who grow up in New Zealand dream of being an All Black,' McCaw tells me. 'Having a dream is important. You have to give it a crack... and I can say from experience they do come true. I grew up loving rugby, but it wasn't until I left school that it went from a dream to a possibility. If you'd said then that I'd be able to go through the experiences I've had, I'd have laughed. It was everything I dreamed of and more. The big thing is to enjoy it. What I say to kids is: "Chase your dreams" because you never know...'

•

It all begs the question of what the planet would be like if we all started our day with a haka. Sean Fitzpatrick now speaks to businesses around the world, doing his best to export the phenomenon. Just before we met he'd been in Miami enticing a bemused American audience – for whom rugby is a foreign language anyway – to give it a try.

'They loved it,' he beams. 'They said: "It's fantastic, we need to develop our own haka before we start work." Most people do have something, like a ritual in the morning which they do either as a family or as friends together. It might be standing over the coffee machine or doing something with your mouse – something that flicks the switch. I asked one of the guys: "You must have a ritual in the morning when you walk into the office." He said yes. He opens his computer and goes "Awww shit."'

Something tells me that man is not alone. Even though some businesses have started cottoning on to the power of the mantra, try telling me the Walmart Chant ever had the same effect. But then some brands inspire a bit more passion than others, not to mention a healthy dose of fear in their rivals.

'The legacy of the All Blacks jersey is more intimidating than any opposition,' adds Fitzpatrick. 'If you're swimming against Mark Spitz, you're going to be saying, "Christ, he's won these gold medals. To beat him I'm going to have to play my best game." As All Blacks we have the same attitude: "You'll have to play your best game to beat us." The biggest problem other teams have is to believe they can beat the All Blacks. So the power of the brand is phenomenal.

'Winning is pretty simple actually, both in rugby and elsewhere in life. Rugby is a complicated game but if you do the simple things well, nine times out of ten you win. The best teams I played in didn't have many superstars, just good players who were powerful as a group because we knew what we were going to do and we knew we'd deliver. If you minimise mistakes no one will beat you because of the pressure you build. The All Blacks don't make mistakes. Teams live with them for 60 minutes or 70 minutes. Then for the last ten minutes they can't.'

Put like that perfection sounds simple, but no matter what colour your jersey it requires total trust. Fitzpatrick reckons what marks out teams that can stay at the top is the will to 'park' success and move on. He smirks at English football's determination to keep celebrating its 1966 football World Cup win half a century later when his own lingering memories from his career are the ones that got away...

'Leadership isn't hard as long as everyone wants to go in the same direction,' he insists. 'As All Blacks we talk of needing to be arrogant to be successful, then you leave it on the field. But sometimes I was involved in a team, like 1991, when we took that arrogance off the field and thought we were better than we were. We were beaten not by better players but a better team. Then 30 of us sat in a room and identified what we needed to win the 1995 World Cup. We wanted to be the fittest and fastest team in the world. That would need total commitment, meaning it was the biggest thing in our lives and everything else had to be second. We went around asking: "Are we prepared to do that?" Everyone said, "We're in." Once you do that it's easy.'

After a dominant tournament, Fitzpatrick's New Zealand side duly reached the final against South Africa's Springboks, going in as favourites thanks to these shared goals and a mighty individual contribution by winger Jonah Lomu. Sadly for them, this was to be the only day in rugby history that the haka has truly been upstaged.

The 1995 Rugby World Cup was the first global sporting event to be held in South Africa since the official end of apartheid – and the last of rugby's amateur era. When new president Nelson Mandela strode into Johannesburg's Ellis Park Stadium wearing a Springbok jersey, it inspired not just the home team but his long-troubled country to unite – at least for the next 80 minutes, plus the extra time it took to knock the All Blacks off the top of the world. No wonder Morné du Plessis, who captained the Springboks for five years before managing them to the 1995 win, is a keen student of the sporting mind.

'All sport has elements of both physiological and psychological preparation,' says du Plessis. 'I see thousands of young golfers breaking par every week at amateur level.

They all swing well and hit the ball a mile but there are 30 guys who win all the time. It's got to be the 30 who are mentally tougher who get their muscles to operate and make the right decisions under pressure. Once you're in the team environment of rugby, luckily the physical decisions come easier. But you still have to get them right the whole time. In today's professional game everybody has the same data and puts in the same physical preparation to get guys stronger, faster, jumping higher, whatever it takes. So the line between good and great is narrowing.

'It's about belief, but overconfidence is something I've seen so many times in my career I can almost predict it affecting a team. After one great performance, as much as you talk to that team about forgetting it and getting on with the new game, it seeps under the changing-room door. You're prepared one week then you go through the same routine for the next game and it's a completely different feeling. In coaching the characteristic that separated the truly great motivators is the ability to keep the guys on that edge between confidence and arrogance.'

This is where the best coaches and captains come into their own, keeping feet on the ground after even the most majestic performances. Du Plessis believes coaches need 'consistency' and 'honesty' to gain their troops' respect – even when the truth hurts. He reckons Manchester United's long-time boss Alex Ferguson had the knack of maintaining exactly the right amount of pressure, whether for places in the team or some other variable, never to let players get too big for their boots. But Ferguson was also a master of what du Plessis believes is the ultimate secret to getting a team into the Zone en masse: he gave them a cause to play for. Suddenly the endless public whinging, perceived injustices and relentless application of double standards makes sense...

'In a team environment you need common values that you all understand and all believe in,' says du Plessis. 'Healthy values are generally more productive than unhealthy ones. It's no good if half of us believe in winning at all costs and we'll do anything including cheat to do it, while the other half believes we won't be doing that. But there is always something special about playing for a cause. Whether it's playing for our country, playing for people who've just experienced an earthquake or just a general feeling, it's great to have a common cause. Then it's them and us.'

●

The motivation needed to bind a team doesn't have to be a grand political gesture, it can be personal. Golf is usually as solitary as sport gets, but the Ryder Cup allows its giants to join forces. In 2012 the Europe team recovered from a seemingly impossible position to defeat the USA on the final day at Chicago's Medinah Country Club. The cause uniting them was the memory of Spain's Seve Ballesteros, whose regular playing partner José Maria Olazábal was captain. Europe's Ian Poulter, who inspired the comeback, told me how he thrives on this rare chance to team up: 'In golf you're supposed to be able to build yourself up and down between shots and find the Zone naturally. If that doesn't happen, something's going wrong. But for me the special moments when I feel at a higher level come at the Ryder Cup.'

'Home advantage' is usually a powerful force in sport as the massed support of fans cheering your every move gives any team a lift. But Dutch football great Ruud Gullit insists he revelled just as much in turning a negative situation – such as walking into an intimidating stadium – into a positive one. Classic 'them and us'…

'Whatever ground you go to, the most important thing is that you absorb and acknowledge the atmosphere,' he tells me. 'Don't block yourself off from it, embrace it. It doesn't matter if it's hostile or friendly. It's important that you feel what the vibe is. Some players just want to block it out but I just wanted to feel it. The big question is: why are they hostile against you? Because they don't want you to win. Are they afraid of you? Oh yes they are – they don't want you to play well. Do I get a lot of energy from that? Hell, yes. Of course I also get a lift from a home crowd. So either way you can't lose. But the secret is to stick together. You need the players to have a strong mental bond. If so, anything can happen.'

Gullit cites Italy's 1982 World Cup team, who were hounded by their home press for underwhelming performances in the group stages before beating Argentina, Brazil and West Germany en route to the trophy. Many of Gullit's finest hours came in Italian club football, notably a golden period for AC Milan in the late 1980s. Tellingly, he came up with a similar description of the Zone to All Blacks head coach Steve Hansen.

'It's like when you go into automatic pilot on the motorway,' he says. 'On a football pitch you're still doing your thing but everything goes blank and you focus. You don't hear anything around you. But it's hard for a footballer to get 100 per cent in the Zone because if it starts to happen the opposition does something. The moment there is an injury that flow is gone, because you stop. That's what they do all the time in sports like basketball with "Time Outs". You see it in tennis too: bounce the ball a bit more, have a discussion with the referee, an injury break… all these little things break the flow of the opponent. That's why people fake injuries in football, because you have no Time Out. So you break that flow or kill it off.

'With a team it's even harder to be in the Zone because it means everybody has to be 100 per cent. But our first Champions League final for Milan against Steaua Bucharest in 1989 (they won 4-0, two goals apiece for Gullit and Marco van Basten) was 100 per cent Zone for the whole game, as was that year's 5-0 semi-final home leg against Real Madrid. Sometimes you do get 100 per cent in the Zone but it's very rare because you need everyone to be in it. If there's one blip, maybe a player who doesn't have it or who's up against a tough opponent, you're already down to 99 per cent, then 98. You think: "How can I help him out of his misery?" Maybe we can work really hard to nick balls from this guy. So there's always a hiccup.'

Whether it's through double marking or sheer mental overload, often even the greats fail to match their billing on the biggest stage. The 2014 World Cup featured football's two hyperstars in Lionel Messi and Cristiano Ronaldo, yet it was Germany's team ethic that won through in style. Gullit has sympathy for the big names' failure to impose themselves on the biggest stage, adding: 'The hard part is that players use up so much energy during their club championships. Because of all the work they put in, it's hard to recharge the batteries because your body needs to rest. It's also a mental thing. You try to peak at the end of the season because it's what you play football for. But if it doesn't happen, all of a sudden the body deflates.'

Gullit was an exception, captaining the Netherlands to a stylish 1988 European Championship, their only major title. But ever since he first dreamed of life in football he had grown used to standing out from the crowd: 'When I was 11 or 12, I played for a team of the best players from Amsterdam, including some from Ajax. I saw I was as good as the rest and sometimes better. So I thought, "Hey..." From then on I never had any doubt I'd make it. I was focused. I was also one of few black kids in that team. If you are the only one, people notice you. So you have to be better than the others. Take advantage of that. It doesn't matter if you're black, have red hair or whatever, you'll get noticed. If you play badly people will see it even more. So you don't want to give them that chance. Now I tell kids to enjoy what they do but don't leave any regrets for later: "If I had done this maybe I could have..." No. There is no second chance. Give 100 per cent to make sure of it.'

No matter how motivated and well drilled a team is, in fast-flowing ball sports the difference often stems from a flash of genius. It seems the Zone is contagious and team-mates can catch greatness from each other. That's according to Marcel Desailly, of the French football team that was the first to hold both the World Cup and the European Championship with wins in 1998 and 2000 – a feat later topped by Spain.

'France didn't qualify for the 1994 World Cup but in 1996 we started to build that new generation,' says Desailly. 'We had natural leaders who showed they could perform at a higher level. We were professional players, focused and dedicated to the game. On top of that we had Zinédine Zidane. When Zidane was there it was different, even in a training session. A star like that brings direct motivation and more responsibility for the others. You wanted to keep the ball correctly, your attention was higher and you were more focused. The concentration and consistency we showed spoke for us. That was what allowed us to last at the top, which is the hardest thing.

'Luckily we were able to deliver collective performances. From 1998 to 2001 we were the world's best team. Then in 2002 we reached the end of the cycle and we suddenly went down. The positive pressure that had allowed us to perform suddenly became scary. I was expecting Spain to have the same when they had nothing more to prove during the 2012 European Championship. They could have started to think they could lose, like a tennis player who's scared to serve out the last game. Instead Spain stayed at the top because collectively they were the best. A collective link in a team is very important and makes the difference every single time.'

•

Ball sports are made for this enhanced state of collective concentration: planning only takes you so far and moments of spontaneous creativity are the key. But from there it is a short step to an even more creative world where improvisation has long ruled.

'The phrase "in the Zone" almost works better for music,' says Nick Mason, drummer with rock giants Pink Floyd. 'What you get is the intuition to know what the other people are going to play. So you know you can do something you've never done before because you can sense what other people are going to do. It would probably be only with one particular song rather than a whole evening – or maybe one solo where someone takes it to a different level or plays something entirely new. When everyone is on it, there's a step up. It's a special feeling.'

Drummers rarely take the plaudits – much like rugby's front row forwards – but for any team to shine every player needs to be in the same moment. Playing live is a more regular environment than recording for musicians to reach the Zone thanks to atmosphere and numbers: months on the road trump their occasional visits to the studio. But they can work every bit as hard as sports stars to get there. Stacey Kent is an American jazz singer with a gentle lilting voice. But the tranquil façade masks her expertise in seeking the ultimate high, a process that starts long before she steps onto the stage.

'Musicians and athletes have a lot in common because you have to perform at that moment,' says Kent. 'The Zone is about being very concentrated, so you work to be in that place. You don't want to peak too soon or be too energetic or lacklustre. So from when you get up in the morning everything is aimed at that peaking moment. If you're not concentrating you can falter so you always watch out for distractions. I take inspiration from tennis players who come back from two and a half sets down because they are so good at looking forwards. The problems start when you think of what has already gone wrong, when you're not losing a match but you are losing to yourself. If something bad happens in the morning it can either ruin the rest of the day or you can stay focused and look for a way to get right back.

'It's not just about physical ability to play tennis or music, it's also having the head and the personality for it. I played tennis as a kid but I would get flustered by the competitive side and I didn't stay concentrated. I didn't have the head for competitive sport but I do have a head for this. We compare ourselves to athletes all the time but the difference here is that there is no competition. There's nobody on your side or not on your side. Everything with music goes together.'

Competition is not a prerequisite for the Zone. It can even be a hindrance. Yet whether we chase perfect performance on a pitch or perfect pitch in a performance the similarities are uncanny, both in preparation and the sensation itself. And there is always something uplifting about the effect of a group finding its wings at the same time.

'Finding the Zone is a learning process and you're constantly striving for it,' says Kent. 'I once heard Andre Agassi say he played a perfect match because he saw the ball larger. That's the metaphor we use. The difference between us and a concert pianist is they are alone. So there's an unspoken place where we collectively find the Zone. After our sound check we try not to talk to anyone outside the band. We find a place where we are very much together. Then we go out and concentrate together.

'On a long tour one of us might be struggling one night, but you find a way to pick each other up and pull each other along. Sometimes you think of things outside the gig and before you know it you're lost. At other times you think too much. It takes an immense amount of concentration not to get flustered if, say, the mike is shaking. But when you're on it it's an amazing feeling. You're concentrating but it must be a different part of your brain. You're carried along and before you know it you're at the end and you haven't thought about where you are. It feels beautiful, but if you can find it collectively with other people in a group, it's an immense feeling.'

•

'Them and us' may be a powerful way of getting a group of disparate individuals to gel, but it leaves room for a tantalising step higher in the quest for a common cause – namely 'us and us'. Such a sentiment may seem quaint and totally out of place in the ultra-competitive world we supposedly inhabit. But there is one high-profile example of a team that has dominated its discipline for decades using this principle. For half a century the world has marvelled at Kenya's pre-eminence in track events from 800m to the marathon. Kenyan Olympic Committee president Kip Keino, who started the domination with gold medals in 1968 (1500m) and 1972 (3000m steeplechase) is happy to share the secret – and, for that matter, everything else.

'We work as a team, not as an individual,' says Keino. 'We share. That's the attitude in Kenya as a whole: we do things together. Today we all help at one house, tomorrow we'll go somewhere else. After we finish we eat together too. Similarly you won't ever find an athlete training alone in Kenya but always in a group of five or ten. One takes over in front and the others follow, then another will take over. This is the mentality of teamwork. That group is the most important thing.

'We train people from all over the world. We share. And we want to see the people who train here beating the Kenyans too. We've had people come from Israel, Zambia and Sri Lanka. We had a boy from Sudan who went home with silver in the Olympic 1500m. Then we had a girl from Sweden who was training in cross country. In the end she beat the Kenyans and we were happy. In this world and this sport we share. Win or lose you shake hands with the winner.

'When you are here we want you to maximise everything

about your training. The idea is to bring out the best you can do and make sure that when you leave you've improved your personal best or national record. That way your country will be proud of what you have done. We want you to do your best performance. We don't want to deny you that right. Then when you achieve we are proud of what you have done.'

Such a magnanimous approach is refreshing in the dog-eat-dog world of top sport – but it has a limit: it doesn't mean the Kenyans won't do everything in their power to end up on top of the podium themselves as the best of the giant global 'us'. Their haul of 86 middle- and long-distance Olympic medals since Keino's era shows who the real beneficiaries are.

'The group ethic is a massive part of the success the Kenyans have had,' says Richard Nerurkar, a British runner who went to train in Kenya in the 1990s. 'My motivation to join them was the same: it's easier to train hard if you have training partners who are like-minded. I'd loved training in a group since I started running at school but it's not in the psyche of European athletes like it is in Africa. In Ethiopia if you're running on your own they'd think: "Is there something wrong?" One factor is security, but you don't train on your own because you do everything together anyway. It's that kind of society. I loved training in Kenya. There is no language barrier, they are very open, smiley and welcoming right from the start.

'The challenge for a British-born athlete is that you live life at sea level. You don't have the same physiology because you haven't lived at altitude. Most European runners would now say it's more beneficial to start a group of their own, because the training you hear the Kenyans and Ethiopians are doing is almost beyond what is sensible for a European athlete. It's amazing...'

The benefit of growing up in this part of the world isn't limited to physiology. Olympic marathon champion in 2016, Eliud Kipchoge ran 20km a day from the age of eight just to get to school. Such feats have become a cliché, but if you can manage it the power that results is not just in the limbs but where it really counts: up top.

'When you train with a group an athlete's mind can work more than when you are alone,' adds Kipchoge's training partner Emmanuel Mutai, winner of the London Marathon in 2011. 'If you can't see anyone ahead and nobody is chasing you, when you say you're tired your mind won't know any different. But in a group when the mind gets tired you might see a runner behind, closing the gap. Suddenly you say, "No, I can maintain this pace." That's when you get more energy and your mind works harder. Then you strengthen your mind.

'The mind controls everything. Sometimes you feel pain, but even if you are getting tired the most important thing is that once you've started you'll fight until the end. When you say "I'm tired now" it's the end. That's how to lose. If the mind says: "No you're not tired, just keep going" you'll find the strength. So your mind needs to be strong to control the body. At the top we all run to the same level so what matters is how strong your mind is compared to others. If you are getting tired but you move two steps ahead so your rival realises he's tired and has to slow, you'll win. But while it's important for joy to come when you do, if you lose a race it doesn't mean you lose anything, because whatever you have achieved on that day, that is your success.'

Of course not every member of a Kenyan group will make it big in athletics, but the strike rate is impressive. The rewards on offer mean some have been caught taking short cuts with drugs in recent years, tainting the sport of endurance running. But for those who run clean the real secret is surely this group dynamic. This prepares individual minds to find the extra push in the closing stages when their every sinew is telling them to stop imposing this torture on their bodies.

'Seventy-five per cent of distance running is mental,' says Kip Keino. 'When you are training you are building your mind towards that event. If you think you can't do it, you've already lost. So you need a mental way of fighting. You can't do mental preparation at an event so you do it before. You read your competitors and make plans for whoever you're running with. You have to know what their tactics are and when, so you plan your own. In the event itself, if he moves, you go too. You never know whether he could be finished in another five yards. So the mental side is to make sure when they go, you are there. Everyone trains hard for the Olympics and you don't know what is coming. So you prepare yourself mentally and know if anything happens, you have something extra.'

For those who do find that something extra, a surprisingly frequent choice is to forgo the fortune that accompanies it. Instead many opt to give something extra back. There has been a marked effect on the economy of parts of Kenya such as Eldoret and Iten thanks to reinvestment of prize money into schools and other infrastructure. For over 50 years Kip Keino has run a farm offering shelter and education to orphans. In that time he has looked after over 600 youngsters, who have become a giant family of their own. They are brothers and sisters to each other, and even those who have grown up and moved on still call him 'Daddy' when they return home.

'We do this for the needy members of our society,' he says. 'The orphans need shelter, education and love. Sometimes a child is really desperate or brought to us by the police. Some come to us at just three weeks old if their mother dies in childbirth. Yet some have gone on to university, then they get a job and start their life – not just in Kenya, some are in the USA, China or other parts of the world. We learn by seeing and by imitating. People do what they think is right. When someone has knowledge it is important they can use it. That's the main thing. I came to this world with nothing; I will leave with nothing. If I can do something for humanity in the meantime...'

•

The power of 'them and us' has been exploited for millennia far away from the sports field too, to promote war, conflict and upheaval. To divide and rule the first step is to declare 'them' less worthy than 'us', so they deserve whatever we are going to throw at them. Former world marathon record-holder Tegla Loroupe is another Kenyan distance runner who has turned to education on this very issue in a bid to right such wrongs – using an approach directly tied to the sport that made her great. In 2003 she founded a Peace Foundation that organises marathons in areas of Kenya, Uganda and Sudan that are plagued by tribal rivalries – all in a bid to use the 'pretend' version of competition to show the flaws in the real one.

'I grew up in a conflict area myself, where the parents would always tell their kids that so-and-so is the enemy,'

Loroupe tells me. 'But I saw that when the kids did sport, the parents from the different communities just exchanged fun and words. So I realised the only thing that can bring the community together is sport. If politicians call for a rally no one listens, but we as sportsmen and women can make a platform to talk to the people. I want to help them grow together to understand we belong to one family and we are not enemies.

'To live with one another we have to have trust, live in total respect and harmony – and start it together. You respect somebody and let the other person respect you the way you want. When you point a finger at someone your other fingers are pointing back at you. But when you have love for others, you don't point a finger, you reach your hands out to them. When you give out love to somebody, it comes back to you.'

This is what true confidence can produce: an impact from a 'mere' sports star on the 'real world'. Like many of Kenya's great runners you are struck by how slight Loroupe is, masking the mental power she hides within her slender frame. This can be taken off-track too. She led a group of displaced athletes making up the first Refugee Olympic Team at Rio in 2016, having trained half of them at a camp in Kenya. She has also founded a school for 400 children. Once your reach stretches far beyond the limits of sport, you can see how the importance of silverware pales in comparison. For Loroupe that includes all the traditional goals of a materialistic world.

'We cannot take all our wealth with us,' she says. 'We are all naked when we die. So why always seek to have more? Some people fight for resources, but I'd like to see them start sharing to empower the poor communities with education. There are poor people both in developing and developed countries. But while it's like this the rich will never have protection: when there are riots, the poor don't lose anything; only the rich lose because they have so much. So I would like to see people come down to the same level and share, especially when it comes to educating kids.

'The same applies on a global scale. The more you make problems for others, the more the problems come back and follow you around. So people should look for brothers in the world and try to be an example of giving peace to others, not to use military force. That will never help; it always breeds more hatred. If we can use the money we are putting into the military to solve a problem in a good way, we will save lives and reclaim what we call "trust" from other people.'

Loroupe surely personifies the ultimate aim of the mantras and techniques for positive thinking that feature in this book. To chase a gold needs one level of courage, to step into a boxing ring needs another. But to stick your head above the parapet and speak out for what you believe in – particularly when it is bound to incur the wrath of those who disagree – is a higher aim still, requiring correspondingly greater levels of bravery. Whenever you meet someone with the gentle magnetism and drive of Tegla Loroupe you can't help but come away with a spring in your step.

'I'm just one example of how one person can start something,' says Loroupe. 'But when you plant a seed you don't just reap one seed, you reap more. On the way of a marathon you are not running alone. You bring other people in. That's what I'd like to see: other sports people, other business people coming in the name of peace so our work today can change things a little bit for tomorrow.'

9

PASSION

K nown by the enchanting title of the 'man-killer', the
400m hurdles is one of the most brutal disciplines
in track and field, requiring a mix of raw speed, endurance
and technical ability. Yet one man found a way to dominate
the event so completely in the 1970s and 1980s, he went on a
run of 122 straight wins against the (next) best in the world.
For nine years, nine months and nine days, he killed off the
man-killer. His name was Edwin Moses.

Far from your 'average' champion, Moses started off as an
engineer, earning a degree in physics. The American made
his 400m hurdles debut only months before he took Olympic
gold at Montreal in 1976 with a new world record. Even then
he didn't focus on athletics full-time, coupling his work in
aerospace with a punishing regime – up to eight hours of
training before his working day even began. He made the
most of his scientific knowledge, becoming a pioneer in

applying biodynamics principles as he sought every possible sporting improvement. Back when computers had just 16K of memory he used them to measure everything from respiration to heartbeat patterns. He developed a pattern of 13 strides (of 9 feet 9 inches each) between each hurdle for the whole race while his rivals could only keep that up for half the lap.

I was so intrigued that I was soon chasing Moses myself – round Asia, South America and Europe – in a bid to hear more. Some people really are worth the effort. It turns out the secret to his run of glory was not in his body or his legs. When I asked Moses if he had been ahead of his competitors on a mental level, he nodded. What he said next made my heart hurdle several beats.

'I lived in the Zone,' says Moses. 'It's more than just trying to get there for a race or a day; it's a state of mind. Your whole life is in the Zone, everything that you do. All the time…'

The Zone is typically associated with the peak experience, a brief moment of magic where everything goes perfectly, often under the most extreme pressure. The idea of making a home at that level seems less human and more, well, Jedi. Then you start to assess the full extent of what Moses has achieved both on and off the track and it all starts to fit. The theme that links it all together is passion.

Moses' father was a school principal and his mother was a teacher who ran a summer school for young kids called Head Start. Edwin worked there while he was at high school, developing an early affinity for education and volunteering. With such a background, coupled with a life in the Zone, retirement from athletics can only ever be a blip. After aborting a business career because money was not his motivation, in 2000 he was elected chairman of the Laureus World Sports Academy – a non-profit foundation that uses sport and its heroes as catalysts for social change in some of the most deprived areas of the world. It has come a long way since and Moses is glad it now supports too many projects for him to list by heart. This is no ego trip or vanity project; neither Moses nor the 60 sporting deity Laureus Academy members – many of whom have featured in these pages – have anything left to prove to anyone.

'When you've achieved at the highest level you're so confident that you don't have to be confident any more,' he deadpans. 'It doesn't really matter that much what people say about me. I don't wake up in the morning thinking: "I'm Edwin Moses and I won 122 races." I just like to wake up and be breathing every day. I'm just glad to be alive and make a difference in the world and do whatever I'm going to do.'

Moses speaks in a low monotone but his every word is crafted by a burning intelligence, leading to an intense charisma. He was struck by the world's inequality while he was competing, once watching a pair of Kenyan kids playing football; one had the left shoe, the other had the right. Moses admits he was a mere 'tourist' back then as his career meant he didn't have the time to act. But he now ploughs as much energy into the project as he expended on the track, following through on his goals with similar dedication. Moreover, he's learned to stay ever in the moment.

'I still live in the Zone today,' he tells me. 'It becomes easy after a while; it's not like you have to try and do it. I'm always in the Zone – in anything I do. For most people it starts young, when you feel like you just don't have any barriers. You feel like you can do things and you feel you want to be good in areas that you might not be best suited for. I was good at other things before I became good in sport. I was a good student, even as a kid.

'Then when I competed I just thought about things. Just like you sit and think about what kind of questions to ask, people like me think about what we're going to have to do to become faster. Sport is no different to being an artist or playing music or being a lawyer or a doctor. It depends how good you want to be at what you do. Everyone has choices they make all the time, but some people put in more work to be able to attain a higher level. I think everybody goes through the same thing but most people don't realise what potential they have. Not everybody is lazy. Some of us are just the opposite.'

When I asked Moses how many people he had known who had reached this level, he didn't have to think very long. Such was the degree of the sporting royalty assembled for that week's Laureus World Sports Awards in London, a certain Nadia Comăneci happened to walk past at that very moment. Moses answered: 'Laureus Academy members: people like Nadia who are not afraid to work…'

•

Malcolm Gladwell's 2008 book *Outliers* – about the influence on success of factors such as upbringing – popularised a 1985 study (by psychologists RH Barnsley, AH Thompson and PE Barnsley) showing the NHL Ice Hockey draft is dominated by those born in the first three months of the school year. It seems there is an advantage in children who grow up as the oldest and biggest of their peers. The boost is not just physical but mental due to a self-belief that brews and amplifies over the years. The younger children eventually catch up their missing months in terms of size and maturity, but as they aren't selected so often early on they lack experience and, crucially, never get to let rip on lesser opposition.

Believe it or not we owe the career of sporting giant Moses to the fact that he was anything but a giant during his schooldays. As his birthday was at the tail end of his year group, he recalls being overlooked by the American football coaches as they went down the line picking the teams – despite the fact he was not afraid of tackling the bigger kids. It was the same story in basketball, even though he'd travel all over the city playing and winning two-man tournaments against much taller opponents.

'I was the last one to start growing,' says Moses. 'When you're 12 or 14 years old that makes a significant difference. I was as tough as the big kids and everyone knew that, I just didn't have the size. So it might not hurt if I tackled you hard but the other guys could hurt me. I often got hurt but I never quit. I never saw myself as a victim and never felt sorry for myself.

'When I ran, size really didn't matter. That's why I stayed with track and field. You can determine your own fate. The first couple of times I started beating kids who were bigger than me, I started to enjoy it. It was all on merit. I was out there every day so I did a lot of running that other kids didn't want to do. That's how I learned how to train, with interval training that gets progressively harder. Along the way I saw what happened to people. I saw kids who were much better than me who didn't like to run, whereas I was still running at the end of the day. Within months I was beating them. Once I beat you, in my mind it was very, very difficult for you. I would just continue to improve. Once I began beating someone I never let them beat me again.'

It would be hard to take a sentiment like that too seriously coming from most people. It's the sort of bluster a boxer might muster to hype a fight. But with Moses it clearly applies for real, hence his relentless run of victories. Nonetheless he insists the ingredients for a feast of success come from a steady diet of defeat.

'Early on I always used to lose,' adds Moses. 'I had to fight my way to the top. High school was like a rollercoaster: up and down, up and down. Once you started winning you faced better competition. Fortunately my trajectory kept going up: I was beaten by better and better people. Then I'd just knock them down, knock them down. Once you beat them, the killer instinct really kicks in.

'In track and field there's no one who hasn't lost a lot of races, it's part of the transition to being a world class athlete. Even a prodigy like Usain Bolt took a while to get going when he hit the world scene. Losing is part of the game and you learn not to take it personally. Even though it later didn't happen to me for a long, long time, the fear of it was a motivating factor for me. That's why I won all these races.'

Moses never let himself obsess over the joy of winning either. Having gone to school on an academic scholarship, sport remained a 'hobby'. Even as he progressed, his all-conquering motivation was not results but an endless quest for improvement.

'I never dared to think about winning an Olympic gold medal,' insists Moses. 'The ones who do think about trophies probably don't get as far. A lot of those people quit sport early because they can't win any more and they get frustrated. I don't wake up thinking: "I'm a bad dude, I've run 47 seconds flat and I can beat everybody." You just do what needs to be done. It's a lifestyle – and most of it had nothing to do with winning. You get up and think about how bad it would feel before the sun sets and how you'd get through that process. People said: "You made it look easy." But what everybody forgets is that to win you had to spend so much more energy and run so much harder; that you were the guy who was hurting the worst. Everyone thinks it's the opposite, but to get there first feels worst. You hurt bad…'

•

It is apt that the word 'passion' derives from the Latin word for suffering. It's not just physical pain but the sacrifices and dedication required to push any limits. Even once Moses did finally start winning, he didn't just show up, waltz round, take the tape and go. The American competed for a total of 15 minutes a year but it was the long hours of slog behind the scenes that set up his astonishing run. Most crucially his punishing regime bolstered the thought in his head that no one could ever catch up.

'I always went back to the drawing board in training,' says Moses. 'Whereas a lot of people didn't like to train, I didn't mind. When I got to the top I said: "Now I'm not going to get beaten any more." I was a lot better than everyone else so I shouldn't lose. I did everything I could on a daily basis to make sure. I'd been practising for ten years and every day I knew I trained harder than everyone. I convinced myself my training programme was the best. I put in more time, ran longer, ran until I was more tired, more stretched, more flexible. Nothing could convince me I wasn't the superior athlete. Period. I used to say you have to get up early and go to sleep late. That's what I did every day. I'd prepare like that all day long. That's the difference.

'As the winning streak went on I kept the same attitude and trained exactly the same way. I felt no one could beat me except for some bad circumstances. Meanwhile my competitors all said they were running to knock me off. Whoever did was going to be famous. That's true. But when Danny Harris did finally win a race, he had a hard time running against me after that. Every time he hit the track he set about it knowing I could break the world record, thinking: "Is he going to do it today?" He could never think about racing; he thought about the punishment that could be coming, knowing I could never let him win again. In fact it never happened again.'

Moses kept a meticulous log of his training regime and totalled 26,000 miles – more than a lap of the world. Marathon runners may top that but in his case none of it was jogging. This was all high-intensity running. With a juggernaut like that aiming for the same prizes the rest must have felt like not showing up. Moses could well have become the only track athlete to take gold in four different Olympics but fate reduced his haul. After his 1976 gold he was robbed by the 1980 US Moscow boycott. Moses couldn't watch the race because there was no TV coverage in America, but he barely considers it a race at all as he could have run the winning time in his sleep.

Eight years later Moses reckons he was in such supreme shape for the 1988 Seoul Olympics, he could have beaten his world record. But victory involves staying healthy in the unique environment of the Olympic Village, a multinational gathering ranking alongside a cruise ship as a hotbed for illness – as Moses found to his cost when he suffered food poisoning three days before his race. Timing also dictated he had to run his semi-final at 5pm ahead of the final at 1pm the next day. After drug testing and a visit to a local hospital to find iced water, it was the early hours before he got back to his room – not enough time for such a finely-crafted metabolism to recover. He ended up settling for his first ever bronze in his last ever race.

'I had to be up at 8am, motors running,' he sighs. 'But when I hit the floor in the morning I said, "Oh man…" I just didn't have it in my legs and I knew it when I woke up. I needed six more hours of sleep but I had to get up and get going. I thought: "Oh no, this is not going to be a good day for running an Olympic final." I still ran 47.3s but I'd been thinking about running 46.5s that day; I was in that condition. The worst day of my life in competition. That's how it is. Bad day at the office.'

Ahead of Los Angeles in 1984, by contrast, Moses was fighting fit, even if he insists: 'Your reputation has nothing to do with it. You may have won 122 races in a row but if you lose the 123rd on the night of your final, that's the Olympics. When I went to bed the night before I made sure I had everything covered that I could think of. Even then, with all the things that went through my mind, I was convinced I had forgotten something. Just because it's the Olympics it doesn't mean you're going to be 100 per cent prepared or 100 per cent mentally fit.'

An enduring image saw Moses lying next to his blocks before the final as his rivals contemplated the silver that would be the limit of their ambitions. Yet even the laid-back American was taken aback by what went through his mind as he raced, as I discovered when I asked if he'd experienced any surreal Senna-esque sensations.

'I had something similar in the final in Los Angeles,' reveals Moses. 'There were almost 100,000 people and it was very, very loud. I've never heard that kind of screaming. Because there were Americans running at home, when the gun went off they just went crazy. But after the third hurdle all of a sudden everything went quiet. I could hear the footsteps of the guys on the track behind me above all the crowd noise. All that just went away and amongst it all I could hear guys taking hurdles; I could hear their step patterns and everything. I could hear every one of them when they took off and every one of them when they came back down on the ground.

'Then around the eighth hurdle I said, "There's no more point worrying about what's behind." You look at the next three hurdles and just make sure you don't trip up over those. I took the last hurdle real high. I didn't take a chance or do anything I would normally do in a race. I made sure I went over it. I jumped up into the air and came down. They even closed me down by half a metre but by then it was too late. When I hit the ground after that I felt there was not much that could stop me except someone running out on the track. When I crossed the line the first thing was relief, the elation came later. That was my experience. I've never had anything else happen like that but it happened that day.'

•

Félix Sánchez, another double Olympic 400m hurdles gold medallist, recalls a similar feeling: 'It's amazing: there's always a buzz when you walk into the stadium. You get into the blocks: "On your Marks, Set…" Then there's silence. When the gun goes off I never hear the crowd. I know they're cheering but I don't hear anything until the last 20 metres. It's weird. Maybe it would be different if there weren't hurdles. Unlike other events where you just run, you have ten barriers to manage. If you hit a hurdle, it can go drastically wrong. So you're focused on the hurdles and locked in to what you're trying to do. It's quiet out there… until you cross the finish line when you hear the crowd erupt and hopefully you're the one who broke the tape.'

Sánchez, the Dominican Republic's greatest ever athlete, started his career by breaking the tape for fun: it once even seemed he might eclipse the mighty Moses as he amassed 43 straight wins over four years leading to 2004 Olympic gold in Athens. Then the man-killer bit back. Within a week, a hamstring strain wrecked his run and sparked a chain of injuries to thighs, calves, heels and feet that dogged him for years. Sánchez dragged himself to Beijing to defend his gold in 2008, only for his beloved grandmother Lillian to pass away on the morning of his heat. He failed to qualify.

'In our sport it's very difficult to come back,' he admits. 'You either retire as champion or you overstay your welcome and you leave either from injury or not even making the final. I've had the longest career of any 400m hurdler – 15 seasons takes its toll – but I kept the belief I could get back to the top. There was always a reason I had a bad season: either I was injured or out of shape, so there was a glimmer of hope to get back to the top level, otherwise I'd probably have retired long ago. While I love competing, it was hard because for someone who had dominated for so long to go that long and not win is frustrating. But I'm glad I didn't give up…'

When Sánchez lined up for the 2012 Olympic final, a month shy of his 35th birthday and four further years of woe later, no one gave him a hope. The competitive line-up featured reigning world champion Dai Greene, reigning Olympic champion Angelo Taylor and favourite Javier Culson, who hadn't lost all season. But Sánchez had backup: the word *'abuela'* (or 'grandmother') scrawled on his shoes and a picture pinned inside his number. He had vowed to win one more title for her and ran the race 'with my grandmother guiding me all the way through to the finish line.'

47.63 seconds of blissful silence after the gun went off, Felix Sánchez took his second gold medal – bizarrely in exactly the same time as his first eight years earlier, and the then world record mark Moses set for Montreal gold in 1976. It prompted a memorable, moving Olympic image as his tears poured out at the medal ceremony.

'It was amazing when I crossed the line, knowing that going into the Games I was having a bad time,' he smiles. 'There were so many potential champions and no one really paid any attention to the "old man". I wouldn't say I was lucky because I don't believe in luck – everything happens for a reason – but I was prepared to do my best and that was good enough to win. Then it was just a release of emotions. I didn't know that would come, it was just in the moment. As I got onto the podium they were announcing the silver medal and I just broke down crying.

'I almost took my first gold medal for granted in 2004 because winning came easy. It didn't matter who I was competing against, I knew I was going to win. When you get a chance to dominate and people expect you to win but wait for you to lose, it's one thing. But when people don't believe in you yet you defy the odds and prove them wrong, there's an even greater sense of pleasure. I had to train a lot harder as a 34-year-old with everything that went into recovering from injury and trying to stay healthy. So the 2012 win was quite fulfilling.'

The muscles and bones may have been harder to coax into action but the 'old man' had one major advantage over his younger competitors: 14 years of hard-earned knowledge and perspective stored inside his head.

'Many athletes are overwhelmed by the fact it's the Olympics, worrying about outside influences instead of just focusing on getting to the finish,' he adds. 'Over the years you learn to focus and not worry about the other athletes. In the holding room beforehand the tension and expectation means everyone has their game face on. But it's just a race – and I approach it as that. I try to have fun because it's a blessing to compete at that level in front of so many people. We all want to win but there can only be one winner, so you try to get in that Zone doing whatever allows you to be most comfortable. For me it's to enjoy the moment, ease the tension, laugh, not to be too nervous or stressed at performing. Then in the stadium I like to let the atmosphere stir you up so you go out and do what you've trained all year to do.'

The Zone seems to be a paradox: a state of pure relaxation in the least tranquil situations imaginable. To achieve such inner peace when it matters, the mind needs to be safe in the knowledge that the years of graft are in the bag. The return is a feeling so spectacular and intense that Sánchez has now signed up for the ever-growing band of Zone veterans who would love everyone else to find it too.

'The first thing I like to tell kids is that having won that final, enjoy it,' he says. 'The second: if you have a goal, go for it. Don't let anyone say you can't do it. The reason 90 per cent of people say you can't do it is because *they* can't. If you believe it in your heart, go for it and don't stop until you reach the top. You'll never know whether you can or not if you don't try. So go for it. Over those eight years I had a lot of obstacles in my path. It was a testament to strong will and determination and just never giving up. I've never been the biggest, the strongest or the fastest, but one thing I do have is a heart as big as anyone else's. And I never give up.

'It's just tenacity and the will to win. We all want results quickly. And in life sometimes things come quick, sometimes they take a long time. You have to embrace the process and know what you are getting into from the beginning. The more you put into anything in life, whether you achieve it or not, you appreciate it more knowing all you had to dedicate and sacrifice. If it's greatness you want, you have to be ready to dedicate yourself to that and sacrifice the good things your friends think are fun like partying and fast food. If you really want to become a champion you have to dedicate yourself 100 per cent and surround yourself with positive people that support you, even when the times get rough. Then just keep going.'

•

World-class individual sport is not a solitary pursuit. The impact of the support group was driven home by Sebastian Coe, a double 1500m gold medallist in 1980 and 1984 who went on to head the organising committee of the London Olympics. The Briton ended up taking the credit on both counts but insists he could have achieved neither on his own.

'When you cross the line in the Olympics the overwhelming sensation is relief you haven't let people down,' insists Coe. 'In the career of an athlete you've probably devoted over half your young life to what you do, but it's not a one-man mission. You have coaches, inspirational teachers and families making sacrifices in the background. You have clubs and volunteers who have been on that journey with you but are never interviewed or photographed, they're anonymous behind the scenes. So the least of your concerns at that moment is for yourself. That's how I felt when we got through the London Games. I worked with some talented and passionate people: I'll probably never work with another group with such extraordinary focus. So the first instinct is relief that you hadn't let down the thousands of people in the organising committee, the hundreds of thousands working across London, the millions in the UK and around the world. Then you allow a couple of other feelings in further down the line.'

Coe admits he never used the expression 'in the Zone' but that might just be because he was a member of the Edwin Moses elite who simply never left it: 'It's being entirely prepared for the moment,' he tells me. 'But if you've done everything needed in training and there was nothing else that really mattered in your life, you got to the Zone anyway. It is a mistake to think you can turn up to an event and suddenly switch it on and off. If you like, I was in the Zone for 30 years. You live there all the time. Every day you're trying to figure out how you can be better than the day before, and every hour better than the hour before. You're so focused on everything you need to do to deliver, I tended to be pretty oblivious to the things around me – and sadly on some occasions even to my competitors...'

When I asked Coe what separates the kind of people who live out their dreams from those who don't, he picked on two particular qualities: 'They tend to be imbued by a massive curiosity. My whole athletics career was based on an insatiable curiosity to know what's round the corner: wanting to understand a lot more about me and my event next year. It was never based on simply wanting to win medals or break world records. It was trying to understand much more. Then there's just the passion. People talk about talent identification but it's more about passion identification. I've known lots of people with great talent who sometimes haven't really had the passion to do it. The greats of sport share that insatiable curiosity and passion for what they're doing.'

•

When it comes to passion and curiosity, the greats of the 'man-killer' make a worthy archetype. As a student, British 400m hurdler David Hemery would log his daily 500 sit-ups and count each step from his college dorm to his lecture room. Before the 1968 Olympics he later trained in the US city of Boston, whose winters are famously harsh. When his running track was hidden by snow, his coach Billy Smith sent him out with a shovel to clear what he termed 'the road to Mexico City'. Hemery took on this extra commitment as 'sometimes the hardest way is the best way.' It all led to a surreal experience at Oxford in 1970 during training over the shorter 110m sprint hurdles.

'I'd put the hurdles on the long jump runway because it wasn't an all-weather track,' Hemery recalls. 'I was moving at roughly ten yards a second and going over a 3ft 6in hurdle every 1.1 seconds. Yet even though it was very fast motion it was all utterly slowed down – and it was as if I was outside of myself watching in. While I was going over the hurdle I was able to slightly adjust my hand to be in better balance and synchronisation. It was rare that that ever happened, it was just such an extraordinary slowing down of time. To be able to see yourself while actually running at that speed and feel what needed to be changed, was a really exceptional experience.'

Hemery was just as scrupulous with his mental work. This included rehearsing every lane draw, weather condition and wind direction. He predetermined the pace he needed to run in heats and semi-finals, sticking to his game plan for leg speed and stride length regardless of anyone else going off at unexpected pace. When he went through these visualisations in bed, the detail was such that his pulse rate and breathing all but matched the physical sensations he faced while running for real.

Sure enough, though Hemery went into his Mexico final with only the seventh fastest time of the eight competitors, unbeknownst to any of them he had it in his head that he would break the world record in a time of 48.4 seconds. He had miscalculated. After a display of pure athletic alchemy, Hemery took gold by almost a full second in 48.12 seconds – at a time when British track medals were a precious, rare commodity.

It was only when Hemery returned to defend his title four years later that he discovered the full power the mind has to dictate events. Heading to Munich, he just couldn't shake an image of blasting off at world record pace for 300m before running out of energy on the final straight. The conventional wisdom of the time decreed that athletes peaked at 24 years old so he thought it was a sensible precaution to prepare for the worst now he was 'past it' at 28. By filling his mind with negative imagery he now reckons he pre-programmed the outcome. In fact he was in great shape – the clear favourite – but when he came out on track he didn't feel his usual pre-race nerves. In a desperate bid to gee himself up he started digging his nails into his hands. Too late. True to his prior vision, he went out too hard before flagging and settling for bronze.

'In 1968 it was a classic sensation of being in the Zone,' Hemery recalls. 'My body, mind and spirit were all integrated – only for the time leading up to and in that race. It sounds odd but it's a fantastic feeling to be that integrated and balanced. Then in 1972 I had my mind do exactly the opposite, working against myself. I thought it was common sense to rehearse the option of losing. But rather than saying, "Yes, but what's the best you could do?" I became numb to the possibility: it wouldn't be the end of my world if I lost.

'Physically I'd worked even harder than I had in 1968 so it's really frustrating to have the mind... not override it, but negate some of that. By taking away the fear of losing, the adrenalin wasn't there – and adrenalin allows us to run faster. If there was a dinosaur chasing us, or someone with a knife, it doesn't matter if you've trained, the adrenalin would flow and you'd run faster than you otherwise could. It's an automatic reaction but we can do a lot of that with our heads.'

One of the books Hemery read before the 1972 Olympics was Richard Bach's *Jonathan Livingston Seagull*, then at the top of the American bestseller list. It's the tale of a bird who just won't settle for using his wings merely for the daily grind of scavenging for scraps that happily engrossed the rest of his flock. Instead he sets out to explore the joy of pure flight, pushing himself to the absolute limit to find out what could be achieved – eventually transcending the very laws of nature.

'That book is well worth a read because it's actually raising the limits we put on ourselves,' insists Hemery. 'There are limits, actually: I discovered you can't run flat out all the way in the 400m hurdles. I didn't relax anywhere in that 1972 race and I did try to run flat out. I got to about the eighth hurdle before it started to pay. But we have the power to affect our own futures almost entirely. With our mental focus we get what we expect to get. It's like a self-fulfilling prophecy.

'I do believe the mind is key. The mind is our gift. So whether you do well or not, people say, "Oh well, it's luck." But to a certain extent we make our own luck. If we visualise and rehearse the best we can do and prepare for that, we're more likely to have it happen. It doesn't mean living in a fool's paradise, it just means, "What is the best I can do under this circumstance?" If you prepare for the worst it's more likely to happen. If we dwell on the negative or on sickness, that's probably what we'll get. It was Virgil who said: "They can if they think they can." It's absolutely true. We prove ourselves right. If you think you can't then you will prove yourself right too.'

The fact that this maxim – later famously adapted by Henry Ford – dates from Virgil's *Aeneid* begs the question of why it still isn't routinely taught to kids. Hemery has created the charity 21st Century Legacy in a bid to take this knowledge to a wider, younger audience. So passionate is he about spreading the word, he has been writing books about this subject for decades.

'The top firms now realise that to get the best out of people you have to coach them, recognising the power of a goal of which the person can take ownership,' adds Hemery. 'Eventually I hope this will be open to all in education too. You won't spend time practising something which is not a passion of yours. So we've got to let children identify what their passion is, then ask: "What are your first steps to start work on it?" This can work with anything: health, fitness, relationships, values, business or sport. If we work hard at something we're passionate about we can become exceptional.

'The quest is to challenge young people to follow their dreams. Whether they have some kind of disability or they're a genius, kids often get goals imposed on them: if you're bright you should be a doctor or a lawyer, pass your exams, get to university or whatever. If you can prompt a child to choose their goal, you engage them because you're on their agenda, not just pushing the adult agenda. I'm trying to bring that into education, helping kids recognise that if they take ownership of their goals – it's not the sky's the limit, but you can literally "Be the best you can be."'

•

Few fields have the lines between success and failure marked out as clearly as sport, but there is compensation for Olympians who have only one chance every four years to get it right. For anyone who does nail it in the crucial moment the impact in terms of fame and fortune can last a lifetime. Elsewhere it can take a lot longer. That's why the pure passion for doing what you love should always trump any external rewards.

In 1976, as Nadia Comăneci took 20 perfect seconds to soar into global consciousness, an even younger teenager – just 13 – won the world windsurfing championship. Robby Naish was still winning titles decades later, before switching to kiteboarding in the 1990s and dominating that too. For those who battle waves and wind Naish is a legend. Yet as his sport is considered 'niche', even sports fans might not have heard of him. Thankfully for Naish, it's not about glory. The key to retaining the motivation to scale peak after peak is very human. You can set up home at the top of your field only if there is nothing on Earth you would rather be doing.

'A lot of athletes are goal-oriented: they reach their goal, then they're ready to move on to something else in their lives,' Naish tells me. 'I was never goal-oriented; it was the experience that I always loved. I was never trying to achieve any single thing. I didn't want to become world champion then go and become a chef or take up golf. I realised this was what I wanted to do more than anything, and for as long as possible. It's about the process and the enjoyment of everything that goes with it.

'I'm lucky that my sport puts me in this pretty pleasant environment – but not always. Our events can be in miserable places like the North Sea when it's bitterly cold. But it's taking that and enjoying it for what it is. I did that better than a lot of athletes. They'd be standing on the beach miserable and I'd just think: "Give it to me!" I loved being there. I've always been really appreciative that someone was actually paying me to do this so I've been able to make a living. That realisation helped me continue to push myself to stay in the Zone for all those years. It's still going: people still pay me to go surfing. I'm not competing any more but in my eyes I'm still a professional athlete. I realise the whole life of being a sportsman is profoundly lucky.'

Before we start painting any picture of Naish as a happy-go-lucky type just out for a good time, there are familiar factors leading to his ability to maintain the heights. Like Comăneci he started with a childhood of practice – albeit in sunny Hawaiian surf rather than an austere Romanian gym – before an adulthood of total commitment.

'In our sport the build-up to competitions starts before you get to the beach,' says Naish. 'You have a lot of equipment so you get your gear together and drive to the beach, then there's the lead-up to a race. Throughout my career I was always the kind of guy who would go to bed early to prepare. Then I'd want to be at the beach before everybody else so when they showed up they'd see me and think: "Oh no, he's already here." All those elements helped me know I was ready mentally, physically and equipment-wise – and that I'd done everything better than everybody else.

'I was lucky that personality-wise I was drawn that way. I hated losing so badly that I wanted to do everything possible to make sure I didn't lose. It wasn't so much the thrill of winning; it was doing everything I could to avoid that feeling of losing. For me competition was everything. It was mind, body, spirit, 100 per cent focused. The enjoyment of that feeling was worth sacrificing any other things in life. Whether it was partying with my friends or whatever, it was no issue to sacrifice that to be as prepared as I could possibly be for competition.'

Naish sure doesn't sound like your archetypal chilled-out surfer dude. Indeed his latest heir, Germany's Philip Köster, another multiple world champion, is another with the same meticulous approach – and similarly dazzling results: 'I'm always first on the beach and first on the water too. I really love this sport so I'm stoked to be on the water anyway, but

I'm really focused and when I'm in the Zone everything goes right. I get into a rhythm, everything flows and I can just have fun. When you get in the Zone nothing in life can compare… it's a perfect moment.'

Now all the extra effort of getting up early and forgoing the good life makes sense: the Zone is so special it is worth any such sacrifice. What's more, if you find yourself facing anyone who finds it, that would be a good time to start scrabbling for 'luck'. While Naish demoralised his opposition, that wasn't the main point behind his painstaking work ethic before his events. The most crucial effect was that it combined to put him into the right mental state to compete, turning him into one of the elite who found a way to access the Zone at will.

'Different athletes have different ways to put themselves into that Zone: little rituals they need to bring them to that point,' says Naish. 'I never figured that out as I didn't have to count crows to put my mind into that space. It would come naturally. But I've always been really nervous, internalising it, to the point that knowing I was nervous meant I really wanted it. If it is comfortable and natural, someone who wants it more will beat you. If I was lackadaisical it would be time to do something else.

'So I never had to think about it – until the times I wasn't there and I'd realise what it feels like not to be in the Zone. Fortunately it didn't happen often: through my entire career I was there 99 per cent of the time. But it was profoundly obvious when I wasn't. When it didn't come together you'd sit there knowing you weren't quite there. You'd never figure out what happened or why. Occasionally you could click yourself back into the right state but when you couldn't, you'd have a bad day.

'Part of being in the Zone for an athlete is being able to put all your baggage aside. Whatever is going on in your life that morning, yesterday or last week, or that injury that is nagging you, you have to put it completely out of your mind. It's about cutting everything else out so you can focus 100 per cent on the job in that second – or the eight minutes of the heat or the half-hour, whatever the contest is. Everything else in the world disappears for that moment in time.'

•

American psychologist Abraham Maslow spent his life exploring what makes us tick. His quest is most famous for his 'hierarchy of needs', a simple diagram of a pyramid categorising our every requirement and craving in order of importance. The bottom layer features raw essentials including food, water, sleep and sex – all of which apply to every animal on the planet. The next level is 'safety': health, employment, shelter and general resources. Then comes 'love and belonging', such as family and friends. Only once those basics are in place can we start to exploit the areas that set humans apart, notably 'self-esteem', plus achievements and respect for and by others. Rising even higher we can explore the aesthetics of our environment, stimulating ourselves intellectually and fulfilling our need for harmony, order and beauty.

The top of the pyramid is reserved for 'self-actualisation', where we ditch all prejudice and find morality, creativity, spontaneity plus an ability to solve problems. This is where humans achieve our full potential and chase our dreams; life becomes playful yet honest, individual yet integrated, honourable yet effortless, rich yet simple. This summit is where we are most likely to find 'peak experiences', those profound moments of love, happiness or insight where we feel most alive and connected with the universe. This is as good as it gets. The Zone.

Given that we have to build up a solid foundation of all the other layers first, it's no surprise that the Zone is so hard to reach and most experiences are so fleeting. Much of the world's population is stuck in a daily battle for the essentials for survival. It is possible to peak in such circumstances, but it's at the level of an animal.

Maslow was adamant it shouldn't be like this. The top should be the norm not the exception: not about having something 'extra', but rather having nothing taken away. He reckoned our ultimate goal is to attain personal growth; indeed this very process is the path to true happiness. Yet to reach these higher peaks, he knew certain conditions must be in place, such as the freedom to seek new knowledge and to express ourselves without constraint. That rules out dictatorships and other subtler forms of oppression. But Maslow realised even the lucky souls who have in place all the preconditions and lower layers of the pyramid do not always seek to reach their full potential.

Until the mid-20th century, the science of psychology was influenced by psychoanalysis founder Sigmund Freud; it was a study of 'damaged' minds, striving to make them 'normal'. When Maslow coined the term 'positive psychology' it had a different remit altogether: to take 'normal' minds and see how much higher we can all go.

After Maslow's 1970 death, positive psychology found a new figurehead in Mihály Csíkszentmihályi, a Hungarian who had embarked on his life's work after experiencing the end of World War Two as a child – and with it enough evidence to conclude adults had got life very wrong. Any passion on display was very much limited to the original meaning of the word: suffering.

'Most kids cope with such things with denial, waiting for it to go by and living in a pretend world where everything is OK,' he tells me. 'I did that too, except I also tried to learn activities that were not related to the situation, but let me feel in control. While the bombs were falling in Budapest and people were dying in the streets, that's when I learned to play chess. On a chess board I made my moves and felt in control. I might lose to a better opponent but it was logical: both parties played by the rules so I earned what I deserved. My opponent couldn't just throw a rock at my pieces or pull the board away if they lost. So it was a logical world whereas the "real world" outside was falling apart into meaningless violence.

'I was also helped by hiking and going out in nature, until the last years when it couldn't be done. Some people learn a language or become versed in philosophy or religion. If you can find something to do that is under your control, it's like an escape, not into meaningless consumer activity but into a world where rules make sense; you can learn them and you don't suffer physically if you lose.'

Csíkszentmihályi reckons these tactics – taking back real control of our inner world – can arm us with the capability to face even the worst forms of suffering the outside world can throw at us. 'In Aleksandr Solzhenitsyn's *Cancer Ward*, where he describes what people do to survive in horrible hospital conditions, it's similar,' adds Csíkszentmihályi. 'You get by if you can find an activity to forget the reality outside. It's not easy but it can work. Somehow even the knowledge you may die of cancer is, temporarily at least, put into abeyance. The alternative is to feel sorry for yourself or drug yourself so you don't feel anything.

'In Victor Frankl's depictions of the Nazi extermination camps, even there it was possible to carve out a little reality of your own by paying attention to people and being helpful to them. You remember the life you had outside and think maybe there is a possibility of returning to it one day. As long as you do it actively, it can help you overcome a lot of things that happen around you in real life. The important thing is to realise that to a large extent you are in charge of what happens in your mind.'

After the war Csíkszentmihályi sailed to America to study psychology after being inspired by watching a Carl Jung lecture. His seminal work *Flow* details how we are most alive when we're fully engaged in what we are doing, whether it's work or play. In the flow state we are not moved by outside goals, but rather everything comes from within: what he terms 'intrinsic motivation'. In flow we live totally in the moment and are so absorbed in our task nothing else matters. We lose all sense of time along with real-life concerns such as hunger, ego and money – allowing our true self to flood out, along with any skills we have acquired along the way. Csíkszentmihályi first felt the sensation for himself in sport, rock-climbing as a teenager. He later found it painting, writing short stories and through decades of scientific research into his passion, which is to get us all living our dreams and finding flow for ourselves – throughout our lives.

'Of course you need to have something to live from,' says Csíkszentmihályi. 'If you are on the edge of starvation it's more important to secure a good meal than to be proud of your musicianship or chess-playing ability. But assuming your livelihood is taken care of or you have a job, the added value of living comes from self-chosen challenges. That builds up your notion of who you are and what you can do, and it seems more conducive to a well-lived life than external or material success.

'In my case climbing, painting and writing used to be almost all-consuming activities. Now I get most of my flow from my work and family. Luckily my wife and I have been married for half a century, we still enjoy doing things together and spend as much time as possible with our children and grandchildren. In the summer we go to a mountain retreat to go hiking, cook, talk, listen to music and make music. I also still like to write and do research with a good group of students. A lot of this is preparatory work, but once the data starts coming in and you start figuring out how to interpret the results it's very enjoyable. So there are lots of sources of flow, none of which I chose because they were flow. I only started cooking because I had to – when I was living alone and had no money to go out. But any activity can become enjoyable if you try to do it well. Then it becomes a flow activity.'

The good news is that we can all find this flow in anything from washing-up to playing the piano. Then as we develop our own passion for certain fields we 'achieve' simply by keeping them up and revelling in the pure process of doing what we love. Often that's enough, all by itself. But if we later get the urge to do something well we can push our limits further. When we add quality to any pursuit we gain expertise on the way, leading to inevitable improvements. Finally we start to find this state of flow at ever higher levels, at which 'flow' tends to go by its namesake: yep, 'the Zone'.

CONCLUSION

'There is so much untapped potential in people it's just incredible. It's almost beyond belief, really. I feel it and I sense it through what I've experienced in my own journey. I'm from a humble beginning but the message of my story is that great things grow from small things. The magic lives inside every one of us, despite our environment, our struggles and our doubts. It takes courage to realise what that magic is, then to actually go out and try to achieve it. It's the power of loving yourself, I suppose, and giving yourself a chance.'

In my years of researching the human being at the limit I've been privileged to meet many of the world's biggest sports stars. But every now and again one of them sends me away with my head swimming. This time it is Australia's national treasure Cathy Freeman, who has just summed up this entire book in a hundred words.

The magic of elite performance is that it always starts out

small: with a dream. By nurturing it, crafting it and loving it, sport's champions show us all the untapped power of the human mind. When we believe in what we conceive, the Zone can guide any of us to achieve anything. And it's not just about sport.

More than simply a cliché, the Zone is the mental state required to perform at our own absolute limit in any field. This is the home of 'genius': where artists are at their most creative, where musicians produce their most sublime performances and where scientists make their breakthroughs. This doesn't stop with the stars. Whether you're a teacher, a chef, a nurse or an astronaut, if you're taking an exam or cracking jokes in a pub, to find the Zone guarantees you hit your absolute best. You may not even recall how or why it went so right. Put simply, it all goes like a dream.

Along my own road towards tracking down the Zone, what has become clear is that there is no single definitive experience. Even if there are common themes, the precise nature of the sensation varies for each individual in every situation. Indeed the more I explore, the less possible it gets to tie it down. That's the best part: life is rich enough for countless different ways to live it – and the reward of looking deeply into any big subject is to realise how little anyone knows about how it all works. But what the Zone does consistently show is that we underestimate what we really can do.

The Zone can kick in at every level from a kickabout in the park to the World Cup Final. It is just a blissful state where all internal chatter disappears and we truly go with the flow. We assume conscious thoughts drive us on, but it is when we give our subconscious free rein to do its natural thing that we truly shine. That often leads to a performance at the maximum of our potential, albeit beyond what our conscious minds ever imagined possible. This limit rises in proportion to the hours of practice in the bank and the intensity of the occasion. Blend the Zone with supreme ability and a packed, expectant arena and you get fireworks. This book features plenty of those, but the good news is that we all have enough spark to match any of them, if only we take the trouble to live the dream.

•

'The great achievers, winners, inventors, musicians and painters have all been great dreamers,' says mind coach Don MacPherson. 'What's exciting is that anyone can visualise. We can use it in life's everyday challenges like school exams or a driving test. If you have to make a best man's speech, first picture your audience in as much detail as possible, using all your senses: sight, hearing, smell, touch. See yourself delivering your speech feeling relaxed and confident. Hear the audience laughing and clapping, then coming up to congratulate you.

'These mind movies turbo-charge your confidence because the subconscious doesn't know the difference between the real thing and something imaginary. Like all skills, the more you practise the better you get. But your brain loves a target, so give it a big one like a great success. When you have it burned into your subconscious mind, switch focus to the process by visualising how you're going to get there, step by step.'

The first step towards any dream is always to conceive it, but it's not always easy to truly believe in it. Step two, then, is to stick with the scheme. This is a battle not of the body but of the mind. Some quests can take years or decades of persistent, single-minded toil inconceivable to anyone looking in from the outside, bordering on insanity. Even the most apparently invincible stars must first endure a diet of defeat and punishment too. They, like all of us, have a voice in their heads nagging them to quit. The 'you can't do that' refrain is endorsed by often well-meaning family and friends and reaches a crescendo when they're at their lowest ebb.

When the idea of 'Little Me' does reappear in our minds, it can be comforting. It offers the tempting chance to lie back and let ourselves be battered by the slings and arrows of outrageous fortune. It's all too easy to forget that the vastness of unlimited creative ability is in each of us, just like the champions in these pages. They have to battle for this simple truth too – and it starts young.

Multiple F1 world champion Lewis Hamilton makes a good example, insisting: 'I tell kids if they have a dream, don't let anyone tell them they can't do it – because I had that so many times when I was a kid. Grown-ups like teachers would tell me, a ten-year-old: "You're not going to succeed." I disagreed. Now I have a huge smile on my face when I think of those moments – because I'm sure those teachers now watch TV saying: "I told you he'd do it." So I tell kids to have that full belief in themselves.

'What separates remarkable people from those who perhaps have not achieved to the same level is drive. When I watch Novak Djokovic or Lionel Messi you can't imagine they could get better, but they are just constantly growing. It's single-minded focus on getting somewhere that's beyond the norm. But every single one of them has had some great people with them, whether it be a team or their family.'

CONCLUSION

If you are old enough to have read this far, your chance to win Wimbledon or the World Cup might have gone. Even if so, we are all a team or a family to someone who still could, so we have the chance to help them rather than hinder. Children start life with an empty subconscious that gradually fills with whatever they see and hear. Australian cricketer Steve Waugh insists: 'Kids thrive on positive feedback so it's about letting them know they're doing well and they've got plenty of potential: "If you keep training you can achieve whatever you want."'

The truth behind this maxim was finally confirmed to me by a man who lives by the motto 'anything is possible' and can claim the title of the world's most famous wannabe cricketer: Usain Bolt.

'My role models were my parents, who pushed me to do whatever I wanted to do,' says Bolt. 'But I started out playing cricket. I didn't know about track and field – and I didn't even care because I was so in love with cricket. Then when I started track and field, all I wanted was to go to the Olympics and win one gold medal. Suddenly I was a triple gold medallist and it started: I wanted more. I worked hard and even when I got injured I never doubted myself. I've been injured so often, I expect to get injured and I know it's going to happen. But I had a great support group, I kept pushing and I'm satisfied with what I've done in my career.

'Now I keep reminding kids: the road is hard, but if you really want it, as I did, you have to push on, be strong and just be focused. That's key. When I'm in the 100 metres I can tell you everything from the start to the finish because I'm that focused and aware of exactly what's going on around me. It's a great feeling to think back to those moments –

and especially when you watch the race, because you know exactly what's going through your mind and exactly where you are.'

•

Sadly we're not immune to doubt even as adults, though the sabotage is more often self-inflicted. Most of us have some idea of what we would really love to do if we were free of all ties and concerns, financial or otherwise. You'll recognise it when what initially appears a flight of fancy won't stop gnawing away at you. That's your dream right there. But going for it for real involves major complications, which our inner critics dutifully itemise day after day, night after sleepless night.

The first few come under the banner of survival. Our inner voice is only too happy to take these often very serious points and dream up terrifying consequences of failing to pay the bills. Then comes a subtler secondary attack based on whether we are really good enough, plus the price of failure. Part three drums up pre-emptive peer pressure, imagining negative reactions from family and friends. Given the inner voice has parts four to 99 of this epic manifesto lined up, it's no surprise we generally lose the debate.

The mark of the champion is that they don't listen. Their belief in their dream is sacrosanct and they justify their mission with an understanding that no meaningful goal ever arrived after an easy ride. Hardship, then, is an inevitable part of the process but one they know won't last for ever. Far from being buffeted helplessly about, they show what happens when you take control of your own path. Bolstering their belief with positive thoughts, the greats force their way over or straight through all hurdles blocking their own private dreamland.

This is why we are so happy to celebrate pioneers, champions and other great achievers: they win the argument we lost. Then they keep winning for all the years or decades needed for their chosen path, even through countless painful setbacks. When I asked motorcyclist Jorge Lorenzo about the factors that turn a racer into a champion, he replied: 'Never, ever give up. It's about having a positive attitude to failure. When you have a failure and you have a positive mentality you will win in the end.'

There's a massive difference between having a failure – as every champion in these pages has, time after time – and being one. Yet this battle between negative and positive rages on in seven billion heads out there. So here's the rub: any one of us can take control of the debate any time we like. Just dream bigger.

'If you stay in your comfort zone you won't gain much,' says 'Fearless' Felix Baumgartner. 'It doesn't matter what you want to do. People think: "I've never done this before so I can't." But it's not about what you've done before; it's how smart you are and whether you're willing to go the extra mile. I've met a lot of people in my life – Neil Armstrong, Muhammad Ali, Sir Edmund Hillary – and it wasn't easy for any of them. When they came up with their idea everybody looked at them like "What the hell is wrong with you? This is impossible. You can't climb the highest mountain in the world, you can't break the sound barrier..." But people should understand if you want to accomplish something big you have to leave your comfort zone.'

If the Zone begins where the comfort zone ends, perhaps

it's time for us all to rethink which is really the bigger gamble. If we chase after a dream it certainly comes at the risk of losses. If we 'play safe' and ignore it we get to stay nice and cosy in our comfort zone. Then some day that comfort zone crumbles anyway and we're left with the knowledge that we once had a golden chance but didn't even give it a go. Let's try that little conundrum out on our inner critic and see what it comes up with.

'If we didn't have a Monkey Mind there would be no "I am": we'd be egoless, just being,' adds Don MacPherson. 'We would feel detached from reality, living in a fluid world – always in the here and now, no fears, no worries, no inhibitions. You'd just be hanging out, fully connected to all the beauty of the Universe. It sounds great but there is one big problem: if you lost your Monkey Mind you would not be safe.

'It is this voice in your head, your conscious mind, which filters all the data coming at you from all angles. What should I do next? Run or fight? Stick or twist? Questioning, worrying, judging, calculating, predicting, the Monkey Mind has jobs that are essential for life. It is also responsible for logic and awareness, without which you can't gauge performance and learn how to progress. Unfortunately he can get too big for his own boots. He has a tendency to interfere, doesn't know when to shut up and errs towards caution and analysis when just doing it would be better.

'The Monkey Mind likes you to stay nice and cosy at home, especially if you are threatening to do something risky or dangerous. So the only way to progress is to practise frightening him, taking him for regular trips out of his comfort zone. This lets your brain rev higher, increasing its capacity and performance. When you truly trust your skills the Monkey Mind relaxes and lets your subconscious autopilot get on with the doing. Now the Zone beckons.'

This doesn't have to mean throwing ourselves out of a plane or quitting a job. Many would find it equally terrifying – and beneficial – to throw their smartphone in a skip and smell the roses instead. Wherever our comfort zone ends, that's where our journey to dreamland takes off. Olympic heptathlon champion Denise Lewis is in the athletic army hoping to inspire us to aim higher. 'It's about unlocking that potential in your mind,' she says. 'The first step is not to put any limitations on what you think is physically and mentally possible. If you could engage that philosophy every time you woke up, when you go about your daily business at work, you'd think: "Where did I generate that many hours in one day?" We do underestimate ourselves and I'm really passionate about instilling that in young children: learn not to limit yourself. We all have negative chatter but it's trying to minimise that. It's about having a go...'

●

Of course, none of this is compulsory. In a book almost entirely about winners, it may come as a shock to hear the phrase 'winning isn't everything' at this point. But sport's champions all perform in environments with a clear concept of victory, whether it's Olympic gold or anything else. Everyday life is not so straightforward and success is much less defined. If you work in an office, what really constitutes winning? Rising through middle management by stabbing the most backs?

The single-minded focus and dogged determination

needed to climb to the top of any field can come with drawbacks too – not least with relationships. To give it all for a single cause can be inherently selfish: such drive means ignoring all distractions irrelevant to the quest, human or otherwise. By contrast most of us have more than one dream on the go, routinely juggling family life, relationships, career and hobbies. Then there are life's sudden twists that radically overhaul our sense of priorities.

Thora Rain works as a health and well-being practitioner in the UK city of Cambridge. This Icelander specialises in medically unexplained 'Sherlock' symptoms, having suffered with ME and fibromyalgia for six years during her studies. Rain made a full recovery and now uses her experience to help people find this state of 'flow', from business high-flyers to anyone who has been ill and now just wants to get by.

'Flow is when our focus, our body, everything is in alignment,' Rain tells me. 'We hit upon that state sometimes just because it all comes together. But the question is how to bring it about again and again. The higher up Maslow's hierarchy of needs we go, the more we have access to it. It's easy to be in flow when things go well, but when you feel like shouting, "Aarrggh..." that's when we need to understand how to stay as present as we can. If you're in high levels of pain, starving or freezing, being in flow is a lot harder. It can be done with a lot of practice, but you can't jump straight from despair to flow. You have to do it step by step.'

Intriguingly, Rain reckons most religions and spiritual practices are all aiming towards flow, 'that sense of ease, harmony, peace and interconnected love'. But none of us lives a life of ever-present bliss, so this flow state is not just about performing to the limit. It can also be a crucial crutch when life is at its most challenging.

'There is a drive with anyone chasing that high-performance ideal,' adds Rain. 'But people who have come through a recovery may just want optimal health, which involves a much slower pace of living. That is completely fine. So the key is "optimal performance". If you want to potter around on your allotment for the rest of your life, that's optimal to you. It's about keeping motivated while giving yourself permission to collapse in a corner when life is too hard. Some patients have this illusion that once you've recovered everything will be perfect. But life still happens... you still get flu, you still wish you had more money, someone in your family will be ill. So I think we should actually cut ourselves a bit of slack.'

•

Pieter du Preez was an aspiring triathlete competing for South Africa at Under-23 level – until he was hit by a car while cycling in 2003. The crash broke his neck and left him paralysed from the chest down. The first time he tried getting dressed it took him 15 minutes to put on a single sock. That's when the 'can do' instincts of life in sport kicked in, coupled with a healthy obsession with numbers from his day job as an actuary, and he began setting himself unrealistic challenges in his quest for a regular life.

'When I got home I timed myself getting fully dressed,' says du Preez. 'It took 51 minutes and I was dead tired. I told myself it's not functional to do that every day so I set a target to be fully dressed in 15 minutes. As a C6 quadriplegic that would be OK. So at first I'd dress for 15 minutes then stop and someone could help. I timed it every day, slowly I got closer, then a month later I did it. But I wasn't going to stop there. I set myself an "impossible" world record time of seven minutes, without really thinking it would ever happen. But I opened my eyes one day and I'd done ten minutes, then about two months later seven minutes.

'As I got faster I couldn't actually move more muscles but I got better with living my life with what I have. People telling me "you can't" do things also helped because for me it was like: "Screw you, I'm going to show you how I'm doing it…" I don't time myself every day but my current record is 2 minutes and 41 seconds, three times faster than what I thought would be impossible. That showed me anything is possible. It's OK to see a barrier but it's there to be smashed through.'

Du Preez has no hand grip or finger movement and his strength comes only from biceps and shoulders. He admits his background as a sportsman helped him cope with the extra physical demands of a life where 'everything is an effort'. As such he is full of empathy for the greater struggles faced by others with similar disabilities. But once he had started to conquer everyday life, why stop there? Why not get back to what he knew best? Although he can swim only with a kind of double-armed backstroke, the unfeasible idea soon hit: to be the first quadriplegic to do an Ironman.

'The guys in my situation will tell you it's impossible,' he says. 'They don't believe it and say I must have more muscle function than I do. But it's the same as getting dressed. It's this untouchable dream – and you don't make a jump all the way there. You put small goals on the way to big ones. If you keep trying, step by step, the more you train you slowly but surely get up that mountain. Then you start believing more and more. When I did my first half Ironman, I did it in such a fast time I started to think maybe I can do the full one. Then it's amazing how the mindset just changes. Once you've done something "impossible" it's suddenly possible.

'I know how to get myself in the Zone and I've had many "Zone" moments in sport – but none compare to that first Ironman. It wasn't just on race day; I was in the Zone for six months. Everything was just about reaching that dream. I've never been so focused. It was a meditational, spiritual thing. I'm a man of faith so for me this was a journey with God as well. I can't explain how special that feeling is. If you can ever get in the Zone it's a special feeling. You will know when you are in the Zone...'

So immersed was du Preez in this ultimate long-term version of heaven on Earth, he wasn't even knocked out of it when the unthinkable happened. Six weeks before he was due to race he broke his forearm in three places when another cyclist did a sudden U-turn ahead of him. There was no time for it to heal so his doctor put in a plate. With over 200km of pure hell awaiting du Preez, it was time for more number-crunching.

'I do everything with my arms,' he smiles. 'So obviously everybody said you can't do it. But I read up on every single muscle I use, how I use it, what I do and how I do it. I took an X-ray every week and upped my training to see if it was still fine or if I was doing any damage. Then we made a call two weeks from race day and said, "OK we're going for it." I took a risk, but it was calculated. An Ironman is always a mental battle: that's where the big fight is. Everybody knows that but only once you do something seriously do you realise how much of a mental battle it is, fighting off those negative thoughts: "You're not going to make it, you're not going to do this…"

'With everything I have and a broken arm, it's insane. But it was a journey of faith. If you do things in the right way and you do it clever, anything is possible. The weather was perfect and everything just panned out as it was supposed to be. Still, it wasn't easy. I couldn't put any weight on it. But I did my first Ironman. With a broken forearm. That's how insane it is. If you understand how impossible it actually is… and I did it. It's a miracle.'

No one could argue with that – but it's a specific self-inflicted kind of miracle, born within the mind of a human being who just won't take no for an answer. To turn impossible dream into miraculous reality there's also the minor matter of 40 hours of training a week, just like the professionals. Such a 'process' sounds like it takes pain to new levels, yet this is what du Preez treasures most.

'It's all about the climb,' he insists. 'Yes, the cherry on top is great, but the nice part is your whole journey all the way up. We should live life fully and chase our dreams but the process is the most important thing. "Live your dreams" is a cliché but people need to realise what they're saying; it's like "I do" when you get married. You need to go for it, keep trying and don't be scared. The lifestyle includes having it all balanced with what's important to you, not forgetting family, friends and everything. Then even if you never end up getting to the dream it won't be a disappointment. And you'll be a hell of a lot closer than if you never started down the road of trying.

'After my accident everybody told me: "You've got a second chance in life". I completely disagree because I didn't do anything wrong that day. I didn't cause it and I wasn't doing anything new. I could have chosen to leave my house one second later and it wouldn't have happened. So I don't think the accident was necessarily meant to be. But a lot of things happened that year, culminating in my accident. Spiritually and mentally I couldn't have been better prepared. Before I was living life fully and going for it. Then I just kept going for it – with a slightly changed body. So it's not a second chance, I've just carried on.

'That's why I really believe I was born to be a quad. Maybe this is how it was supposed to be. I can't say I want to be in a wheelchair. I love the freedom of running, it was my favourite thing, so when I see people running… It's not that I don't miss stuff, but I've adapted. I'm carrying on with life and living the dream. The amazing thing is that I've not had a bad day sitting in this wheelchair. I didn't change. Pieter du Preez just got stronger and stronger. And I've learned so many more things in life.'

Du Preez is determined to keep learning in the face of anything life throws at him. He already has a new challenge lined up as he is 'busy going blind' with an incurable degenerative eye disease – inherited, not linked to his accident. 'SupaPiet' admits he is therefore in a race against time to keep up his competitive sport, but he has plenty of dreams, including a sub-12 hour Ironman, a marathon world record and becoming the first quadriplegic to swim the English Channel.

The coming pain is worth it because du Preez is not his only intended beneficiary; there's a whole planet to inspire. Indeed he insists we can all apply these principles to our own lives. It's not about chasing medals, firsts or any other glory. It's every living moment, no matter how pathetically insignificant it may seem at the time. Whenever we come into contact with another living thing we have the chance to make our mark. When we pay real attention to our intention, that's when true greatness beckons.

'I feel I was born to be a quad because the amount of people I'm helping now is way more than before,' he adds. 'Yet even before the accident I made an impact on many lives without realising. I didn't know half the people who came to the hospital and I wouldn't have done the same if they'd been in an accident. I feel ashamed to say that but it made me realise what an impact we make in people's lives on a daily basis and how we influence and inspire each other without knowing it. That should make us all wake up because we should think about what we're doing in every moment. Sure, it's nice to do stupid things sometimes but think about the impact you have on people.

'It's important to realise we all have the power to inspire, able-bodied or not. Everyone tells me how inspirational I am but they don't realise how much they inspire and motivate me by coming up and telling me that. So we all have that power. When I have a tough session and I'm really struggling I wonder, "Why am I doing it?" But I'm doing it for other people because we inspire each other. That guy sees me today and I inspire him. Him seeing me then inspires me and helps me train harder. It's a complete circle effect, all interlinked.

'My favourite saying is when a bad thing happens it's an opportunity to be great. Inspiring people starts within yourself. First you need to fix it within yourself. Doing the positive thing often sounds the hardest one when it's a tough day and things are not going your way. It's not an easy choice and it takes time. But the more you do it, it becomes second nature, a habit. Then the negative choice turns into the hard one. People think they need to be a world champion to inspire, when it's really about being nice to the person at the supermarket till. Everyone's tired and in a hurry but for that moment you give them a smile. You may not think it's inspiration, but it changes their day. Being nice to people is a simple thing. So you don't need to be a superhero to inspire. You can be a normal person with a smile...'

•

This book has drawn on the testimony of the cream of the world's brightest dreamers and most focused schemers to show we all have a chance to be a magician. Anyone with a dream can follow these greats all the way to the top of the world by setting their mind unflinchingly on their own specific quest.

How do champions think? They don't. The original dream comes not from the head but the heart: conceive. No matter how long it takes, they don't think they can, they know they can: believe. Finally, to truly peak they stop thinking at all: achieve.

We all have this potential if we can stop suppressing it ourselves or believing others who haven't yet learned this universal truth. When we finally pay dreams the attention they deserve, the payback is a sea change in everything from self-belief to self-discipline, self-knowledge to self-esteem. Then a realisation dawns that buried within each of us is the power to make any dream come true, even if the process may initially seem more of a nightmare.

Bear with me, I'm not entirely delusional. We've created an unequal world where many are so focused on survival they have no chance of living the same dreams as these stars. It is no coincidence that Great Britain's Olympic medal haul went into orbit with the advent of lottery funding, letting hopefuls train without spending every hour worrying about paying bills. But most dreamers aren't offered a pot of cash to lift them up Maslow's hierarchy of needs; we just have to clamber up by ourselves.

Even those with the luxury of spare capacity to dream big should do the math: every champion leaves countless seemingly unsuccessful dreamers in their wake. No matter what dream we try to live, we could do everything by the book and still end up facing a competitor whose mental strength is in another dimension: an Edwin Moses, a Nadia Comăneci or an Alex Zanardi.

To set out in pursuit of just one dream seems a gamble too far when it comes without a guarantee of eventual 'success'. Obstacles are thrown into every dreamer's path too, any of which could prove terminal, particularly for anyone who still believes the myth of 'Little Me'. While it's tempting to assume everyone from silver down has failed, there is no shame in any such 'defeat'. Whether our passion is for art, business, family or 'mere' survival, the secret is to revel in the process of being the best we can be, secure in the knowledge nothing ever goes to waste. No matter where we direct all our efforts, every investment leads to a return – often with interest. If the examples in this book are anything to go by, the universal law of conservation of energy applies to far more areas of life than physics alone.

Fortunately there are as many different routes to living the dream as there are living things. What links the champions in these pages is that they've learned to tame their minds and clear out any excess negative thoughts. They keep dreaming against rational odds because they know the true thrill of this game is the chase, not the catch. Those who do land among the stars often later rate the journey – no matter how brutal it seemed at the time – as a source of greater satisfaction than the glittering rewards of the destination that inspired it in the first place. And nothing can trump the inevitable visits dreamers make to the Zone along the way.

So maybe it's time to give dreams the respect they deserve. They are easy to ignore – temporarily, at least – but they won't be fooled into giving up on us. That's because dreams have an uncanny knack of guiding us towards true purpose. There is even room for billions of dream machines to speed in all directions on this open road where there really are no limits – and it doesn't have to end in mass road rage.

If your own dream machine ever stutters there are plenty of others desperate for a push start. The brightest dreams always nudge us towards helping others rather than the self-motivated chase to become a champion. This is not about living our own dreams through anyone else, it's letting their dreams live through us. When this happens the result is invariably about helping ourselves too.

What the likes of Cathy Freeman show is that the primary backing we need to cement the courage to start dreaming is not money but love. This is the foundation of the resilience to see it through too. Just as the lucky ones who grow up surrounded by love aim to pass it on to their children, the dreamers among us are determined to get the next generation dreaming. They know the 'lucky' ones are those blessed with the greatest honour of all: the chance to be a part of someone else's dream.

That's all of us, by the way. We don't need an Olympic medal to generate the confidence required to get started. Whether you are a parent, a friend, a teacher or a total stranger, you have the chance to help or hinder the dreams of everyone you meet. Every day. Like it or not, we are all destined to be accidental hypnotists so we may as well be positive ones. Make them smile and you both go away winning.

ACKNOWLEDGEMENTS

This book is based on hundreds of interviews, so my largest debt by far is to the sports stars who gave their time to speak to me. I will never lose the thrill of meeting people whose feats have awed me throughout my life, so to have them share their thoughts so generously on this surreal subject was a privilege indeed. Some of the heroes in these pages are sadly no longer with us – so I dedicate this to the memory of Hannes Arch, Sid Watkins and Dan Wheldon.

The Laureus Sport for Good Foundation deserves the biggest vote of thanks. I visited their annual World Sports Awards ceremony when it first came to London and that's when my collection of superstars began in earnest, starting with the members of the Laureus Academy, real legends all. I have travelled to the event in five different cities around the world because it is paradise for a sportswriter. Special thanks to everyone who has helped me secure so many interviews – most notably Aby Hawker, David Alexander, Nadia Nightingale, Mark Baldwin and Roger Kelly.

Another outstanding venue for meeting the greats was the Goodwood Festival of Speed, thanks not least to the kind help of Gabby Zajacka, Sarah Alexander and others. I also hunted down legends at events including the Red Bull Air Race, London Marathon, Autosport International Show, Race Of Champions, Cross Sports Book Awards, IndyCar Series teleconferences and Team GB's Olympic Preparation Camp.

In *Overdrive* I shared a large list of people who helped in my decade working in Formula 1. My thanks still go out to all of them because this was where I learned my trade as a sportswriter – but particularly once again to Gerald Donaldson for his mind-blowing interview with Ayrton Senna that set me on this road 25 years ago.

Since *Overdrive*'s publication I have also met some of the delightful people who work as sports psychologists and mind coaches. Don MacPherson features most extensively in this book and I owe Don huge thanks for expanding so colourfully on the workings of the mind. Given the large amount of different sports stars featured, I decided to limit the insights from mind experts, but I met others who shared the fruits of their work – including Thora Rain, Mo Costandi, Enzo Mucci, Ben Chell, Robert Bailey, Gavin Gough and Linda Keen, who kindly offered me her quotes from Alex Zanardi. Finally there's the 'Godfather of Flow' himself, Mihály Csíkszentmihályi, with whom it was an honour to speak about his life's work.

Over the course of seven long years of work on this project I've received help from far too many others to name here, not least the lucky souls from all walks of life who told me of their

ACKNOWLEDGEMENTS

own private visits to the Zone. Not everyone has made this final draft; indeed there are some big names who have fallen by the wayside in the interest of flow. I have quoted everyone in good faith and trust that I have not misrepresented any views. The conclusions drawn are all my own, however, as are any errors.

Special thanks to Jon Elek and Millie Hoskins of United Agents, who instantly grasped what I dreamed of achieving and brought this book to the attention of Blink Publishing's Matt Phillips. After self-publishing *Overdrive* I can't overstate the joy of working with industry professionals – not least Oliver Holden-Rea for his insights and patience during the editing process, along with Nicky Gyopari, Madiya Altaf, Beth Eynon and Amy Llambias. Special thanks to Nathan Balsom and Emily Rough for creating such a beautiful cover design and to Lizzie Dorney-Kingdom and Ellis Keene for spreading the word and helping this book find its way to you.

Seven years is a long time to spend on any project without funding – and for the first six of those I had no idea if this book would ever find a publisher. During that time my family were the ones having to put up with my interminable hours in libraries and on trips, all for no payback. I remain eternally grateful for their love and support, without which this could never have been written.

Throughout this book I've emphasised that living the dream isn't easy, but it can be done. Thankfully if doubts ever seeped in, I only had to re-read the thoughts of the superstars in these pages to set me back on track. My own dream was always very clear: it was to have you read this far. Thank you for making that happen. Now I hope their wisdom will prove just as inspiring to you, wherever your dream takes you.

ABOUT
THE AUTHOR

Clyde Brolin spent a decade working in Formula 1 before moving on to the wider world of sport. His first book, *Overdrive*, was shortlisted for Best New Writer at the British Sports Book Awards.

INDEX

Agassi, Andre 248
Ainslie, Ben 212–15, 216, 217
air racing:
    Arch, Hannes 77
    Bonhomme, Paul 178–9, 180–1
    Dolderer, Matthias 180
    Hall, Matt 181–3
    Kindlemann, Adilson 179
    Lamb, Nigel 180
    McLeod, Pete 44–5
    Muroya, Yoshihide 179–80
Albuquerque, Filipe 23–5
Ali, Muhammad 51–2, 153–4
Ambrose, Curtly 84
Arch, Hannes 77
Atherton, Mike 187
athletics (see also triathlon):
    Bolt, Usain 17, 133, 167, 262, 289–90
    Bubka, Sergey 135–8
    Carlos, John 154
    Coe, Sebastian 270–2
    Culson, Javier 268
    El Moutawakel, Nawal 154–6
    Ennis-Hill, Jessica 41–3, 165
    Freeman, Cathy 147–53, 155, 303
    Gebrselassie, Haile 133
    Greene, Dai 268
    Harris, Danny 264
    Hemery, David 272–6
    Hingsen, Jurgen 99
    Johnson, Michael 166–71, 172–4
    Keino, Kip 249–50, 252–3
    Kipchoge, Eliud 251
    Lavillenie, Renaud 135
    Lewis, Carl 166
    Lewis, Denise 41, 293
    Loroupe, Tegla 253–5
    Moses, Edwin 257–60, 261–6, 268
    Mutai, Emmanuel 251
    Nerurkar, Richard 250–1
    Prendergast, Tim 223–6
    Redmond, Derek 203–5, 206
    Rutherford, Greg 100
    Sánchez, Felix 266–70
    Smith, Tommie 154
    Taylor, Angelo 268
    Thompson, Daley 97–101

Ballesteros, Seve 242
BASE jumping (see also skydiving):
    Arch, Hannes 77
    Baumgartner, Felix 61–3, 78–9, 291
    Burnquist, Bob 111–12
    Pastrana, Travis 114
Baumgartner, Felix 61–70, 71–2, 73–7, 78–9, 291
Bell, Graham 52–3
Bestwick, Jamie 91–7, 109
BMX (see also cycling), Bestwick, Jamie 91–7
Bolt, Usain 17, 133, 167, 262, 289–90
Bonhomme, Paul 178–9, 180–1
Bowman, Bob 39
boxing:
    Ali, Muhammad 51–2, 153–4
    Duran, Roberto 79
    Hagler, Marvin 79–82
    Hearns, Thomas 79, 80–1
    Leonard, Sugar Ray 79
    Liston, Sonny 153
Brownlee, Alistair 190
Bubka, Sergey 135–8

Burnquist, Bob 111–12
Button, Jenson 15

Caballero, Steve 110
Carlos, John 154
Carter, Dan 237
Chell, Ben 138–40, 216–17
Cherry, Colin 185
Clarke, Darren 127–8
Coe, Sebastian 270–2
Comăneci, Nadia 9–10, 11–12, 13–14, 177, 260, 276
cricket:
  Ambrose, Curtly 84
  Atherton, Mike 187
  Dev, Kapil 84
  Flower, Andy 154
  Olonga, Henry 154
  Trescothick, Marcus 85
  Waugh, Steve 82–4, 85–6, 289
Csíkszentmihályi, Mihály 102–4, 281–4
Culson, Javier 268
cycling (see also BMX; hand-cycling; triathlon):
  Hoy, Chris 140, 142–5 (see also motor racing)
  Pendleton, Victoria 140 (see also horse racing)

Desailly, Marcel 245–6
Dev, Kapil 84
Di Toro, Daniela 227–8
Dietrich, Arne 187
Djokovic, Novak 119–23, 124, 125, 288
Dolderer, Matthias 180
Doohan, Mick 86–8
Doyle, Ryan 104–8
Du Plessis, Morné 240–2
Du Preez, Pieter 295–301
Dunlop, Joey 32, 34
Duran, Roberto 79
Dweck, Carol 225

El Moutawakel, Nawal 154–6
Ennis-Hill, Jessica 41–3, 165
Eustace, Alan 75

Fanning, Mick 199–202
Federer, Roger 120, 124
Ferguson, Alex 241
Fittipaldi, Emerson 3–4, 191–4
Fitzpatrick, Sean 231–2, 233, 238–40
Flower, Andy 154
Franchitti, Dario 186
Franklin, Missy 156–7
Freeman, Anne-Marie 151
Freeman, Cathy 147–53, 155, 303
freerunning, Doyle, Ryan 104–8
Frodeno, Jan 188–91
Fullerton, Terry 195

Gaisli, Leon 209–10
Gebrselassie, Haile 133
Geistdörfer, Christian 48

Gervais, Michael 66
golf:
  Ballesteros, Seve 242
  Clarke, Darren 127–8
  Nicklaus, Jack 43
  Olazabal, José Maria 242
  Poulter, Ian 242
Goolagong Cawley, Evonne 151
Grainger, Katherine 164–6
Green, Andy 53–8
Greene, Dai 268
Grey-Thompson, Tanni 220–1
Grobler, Jürgen 162
Gullit, Ruud 242–5
gymnastics:
  Comăneci, Nadia 9–10, 11–12, 13–14, 177, 260, 276
  Whitlock, Max 12–13

Habana, Bryan 236–7
Hagler, Marvin 79–82
Häkkinen, Mika 22–3, 133–4
Hall, Matt 181–3
Halliday, Liz 140–1 (see also horse racing; motor racing)
Hamilton, Lewis 22, 134, 288
hand-cycling:
  Gaisli, Leon 209–10
  Zanardi, Alex 207–10 (see also motor racing)
Hansen, Steve 234–6, 237
Harris, Danny 264
Hart, Clyde 169
Hawk, Tony 93, 108–11
Hearns, Thomas 79, 80–1
Hemery, David 272–6
Henry, Graham 235
Hildebrand, JR 1–2, 4–5, 6
Hill, Damon 195
Hingsen, Jürgen 99
Hintsa, Aki 133–4
Høgh-Christensen, Jonas 213
Holden, Will 134
Holmes, Andy 162
Holmes, Simon 163
Homan, Korie 228
horse racing:
  Halliday, Liz 140–1 (see also motor racing)
  Pendleton, Victoria 140 (see also cycling)
  Hoy, Chris 140, 142–5 (see also cycling; motor racing)
Huff, Rob 134–5

Inanga, Glen 197

Johnson, Michael 166–71, 172–4
Jordan, Andrew 132–3

Keen, Linda 208
Keino, Kip 249–50, 252–3
Kent, Stacey 247–8

INDEX

Kimball, Charlie 1
Kindlemann, Adilson 179
Kipchoge, Eliud 251
kiteboarding, Naish, Robby 276–8 (*see also* windsurfing)
Kittinger, Joe 63, 65, 67, 71–4, 75
Klammer, Franz 49–52
Knievel, Evel 113, 118
Köster, Philip 278–9

Lamb, Nigel 180
Lampkin, Dougie 184–5
land speed records, Green, Andy 53–8
Lauda, Niki 49
Lavillenie, Renaud 135
Lendl, Ivan 124–5
Leonard, Sugar Ray 79
Lewis, Carl 166
Lewis, Denise 41, 293
Liston, Sonny 153
Loeb, Sébastien 25
Lomu, Jonah 236, 240
Lorenzo, Jorge 184, 291
Loroupe, Tegla 253–5

McCaw, Richie 232, 233–4, 238
McFadden, Tatyana 221–3
McGuinness, John 31–6
McLeod, Pete 44–5
MacPherson, Don 43, 129–30, 131–2, 183–4, 186–7, 210–12, 287, 292–3
McRae, Colin 144
Maddison, Robbie 113–18
Mandela, Nelson 240
Mansell, Nigel 195
Márquez, Marc 88–9
Maslow, Abraham 280–1, 294
Mason, Nick 246–7
Melzer, Jürgen 120
Messi, Lionel 244, 288
Moses, Edwin 257–60, 261–6, 268
motor racing (*see also* land speed records):
    Albuquerque, Filipe 23–5
    Button, Jenson 15
    Fittipaldi, Emerson 3–4, 191–4
    Franchitti, Dario 186
    Fullerton, Terry 195
    Geistdörfer, Christian 48
    Häkkinen, Mika 22–3, 133–4
    Halliday, Liz 140–1 (*see also* horse racing)
    Hamilton, Lewis 22, 134, 288
    Hildebrand, JR 1–2, 4–5, 6
    Hill, Damon 195
    Hoy, Chris 140, 142–5 (*see also* cycling)
    Huff, Rob 134–5
    Jordan, Andrew 132–3
    Kimball, Charlie 1
    Lauda, Niki 49
    Loeb, Sébastien 25
    McRae, Colin 144

Mansell, Nigel 195
Pagenaud, Simon 21
Piquet, Nelson 191
Prost, Alain 17, 19–21, 23
Robertson, Charlie 142
Röhrl, Walter 46–9
Rosberg, Nico 184
Rossi, Alexander 185
Rutherford, Johnny 186
Scheckter, Jody 123–4
Schumacher, Michael 23, 195
Senna, Ayrton 17–18, 20, 21, 22, 51, 167, 168, 185, 191, 193–5 *passim*, 222
Stewart, Jackie 197–8
Unser, Bobby 36–9
Vettel, Sebastian 23–4, 44, 134, 143
Warwick, Derek 196
Wheldon, Dan 2, 4–7, 10, 14–16
Zanardi, Alex 205–9 (*see also* hand-cycling)
motorcycle racing and motocross:
    Doohan, Mick 86–8
    Dunlop, Joey 34
    Knievel, Evel 113, 118
    Lampkin, Dougie 184–5
    Lorenzo, Jorge 184, 291
    McGuinness, John 31–6
    Maddison, Robbie 113–18
    Márquez, Marc 88–9
    Pastrana, Travis 93
    Muroya, Yoshihide 179–80
    Murray, Andy 119, 124–5
    Mutai, Emmanuel 251

Nadal, Rafael 119, 120, 125–6
Naish, Robby 276–8, 279–80 (*see also* kiteboarding; windsurfing)
Nerurkar, Richard 250–1
Nicklaus, Jack 43

Olazabal, José Maria 242
Olonga, Henry 154
O'Sullivan, Ronnie 140

Pagenaud, Simon 21
Paire, Benoit 125
paragliding, Arch, Hannes 77
parkour, Doyle, Ryan 104–8
Pastrana, Travis 93, 114
Peaty, Adam 185
Pendleton, Victoria 140 (*see also* cycling; horse racing)
Peters, Steve 140, 142
Phelps, Michael 39–40, 165
Piantanida, Nick 65
Pinsent, Matthew 162–3, 164
Piquet, Nelson 191
Postma, Pieter-Jan 213
Poulter, Ian 242
Prendergast, Tim 223–6
Prost, Alain 17, 19–21, 23

Rain, Thora 294–5
Redgrave, Steve 160–2, 163–4
Redmond, Derek 203–5, 206
Robertson, Charlie 142
Röhrl, Walter 46–9
Ronaldo, Cristiano 244
Rosberg, Nico 184
Rossi, Alexander 185
Rotella, Bob 128
rowing:
    Grainger, Katherine 164–6
    Grobler, Jürgen 162
    Holmes, Andy 162
    Pinsent, Matthew 162–3, 164
    Redgrave, Steve 160–2, 163–4
    Savage, Roz 218–20
    Thornley, Victoria 166
    Watkins, Anna 165
rugby:
    Carter, Dan 237
    Du Plessis, Morné 240–2
    Fitzpatrick, Sean 231–2, 233, 238–40
    Habana, Bryan 236–7
    Hansen, Steve 234–6, 237
    Henry, Graham 235
    Lomu, Jonah 236, 240
    McCaw, Richie 232, 233–4, 238
Rutherford, Greg 100
Rutherford, Johnny 186

sailing:
    Ainslie, Ben 212–15, 216, 217
    Høgh-Christensen, Jonas 213
    Postma, Pieter-Jan 213
    Scheidt, Robert 212–13, 216
Sánchez, Felix 266–70
Savage, Roz 218–20
Scheckter, Jody 123–4
Scheidt, Robert 212–13, 216
Schumacher, Michael 23, 195
Senna, Ayrton 17–18, 20, 21, 22, 51, 167, 168, 185,
    191, 193–5 passim, 222
skateboarding:
    Burnquist, Bob 111–12
    Caballero, Steve 110
    Hawk, Tony 93, 108–11
skiing:
    Bell, Graham 52–3
    Klammer, Franz 49–52
skydiving (see also BASE jumping):
    Baumgartner, Felix 62, 63–70, 71–2, 73–7, 78–9,
        291
    Eustace, Alan 75
    Kittinger, Joe 63, 65, 67, 71–4, 75
    Piantanida, Nick 65
Smith, Tommie 154
snooker, O'Sullivan, Ronnie 140
soccer:
    Desailly, Marcel 245–6
    Ferguson, Alex 241

Gullit, Ruud 242–5
Messi, Lionel 244, 288
Ronaldo, Cristiano 244
Zidane, Zinédine 245
Spitz, Mark 157–9, 160, 239
Spracklen, Mike 161
Stewart, Jackie 197–8
Sullenberger, Chelsey 177
surfing, Fanning, Mick 199–202
swimming (see also triathlon):
    Brownlee, Alistair 190
    Franklin, Missy 156–7
    Peaty, Adam 185
    Phelps, Michael 39–40, 165
    Spitz, Mark 157–9, 160, 239

Taylor, Angelo 268
tennis:
    Agassi, Andre 248
    Djokovic, Novak 119–23, 124, 125, 288
    Federer, Roger 120, 124
    Goolagong Cawley, Evonne 151
    Lendl, Ivan 124–5
    Melzer, Jürgen 120
    Murray, Andy 119, 124–5
    Nadal, Rafael 119, 120, 125–6
    Paire, Benoit 125
Thompson, Daley 97–101
Thornley, Victoria 166
Trescothick, Marcus 85
triathlon (see also athletics; cycling; swimming):
    Du Preez, Pieter 295–301
    Frodeno, Jan 188–91

Unser, Bobby 36–9

Vergeer, Esther 226–30
Vettel, Sebastian 23–4, 44, 134, 143

Warwick, Derek 196
Watkins, Anna 165
Waugh, Steve 82–4, 85–6, 289
wheelchair racing:
    Grey-Thompson, Tanni 220–1
    McFadden, Tatyana 221–3
wheelchair tennis:
    Di Toro, Daniela 227–8
    Homan, Korie 228
    Vergeer, Esther 226–30
Wheldon, Dan 2, 4–7, 10, 14–16
Whitlock, Max 12–13
windsurfing:
    Köster, Philip 278–9
    Naish, Robby 276–8, 279–80 (see also
        kiteboarding)

Zanardi, Alex 205–10 (see also hand-cycling; motor
    racing)
Zidane, Zinédine 245